A Handbook of Adult Education for West Africa

A Handbook of Adult Education for West Africa

Edited by

Lalage Bown
Professor and Head, Department of Adult Education,
University of Lagos

S. H. Olu Tomori
Professor and Head, Department of Adult Education,
University of Ibadan

Hutchinson University Library for Africa

HUTCHINSON UNIVERSITY LIBRARY FOR AFRICA
Hutchinson & Co. (Publishers) Ltd
3 Fitzroy Square, London w1p 6jd

London Melbourne Sydney Auckland
Wellington Johannesburg and agencies
throughout the world

First published 1979

Set in VIP Times Roman by Input Typesetting Ltd

Printed in Great Britain by The Anchor Press Ltd
and bound by Wm Brendon & Son Ltd,
both of Tiptree, Essex

British Library Cataloguing in Publication Data

A handbook of adult education for West Africa.
1. Adult education – Africa, West
I. Bown, Lalage   II. Tomori, Sunday
Hezekiah Olu
374.9'66   LC5258.A3

ISBN 0 09 138810 4 cased
     0 09 138811 2 paper

Contents

Introduction

This handbook is designed to help anyone in English-speaking West Africa who is either engaged in the education of adults or hopes to be so engaged, whether full-time or part-time. We believe that it will be of practical use to persons studying adult education in universities and colleges of education and to persons attending other adult education training courses; we also hope that anyone who has been trained in adult education will keep a copy of this book on his or her shelf, as a reminder, refresher and general reference book.

It has been planned by an editorial board comprising adult education specialists from Sierra Leone, Ghana and Nigeria; and each chapter has been worked over by its author in consultation with the board. A common arrangement has been adopted to make the book easy to refer to. Each chapter starts with a list of main headings, so that the reader may see at a glance what topics are covered; this is followed by an introductory section which explains the purpose of the chapter and the relevance of the topic and summarizes the main trend of the argument. In each chapter, where a subject is mentioned which is expounded in more detail elsewhere, the reader is referred to that chapter. Footnotes have been kept to a minimum, but basic references are given at the end of each chapter and are followed by a select reading list of material regarded as most likely to be helpful to a student or a practitioner in the field.

The first chapter deals with essential definitions, but we wish to preface the whole book with some comments on terminology. First, as will be apparent throughout, we have taken **adult education** in the broadest sense. There is still a tendency in many developing countries to think of adult education as referring only to literacy, or only to formal school-type work as managed by a ministry of education. We believe literacy to be vitally important and we accept the value of remedial school education being made available to grown men and women; but such activities are only a fraction of the whole adult education exercise. Other attempts to increase adults' knowledge and skills or to change their attitudes are equally important and valuable. We hope, therefore, that this book will also appeal to persons involved in agricultural extension, health education, industrial training and public service broadcasting. They too are engaged in tasks which are essentially adult educational, and the development of West Africa depends also on their skills in changing human behaviour.

Secondly, as we are writing in English, we are assuming that most of our readers will be from those West African countries which use English as an official language (Gambia, Sierra Leone, Liberia, Ghana, Nigeria) and those which, for historical reasons, have a significant English-speaking population (Togo and Cameroon).We also hope that it will be of use to persons working in multilingual agencies, whether official, such as ECOWAS, or unofficial, such as INADES, and to persons from French-, Portuguese- or Arabic-speaking West African countries trained in English-speaking institutions in Britain or the USA who, up till now, have had no relevant Africa-based text to turn to. It has been our hope that, in due course, West African adult educators from other official language groups might wish to use this handbook as a basis for preparing something similar in French or Portuguese.

For these reasons we have deliberately called this book a handbook 'for West Africa', and we have accepted the UN definition of **West Africa** as a sub-region of Africa made up of the following countries:

English-speaking: Gambia, Sierra Leone, Liberia, Ghana, Nigeria;
French-speaking: Senegal, Guinea, Ivory Coast, Upper Volta,
   Togo, Bénin (formerly Dahomey), Niger, Mali, Cameroon;
Portuguese-speaking: Guinea-Bissau;
Spanish/Arabic-speaking: Mauritania.

The problems of this sub-region are not divisible by language use; and we have tried to take examples from many different West African countries, as it is always helpful to know what solutions to similar problems are being tried in countries other than one's own.

Having now defined the phrases used in our title, there are three usages in the text which we should mention:

a) As adult education is for women as well as men, we assume that educators and learners may be men or women. When we talk of an educator or a learner as 'he', it is to avoid the clumsiness of constantly saying 'he or she', but does not imply that such a person is always male.

b) It is fashionable at the present time to use the word **learning** rather than **education**. This is to underline the point that from the individual's point of view he is engaged in a positive act of learning and not in a passive rite of 'being educated'. But it is sometimes necessary to speak of the learning process from an institutional, or national, or 'teaching' point of view. Rather than resorting to some round-about phrase such as 'the group learning experience', it seemed to us at such times not only less clumsy but also correct to speak of education. We have therefore not hesitated to use the word when writing from an institutional or an educator's point of view.

c) Similarly we have not been mealy-mouthed about using the words **teacher** and **tutor** when we mean a person consciously assisting others to learn. On the whole, we have preferred the word tutor, as this has a less authoritarian ring. In the formal education hierarchy in some West African countries, a tutor may be someone of less status than a **lecturer**; but in adult education the opposite should apply, since the educator of adults should avoid lecturing and aim at a tutorial relationship, as explained in Chapter 2. We have, incidentally, avoided the word **instructor**, since this also has authoritarian overtones.

Preparing this book has been an exciting piece of team-work and we, as editors, owe thanks to all the editorial board for practical planning and appraisal of work and to all the authors for their thoroughness and patience. All of us, editorial board and authors, are also indebted to Miss Evelyn Nsiah and Mr Frederick Adekoya who typed the various versions of the manuscripts and we would like to express our gratitude to them. The whole project owes its existence to a consultative meeting on adult education training called together by the African Bureau of the German Adult Education Association; at that meeting the idea of a handbook was first canvassed. Afterwards, the Africa Bureau financed the various planning and working sessions and offered to purchase a substantial number of copies of the book for distribution to adult educators in training. We are very grateful indeed to the Bureau and to Mr Werner Keweloh, its head, for an imaginative and practical form of aid.

Lalage Bown
S. H. Olu Tomori

Part One
Starting Points

1 Scope and purpose of adult education in West Africa

Lalage Bown

Adult education as an integral part of lifelong education can contribute decisively to economic and cultural development, social progress and world peace, as well as to the development of educational systems.
From the Recommendation of the 1976 Unesco General Conference on the Development of Adult Education[1]

Introductory

Before settling down to study a subject and before contemplating entering a profession, one wants to be satisfied that it is worthwhile. This whole book is written in the belief that adult education is important for West Africa and that to work in adult education is a valuable and useful thing to do. This first chapter attempts to explain this belief. It states what adult education is, what its significance has been in the past and what kind of contribution it may be expected to make to social, economic and political development in the future. It also indicates some of the advantages and problems of becoming a professional adult educator.

Ideas and aims: what adult education is about

First, what do we mean by adult education? The short answer is:

any education given to adult persons, men or women. But one may ask: what is education? And who is an adult?

Many people think of education as what goes on in a school classroom – a series of lessons on set 'subjects', measured from time to time by examinations and ending in a 'qualification' or ticket to a certain type and level of job; after that, the process is over. From this point of view, anyone who has never been to school is uneducated and without knowledge. Such a view was characteristic of the colonial period, when foreign rulers were anxious to encourage people to absorb a given type of knowledge, sufficient to make them good clerks or storekeepers, and not to go beyond that knowledge to independent thought and questioning.

In the post-colonial period, both developing and developed countries have begun to conceive of education as something broader. It is now being emphasized that all human beings in possession of their faculties are learning all the time and throughout their lives. Some learning is **informal**; that is, gained incidentally and casually, from conversation in the market or a commercial on the radio or the sports page of a newspaper. When learning is consciously promoted, it then becomes part of the process of **education**. The rediscovery that education can be **lifelong** is due to the accelerated pace of change in the twentieth century. With constant developments in science and technology, with new means of communication such as radio and television, with major alterations in political institutions, any person 'who does not keep up-to-date is condemned to be overtaken'.[2]

If education is lifelong, it follows that it can be pursued at any age, though it is recognized that some types of learning, particularly of skills, may depend on youthfulness; for example, one cannot easily imagine a person of sixty starting to learn football. And some ways of teaching or promoting learning may be more suitable for children and others more suitable for adults.

Formal attainment of adulthood is often marked by special ceremonies and rituals, varying from traditional initiation to a twenty-first birthday party. It is also recognized in law, which sets a given age at which a person begins to take on responsibility for his own affairs. Human beings, however, develop gradually; and although in custom and law there may be a set day on which a person becomes an adult, in actuality there is no sharp dividing line between childhood and adulthood. The 1976 Unesco *Recommendation on Adult Education* (see Appendix 2) refers to 'persons regarded as adult by the society to which they belong', but it may be helpful to look more closely at the attributes which are accepted by society as those of an adult.

These attributes include physiological maturity, the capacity for marriage and parenthood, at least the potential for earning a living and contributing to society by the work of hand or brain and the recognized right to exercise whatever civic duties the political system allows (such as tax-paying or voting). Perhaps the essence of adulthood lies in the word *responsibility*; an adult person is expected to take full responsibility for his actions, for any debt he incurs, for any agreement into which he enters (such as marriage or a business partnership) and for the orderly conduct of his life within the laws of the land. A simple practical definition of an adult, which incorporates or implies these points is:

> A person (man or woman) who has achieved full physical development and expects to have the right to participate as a responsible homemaker, worker and member of society.[3]

It is necessary to remember that even in custom and law, recognition may be given to *stages* in the attainment of adulthood. In many societies there is an age-grade system separating the 'youngmen' from the 'elders', and the laws of several countries may exact some adult responsibilities at an earlier age than others; for example, the age at which a man is allowed to be a soldier may be seventeen or eighteen, whereas the age at which he may vote or join a cooperative or raise a loan from the bank may be twenty or twenty-one.

In educational work, we recognize the special needs of various age-levels in adulthood, and thus we have such concepts as the **young adult** and the **elder,** or senior citizen. At present in West Africa, the young adult is a category of person with which educators are very much concerned. He or she will be someone physiologically mature, who has been thrown on to his or her own resources for gaining a livelihood – having lost or never had access to educational opportunity beyond that provided by the formal primary school. Such people are the 'applicants' and job-seekers whom we all know in the large towns and cities. Although many are not yet adult in law, they are forced into social and economic independence. The age-range we are considering is between fifteen and twenty-five.

We have so far stated that **education** is consciously facilitated learning, that it is lifelong and can affect young and old, and that **adult education** is the education of persons physiologically mature and socially and economically responsible. We may now seek to define adult education more closely. A thoroughly comprehensive definition is given in the Unesco *Recommendation* in Appendix 2. A briefer one, which is also useful is:

The process by which men and women (alone, in groups, or in institutional settings) seek to improve themselves or their society by increasing their skill, their knowledge or their sensitiveness: any process by which individuals, groups or institutions try to help men and women improve in these ways.[4]

Adult education is thus conceived of very broadly. Its content may include education parallel to the school and university system, vocational training and civic education. Education parallel to the first years of the school system is sometimes called **Adult Basic Education** (ABE) and includes **literacy** and **numeracy** (the skills of reading and handling figures). Literacy has been a very important element in adult educational programmes in Africa, and recently there have been attempts to make literacy more immediately **functional** (or purposeful) by combining the teaching of reading with the teaching of another skill, in a programme related to a given community in a given environment and to a given economic and social development plan. Very often the particular skill emphasized is geared to earning a living either as an independent farmer or worker, or as a person in paid employment; this type of functional literacy programme is known as **work-oriented functional literacy**. Education beyond the literacy stage, for whatever purpose, is often called **post-literacy education**, and a newly literate person is known as a **neo-literate**.

Very many adults who are already literate want to improve themselves in their jobs and therefore undergo courses of **training**. Training is more narrowly defined and more specific than education, since it is designed expressly to enable adults to understand their work, perform it more effectively and advance within it, but it may be seen as a part of adult education, since it is concerned with changes in skills, knowledge and ideas, and relies on the same principles.

Education related less to earning an individual living than to being an effective member of society may be termed **civic education**. It can be related to the betterment of one's village (associated then with community development), to the functioning of a socio-economic agency (such as a trade union or a cooperative), or to the political system (learning how to vote or understanding a new constitution).

Whatever the content of adult education, certain approaches may be applied. Probably the most fruitful approach for Africa is that often known as **conscientization**. The word was invented by the celebrated Brazilian adult educationist, Paulo Freire, to describe the process by which learning can particularly help the underprivileged. What it implies has been eloquently described by the president of Tanzania, Mwalimu Julius Nyerere:

... Man makes himself. It is his ability to act deliberately, for a self-determined purpose, which distinguishes him from the other animals. The expansion of his own consciousness, and therefore of his power over himself, his environment, and his society, must therefore ultimately be what we mean by development.

So development is for Man, by Man, and of Man. The same is true of education. Its purpose is the liberation of Man from the restraints and limitations of ignorance and dependency. Education has to increase men's physical and mental freedom – to increase their control over themselves, their own lives, and the environment in which they live. The ideas imparted by education, or released in the mind through education, should therefore be liberating ideas, the skills acquired by education should be liberating skills. Nothing else can properly be called education. Teaching which induces a slave mentality or a sense of impotence is not education at all – it is an attack on the minds of men.[5]

The stress in many African countries on liberation may remind us that liberation of the human being is the true goal of **liberal education** (liberating education), a term often misused to apply to a particular academic subject-range or to non-vocational education. The division between vocational and non-vocational has always been artificial, since one person's vocation may be another person's recreation, and it has been out-dated by such concepts as functional literacy and conscientization, which are based on a view of the human being in a social and community context.

A similar concept is expressed in the phrase used in French-speaking West Africa, **rural animation**: the enlivening, arousing to greater consciousness, or stirring-up of the rural population. An important aspect of the animation approach is that the agents of change, or **animators**, are usually persons from the village community and not professional educators of any sort.

Because of respect for the adult learner's dignity and individuality, another approach is the non-formal one. Sometimes the phrase **non-formal education** is used to cover all education outside the school system (whether for children or adults); but, strictly speaking, some **out-of-school** education may be formalistic in that it duplicates the organization, methodology and approach of the school system. A more accurate interpretation of **non-formal** may be: *unlike school* or *designed for specific individuals and groups*. A class for adults wishing to pass the West African School Certificate (WASC) is likely to be formal in nature, even though not part of the school system as such, whereas a demonstration to a group of farmers on better maize-growing is likely to be non-formal.

The general stress on liberation of the learner and on the avoidance of formalism means that adult education is less *institutionalized* than the rest of the educational system. But there are plenty of adult education institutions in West Africa, as will be seen in Chapter 3. Some of the common terms describing institutional activities should be mentioned here.

Very often we meet the word **extension**. Extension means literally a stretching out and is often used to mean the stretching out of an organization by interchanging intelligence with persons it wishes to influence. If the organization has non-educational goals, then its extension may be less educational than propagandist. Much extension work is, however, a part of the adult educational process; we think most often of **agricultural extension**. Another expression used for the 'reaching-out' programmes of an institution, peculiar to Commonwealth countries, is **extra-mural**; this means 'beyond the walls', and it is used for adult educational programmes outside the institution's normal geographical programmes or outside the range of its staple activities. Extra-mural departments are generally found attached to universities or colleges or other full-time educational institutions, and so also are departments or centres of **continuing education**. This phrase usually implies that the learners dealt with already have had some contact with the school system, and are building on to knowledge, skills or ideas already acquired.

A useful phrase describes the institutionalization of the concept of lifelong education itself. This is **recurrent education**, the organization of the whole educational system so that learners may recur (or come back) to it at will throughout life. This type of arrangement is beginning to be used in industrialized countries, where there are laws about paid educational leave and similar matters.

In describing what adult education is about, we have introduced most of the basic terms commonly used by adult educators in their work. Other expressions, relating to special aspects of the work, will come up in later chapters and will be explained as they appear for the first time.

The history of adult education in West Africa

Earlier in this chapter, I referred to the idea of lifelong education having been 'rediscovered'. This is because in pre-colonial times it was firmly embedded in many West African societies. The content of education was related to community consciousness (official history and literature), common values (codes of behaviour) and skills needed for community survival and individual livelihood (agriculture, warfare). Methods of education were often fairly informal: adult education in West African societies before colonial times was not usually organized in terms of setting aside a time and place to instruct a specified group of people. No special institutions existed solely for the purpose of teaching basic values and morality, and such basic skills as farming, fishing and public speaking. Instead, as a person grew up, he learned informally such ideas, standards of behaviour and skills from members of his family and lineage.

Further, there were some occasions, such as the celebration of births or funerals, when certain ideas and modes of behaviour were emphasized; and persons present could learn new things accordingly, although learning as such was not the stated object of the ceremony. For instance, during the funeral ceremonies for an important chief in Ghana, the history of the locality, dance-forms, songs, appropriate dress and special drum rhythms could be learned, but informally. Such education was not rigidly directed to any one age-group; young and old might listen, for instance, to an official praise-singer and derive the message of loyalty and unity which he conveyed. At major ceremonies, hundreds of persons would participate and all become learners of some aspect of their culture.

The absence of formality did not mean that there was any lack of sophistication. Many peoples had sophisticated mechanisms for lifelong education and for adult education within the lifelong education system. Some groups had a progressive age-grade system, such as that of the Nupe of Nigeria, by which young men gradually learned a code of conduct based on mutual assistance and in which they tried out leadership roles and responsibilities. Others had regimental training, as through the *asafo* companies of the Fanti in Ghana, which competed at various activities and thus encouraged standards of efficiency. Others had traditional organizations through which each generation had to pass and which treasured and transmitted important lore, often concentrating on the initiation into adulthood of adolescent boys and girls; examples are the Poro and Bundu societies of Sierra Leone.

These arrangements affected most members of the community at some time or other. There were some specialized types of education, an example being the craft guilds, common in Northern Nigeria, in which master-craftsmen, such as blacksmiths or doctors, organized training of younger persons into their skills, and in which the leaders might act as advisers to the other members. Another example is the custom among the Akan of Ghana whereby the prospective holder of an important traditional office, such as the chieftancy of an important division, would be in seclusion for some time, during which he would be educated by the elders about the post he was to take up.

All this has been written in the past tense. But many of the types of education described exist, and flourish, to the present day; and, as is stressed in Chapter 3, any adult educator hoping to be successful needs to be familiar with them. New forms of adult education have overlaid the old ones, but the old ones still remain important.

In addition to having inherited these time-honoured forms of adult education, a large part of West Africa has been influenced over many centuries by the religion of Islam, which of its nature fosters continuous education. Since it is a religion which includes both ethical and legal codes, accuracy in the handing down of such standards is important, and scholars derived their own authority from licences to teach passed on from older *sheikhs*. This system, which prevailed over much of the Western Sudan, resulted from the accumulation of a substantial body of knowledge, too weighty to be learnt by the young. It also resulted in a cadre of travelling teachers, or *Malamai*, and in the existence of wandering *talibs*, or 'seekers-after-knowledge' who went looking for the most noted teachers. The Holy Prophet himself was said to have encouraged a person to seek for knowledge 'even as far away as China'.

Islam, because of the central importance of the Holy Koran, encouraged literacy; and Koranic Schools, although primarily for the young, may still be attended by the occasional adult. Moreover, it is one of the five obligations of a Muslim to go on the pilgrimage or *Hajj* to Mecca, and the journey (especially before the coming of the aeroplane) was an opportunity for learning.

West African history has many examples of Islamic scholars whose repute was such that they were teachers of established and mature persons. One such scholar was Ahmed Baba of Timbuktu (1556–1627) who came from a family of learned men and was taken into exile when the Moroccan army crossed the desert to attack the Songhai Empire. As a poverty-stricken exile under open arrest, he taught at one of the mosques in Marrakesh and wrote later that:

Ordinary people thronged around me and followed my teaching, as well as the famous knowledge-seekers of the city.[6]

He gave the names of a number of judges who came to learn from him, including one who was over sixty and 'to whom men journeyed for knowledge'.

In more recent times another religion of a book, Christianity, came to West Africa. Portuguese Catholic missionaries appeared on the coast in the fifteenth century, and Protestants began to engage in missionary work in the eighteenth century. Missionaries included the half-African, Christian Protten of the Church of the Brethren (d. 1769), and the two Ghanaians, Jacobus Capitein of the Dutch Reformed Church (1717–47) and Philip Quaque of the Anglican Church (1741–1816).

The nineteenth century, however, saw the beginnings of major Christian missionary effort. Like Islam, Christianity emphasized literacy; and although there was always an attempt to train up children and establish some schooling for them, evangelism demanded the teaching of adults as well. When John Morgan, a Methodist, went to the Gambia in the 1820s he ran a school for children and evening classes for adults. Distinguished African clergymen such as J. C. Taylor and S. Adjai Crowther (both Nigerians) have left reports of their teaching in public places.[7] Later in the century, women missionaries held classes for women in home economics.

During the nineteenth century, also, the first newspapers in West Africa started up, and many early African journalists saw themselves as educators of the public. It is interesting to read the editorial in the *Accra Herald* of 5 October 1957, written by Charles Bannerman, whom Professor K. A. B. Jones-Quartey describes as the 'first native-born newspaper proprietor and editor of Black Africa'. Part of the editorial says:

In civilised communities, the Press deservedly occupy a high position. The mass of mankind want [lack] either the leisure or capacity to form a sound opinion on most questions of the day – we mean an opinion founded on calm reflection and thorough examination of the subject. Men's opinions therefore, where there is no Press, are often mere whims and fancies, formed on very trifling knowledge of the matter. Their information is frequently incorrect.

It is good therefore for the public that there should be a set of men who devote their time and ability to collecting and distributing general information. And it is good that these men should make it their duty to examine questions of importance and submit their opinions, when matured, to the Public.[8]

In the twentieth century, governments began to take a hand in adult education. The British government's interest was stirred by the Phelps–Stokes Commissions (1922 and 1923), financed from the USA and manned by important lay and missionary educators. They emphasized the importance of the school-teacher as an agent for change in rural life. But the efforts at community betterment which followed were limited by the economic depression of the 1930s.

It was only after the Second World War (1939–45) that colonial governments embarked on ambitious adult education programmes, partly as a result of new currents of thought in the metropolitan countries favouring independence and partly as a result of pressures from the returned ex-servicemen in West African countries themselves. Characteristic of the early post-war period were literacy campaigns and the use of mass education teams moving from place to place (e.g. in Senegal and the Gold Coast). **Mass education** became the fashionable phrase.

In addition to government activity, there were various private efforts at adult education, usually arising out of the popular political enthusiasm for independence. Among them were numerous literary and debating clubs, the work of Old Achimotans in conducting literacy 'Sunday Schools' in Ghana, and the first purely adult educational societies – the organization of extra-mural students in Nigeria and the People's Educational Association in Ghana. The latter appeared in response to another development in Commonwealth Africa – the establishment of university extra-mural departments in the 1940s and 1950s. Later, a similar department was set up at Lovanium University in the Belgian Congo (now Zaïre).[9]

The general characteristic of these immediate pre-independence years was the linking of most forms of adult education with political and social change. The whole colonial period was marked by the growth of many new institutions of adult education; these are described in Chapter 3.

After West African states had achieved independence, the decade of the 1960s was marked by a heavy emphasis on formal school education and individual competition for qualifications, in line with the general goal of economic growth in a capitalist framework. The various states also became members of Unesco (the United Nations Educational, Scientific and Cultural Organization) and were influenced by (as well as being part of) a new trend towards work-oriented functional literacy. In 1964, Unesco adopted an Experimental World Literacy programme; nine out of the original twelve projects were in Africa, including Guinea and Mali, while Unesco also supplied experts to a number of countries, including Senegal and Togo and the People's Republic of Congo, to help them design their own functional literacy schemes. Still greater diffusion of new ideas about literacy resulted from the foundation of the International Institute for Adult Literacy Methods in Teheran in 1968. More is said about literacy in Chapter 10.

In the 1970s it has become apparent that the hoped-for expansion of the school system is likely to be limited in most African countries (other than Nigeria) by the absence of adequate resources, and such countries have begun looking for other ways of spreading education in the population. The World Bank has publicized the idea of non-formal education and governments and other agencies have become interested in schemes to teach alternative technology and also to use correspondence and the mass media for the education of the public at comparatively small cost. A notable example of an organization using correspondence and other new methods to teach new techniques of farming, business and home management is the African Institute for Economic and Social Development (INADES), based in the Ivory Coast. Founded in 1963, by 1970 it had students in Burundi, Cameroon, Central African Republic (now Empire), Chad, People's Republic of Congo, Dahomey (now Bénin), Gabon, Mali, Niger, Rwanda, Senegal, Togo, Upper Volta, Zaïre, and Ethiopia (see also Chapter 8).

Adult education and development

After the limited progress and dependent relationships of colonial times, modern African states have naturally been eager for development. Large-scale plans were started to promote general economic growth and emphasis was placed on physical infrastructure (roads, telecommunications), greater industrialization and a larger gross domestic product.

Education was seen as an instrument for economic development. It could provide the manpower at all levels to increase output, by training people in the needed skills; and it could influence attitudes towards work, productivity, profit-making, etc. ('modernization'). Adult education was recognized as having a contribution to make towards economic development, since men and women could use their newly acquired knowledge at once, whereas years must pass before children reach the stage of using theirs.

The fact that adult education can have a speedier effect than school education is still recognized, but the type of effect now desired has changed in many Third World countries. They have come to question the conventional ideas of the 1960s on the best forms of development; and some African leaders in particular have stressed that the aim of development is to improve the life of human beings (as did President Nyerere in the speech quoted earlier in this chapter). 'Modernization' is now often seen as meaning 'Westernization' and as a brand of neo-colonialism.

According to R. Herbold Green, improvement of life requires the satisfaction of five main types of need:[10]

1 Personal consumer goods – food, clothing, housing
2 General access to such physical and social services as good water-supply, communications, preventive and curative medicine, and education
3 Physical, human and technological infra-structure and capacity necessary to produce those goods and services
4 Productive employment of individuals, families and communal units yielding high enough output and fairly distributed rewards so that they earn incomes sufficient to enable them to benefit from the supply of goods and services
5 Mass participation in decision-taking, including revision of plans, general strategy formulation, control of leadership, and also in the carrying out of decisions

From the point of view of adult education, the last three items are the challenging ones. How do we help people to *learn* how to produce and to use the goods and services? How do we *train* them for productive employment? How de we *educate* them to take part in decision-making; that is, to control their own economic and social destiny, so that they share in the wealth they produce? The last is the most difficult, but without it the rest becomes meaningless.

If adult education can rise to these challenges, it can make a crucial contribution to social, economic and political development of a kind that will benefit individuals as well as communities. It can do this if it is seen as part of the overall national provision for lifelong education and also as part of the overall national social and economic plan. But it must be admitted that, until now, adult education has often been separated from the school system, has also been compartmentalized within itself (agricultural extension officers may not see that they have anything in common with literacy workers) and has not been taken into sufficient account by social and economic planners.

Perhaps this is because professional adult educators have been too burdened with day-to-day worries (counting the numbers on the register, preparing new teaching material, organizing programmes) to think of the broader implications of what they are doing. *But the whole point of adult education is to help people to contribute to, promote and participate in national development.* It is not a fringe activity: adult educators have to take account of national goals, national needs and the system of planning. An attempt by professional adult educators to do this was made (uniquely so far) in Nigeria, when a task-force of the Nigerian National Council for Adult Education drew up a proposal for the integration of adult education into the Third National Development Plan, then in process of being framed.[11] The plan did allocate a good deal more money to adult education than the previous one and also accepted the proposal for a national Adult Education Development Centre.

It has been pointed out, however, that adult education cannot be planned simply in terms of the allocation of existing resources. If we believe it is a tool for change, part of that change may be the unlocking of new resources by enabling citizens cut off previously from development to contribute to it and push it forward. The new resources can in turn be particularly allocated to promote more adult education.

Adult education as a profession

We have mentioned the tasks of 'professional adult educators'. Who are they? And can we view adult education as a profession?

First, let us distinguish between an **educator** and an **educationist**. The former is a practitioner, the latter a theoretician, and while many people who theorize about an activity were once practitioners themselves, this is not always the case. A professor of medicine will be a person qualified to practice medicine, but a scholar who writes about the history of medicine may not be so qualified at all! So not everyone who talks or writes about adult education is an **adult educator** (though he would be an **adult educationist**). When I talk about an adult educator, then, I mean someone who practises adult education.

Secondly, a profession comes into being as people who practise an occupation requiring special skills work out a common basis for training, common interests and common standards. It has a unity, an ethic and an accepted basis for preparation.

Until fairly recently in West Africa, persons who started practising adult education came to it from a background of some other form of education (usually training as a school-teacher) and had to learn by trial and error. The coming of universities brought about the beginnings of professionalization. Those who practised adult education at university level (i.e. those men and women working in extra-mural departments and continuing education centres) began to formulate systematic requirements for adult education work and started to run *ad hoc* training programmes, such as the courses for its own part-time tutors run by the University of Ghana from its beginning, and the extension method seminars organized by the University of Ibadan in the late 1950s and early 1960s. In the same period, voluntary agencies and governments also began to establish training institutions to serve their own needs. There is as yet no complete scheme of adult education training in any West African country, but there is systematic university-level training in Nigeria and Ghana, and sub-university training institutions exist in Ghana, Nigeria and Sierra Leone. It is slowly coming to be recognized by employers that training as a school-teacher is not an adequate preparation for adult educational work.

It is also recognized that a core of full-time professionals has to be supported by a large number of part-time tutors of adults and organizers of adult learning programmes. This is because of the very diversified subject-matter of adult education, so that not all teaching needs could be met by full-time workers, as well as because of limited resources. It is assumed by governments and other agencies that many of the part-time helpers in adult educational work will be school-teachers; and it therefore becomes logical that school-teachers should be introduced to adult education principles and methodology during their training. It has been accepted as national policy in Nigeria that this should be done, and thus the two types of educational professional should be brought closer together.

What is the main work of a professional adult educator? Since the central activity of adult education is *learning*, an adult educator's main job is to help learning to take place. He may do this through some sort of teaching, through programme-planning, through organization and, most commonly, through a combination of the three. The components of his work are thus **pedagogic** (to do with teaching), **facilitative** (making adult learning easy) and **administrative** (doing the necessary planning and organizing). Adult education training has to take account of all three aspects.

If *preparation and training* have brought the beginnings of professionalism, what about the development of *common interests* and *common standards*? The former have been helped by the existence of international professional bodies to which West African adult educators often belong. These include: the International Council for Adult Education (based in Canada); the International Congress of University Adult Education (based at present in Nigeria); and the African Adult Education Association (with its permanent office in Kenya). All these provide professional strengthening through conferences and meetings, journals and newsletters. The most developed national body of this type in West Africa is the Nigerian National Council for Adult Education (see Appendix 1 for address).

No West African country as yet has a professional body recognized by the government, and thus there is little dialogue on the setting of rates of pay, conditions of service or some form of registration for practitioners. An adult education organism analogous to the various national medical councils or institutes of architects would enable agreements to be reached on conditions for adult education workers.

Little has as yet been done about *common standards*; that is, a common ethic. In general, adult educators would probably agree that it is immoral for an evening class tutor not to turn up at the agreed time, or for a correspondence college to take a student's money without supplying the lessons, but there is no agreed code and thus no particular set of sanctions. This predicament is also linked to the absence of a national body with government recognition and a register of adult educators; they are the conditions for professional discipline.

There has still also been little discussion of some of the deeper issues, such as how far adult education is a form of social engineering, or how one draws a line between 'public enlightenment' and propaganda. Conferences and publications avoid them and stick to the beaten tracks of methodology, institutions and national comparison. A full-grown profession is characterized by its members' belief in it and readiness to spell out its basic philosphy.

Adult education is, then, a profession still in the making. Perhaps some of the readers of this book will be able to establish it more firmly in the future.

Notes and references

1. See Appendix 2 for the full text
2. Paul Lengrand, *An Introduction to Lifelong Education* (Unesco, 1970)
3. Cyril Houle, *The Design of Education* (San Francisco: Jossey-Bass, 1972), p. 229
4. *Ibid.*

5. J. K. Nyerere, *Declaration of Dar es Salaam: Liberated Man – the Purpose of Development* (opening address to the International Conference on Adult Education and Development, Dar es Salaam, 1976), *Convergence*, vol. 9, no. 4 (1976), pp. 9–10

6. J. O. Hunwick, 'A new source for the biography of Ahmad Baba al-Tinbukti (1556–1627), *Bulletin of the School of Oriental and African Studies*, vol. 27, no. 3 (1964), pp. 586–7

7. J. C. Taylor, 'Journal at Onitsha', in S. Crowther and J. C. Taylor, *The Gospel on the Banks of the Niger* (Dawson, 1968) and S. Adjai Crowther, *Experiences with Heathens and Mohammedans in West Africa* (SPCK, 1892). In his article, Taylor gives an example of this method of teaching: 'I went around two squares and gave a lecture about the Creation to some young men. . . .' (pp. 253–4)

8. K. A. B. Jones-Quartey, *History, Politics and the Early Press* in Ghana (Accra/Tema: Author and Afram Publications, 1975)

9. L. Bown, 'African universities and adult education', *Journal of the ICUAE*, vol. 9, nos. 1 and 2 (May 1972), pp. 67–84

10. R. H. Green, 'Adult education, basic human needs and integrated development planning', *Convergence*, vol. 9, no. 4 (1976), pp. 45–60

11. Nigerian National Council for Adult Education (NNCAE), *Proposal for a National Adult Education Programme for Inclusion in the Third National Development Plan* (Lagos: NNCAE, 1973)

Suggestions for further reading

Bown, Lalage. 'The education of adults in African societies', in R. Jolly (ed.), *Education in Africa: Research and Action*. EAPH, Nairobi, 1969

Freire, Paulo. *Pedagogy of the Oppressed*. Penguin, 1972

Hall, B., and Remtulla, K. (eds). *Adult Education and National Development*. Proceedings of the Third Conference of the African Adult Education Association, Dar es Salaam, 1971. East African Literature Bureau, Nairobi, 1973

Lewis, J. L. (ed.). *Phelps–Stokes Reports on Education in Africa*. Oxford University Press, 1970

Okedara, J. T. 'Developing an adult education profession in Nigeria', *ICAUAE Journal*, vol. 13, no. 3 (November 1974), pp. 28–34

Prosser, Roy. *Adult Education for Developing Countries*. East African Publishing House, Nairobi, 1967

2   The adult learner
Christian R. Abiose Cole

Introductory

The success of any programme of education for adults will depend on the degree to which the learners are made central to the process. Effective teaching must start from consideration of the needs and interests of the learner. An adult educator should therefore make himself conversant with the psychology of adult learning and establish from it the conditions which will enable the adult learner to benefit from an educative experience. What follows is an attempt to outline some of those conditions. We discuss first the inter-relation of social and individual educational needs, and then observe characteristics of adult learners. The main emphasis in the rest of the chapter is on conditions promoting adult learning, with practical hints on effective motivation, teaching and learning.

Adult learning needs: the social context

In Chapter 1 we have seen that adulthood has a social as well as a personal dimension. An adult is viewed as 'a responsible home-maker, worker and member of society'. In West Africa, he or she is living in and expected to participate in a developing society.

The need for educating adults to play meaningful roles in their societies became pressing after the achievement of political independence and the consequent need for rapid changes in the social and economic structure. Since these changes are for the benefit of the people, it is desirable to involve the mass of citizens in the direction and control of them. It is thus necessary that citizens should know and understand the implications, the arguments for and against, of such changes.

'The first function of adult education is to inspire both a desire for change and an understanding that change is possible.'[1] There is also the need to learn how to participate in and influence the decision-making processes.

In the particular context of Africa, the chance of many citizens to contribute to nation-building, in either family or village, in productive employment or in civic matters is, regrettably, hampered by illiteracy and poor basic education. It is reasonable, therefore, to expect adult educators to endeavour constantly to reach the poorest and least educationally privileged members of society, bearing in mind that without their involvement society will progress, if at all, at a very slow rate.

In the world context, very rapid social and technological change demands constant up-dating and renewing of skills and knowledge for all, to enable new techniques and new attitudes to be absorbed. This is not just a matter of improving the individual's position in society, important though that is; it is a matter of enabling his whole society to survive.

Against this background, the adult educator may view the learners in their various social roles and provide for their needs within those roles and at the various stages of their lives – as young adults, middle-aged adults and elders. Common social roles of interest to adult educators are those of spouse, parent, home-maker, worker, union or cooperative member, neighbour, friend, church member, citizen, club or association member.[2]

Individual learning needs

The implication of all this is that the learning needs of an individual will vary according to his social role. An adult newly arrived at working age will be obsessed with learning how to make a living; a woman with young children will be interested in domestic matters and in the children's education; a member of a church choir will be interested in music.

The individual person, however, has needs *as an individual*. He or she has a need for what is sometimes termed *self-fulfilment*, sometimes *self-realization* (or self-actualization). Some adults may wish to develop skills in their work which will enable them to excel, or other skills from which they may derive satisfaction and recognition, such as in a sport or in a domestic practice like sewing or cooking. Some may wish to enhance their social standing, to gain a sense of importance or to cultivate new social relationships, and feel the need for learning how to achieve such ends. Others, who may have lost some educational opportunities in the past, may feel incomplete as persons unless they fill what they see as gaps in their knowledge and education. Yet others may want to learn how to make constructive use of their leisure time.

Add to all these the objectives of those who wish to become better-informed citizens, as well as those who simply find a creative stimulus in the act of learning. It will be seen that individuals may be interested in learning for a very wide variety of reasons, many of which are personal. How can we meet their needs and harness their interests?

Characteristics of the adult learner

There are still people (including some would-be learners themselves) who, while recognizing the needs we have mentioned, assume that they cannot be met because older persons find it difficult to learn. They say: 'You can't teach an old dog new tricks.' Modern research has disproved this. It has been shown that, given suitable conditions, older persons can go on learning so long as they are not senile, that they may actually be better than younger persons at grasping the implications of certain types of information and that persons who have kept on learning throughout life perform better than those who have ceased to make any conscious learning effort.

Physiological changes

There need be no apprehension about the fact that, with advancing years, the adult goes through a process of physiological change, which may result in his sight and hearing becoming less acute and in some loss in physical dexterity. In addition to what we have just said about adults' continuing capacity to learn, it has been observed that adults also have a capacity for making adjustments to compensate for physical defects, e.g. a person who has become long-sighted (which often happens in middle age) will sit at the back of the classroom.

Nevertheless an adult educator must bear in mind that some of the learners (his students) may have problems of sight or hearing; and he must find ways of overcoming them. For instance, a slightly deaf person can be helped to make up for any part of the programme which he has missed by a written handout or a summary on the chalkboard. Deliberate attempts must also be made to minimize the strain on those with weak eyesight by ensuring a well-lighted classroom and good visual aids (see Chapter 7); printed matter should be clear and in appropriate type. Such efforts to assist adult learners to overcome physiological problems should of course be accompanied by advice, if necessary, on how to deal with their personal physical difficulties. Very often, medical treatment can help, and they should be advised to consult the appropriate specialist. For instance, in rural areas it may be necessary to counsel individuals on what clinics are available within reasonable travelling distance, or even simply to supply the address of an optician's where eyes can be tested, or of a chemist's shop where a solvent can be bought for wax in the ears. As we keep suggesting in this chapter, an adult educator's role includes that of a counsellor and friend.

Sociological changes

As we have seen, an adult goes through life in a series of changing social roles. For example, 'a person in the social role of a father is expected to behave in certain ways as his children grow up, and he learns to expect this behaviour of himself '.[3] In West Africa, as a person grows older, he will command greater respect, from his children and from other members of society.

It is necessary for an adult educator to make allowance for the social situation of the learners. A middle-aged person who is a grandfather, a councillor, or the owner of a large house, will not take kindly to being treated without the deference such a role entitles him to. This should be obvious, but very many people drop out from literacy classes or agricultural extension projects because persons younger than themselves treat them as schoolchildren.

Further, as has been implied earlier, adult education programmes may usefully be designed to help persons perform more effectively in their various roles. Young adults will respond to programmes which help them to start on a career or to set up in married life. Persons with families will want to learn about the relationships between parents and children and about problems in their children's education. Middle-aged adults will seek to know how to handle the difficulties of adolescent children. Elders will want help in overcoming handicaps of old age and disengagement and in taking advantage of additional leisure.

Psychological changes

It must be confessed that many adults' attitude toward formal learning is one of indifference. They may have painful memories of school, they may think that education has no relevance to their lives, they may be afraid that they have lost the capacity to learn. **The first challenge to the adult educator is thus to stir their interest in learning**, to motivate them. This is discussed later in more detail.

The interested adult learner brings to learning two great assets, which a schoolchild does not have. The first is *experience*. In some cases, adult learners may have more practical experience than a young tutor whose knowledge of a subject is gained from a book. Any adult educator must therefore take account of the learners' background and build on their experience. It is useful to find out as much as possible about the learners early on in an adult education course or programme and throughout to link teaching with their own accumulated knowledge and experience.

This is not to say that what the learners have taken in over the years should be accepted without question, since

> in psychological usage, what is learned is not necessarily correct or helpful. . . . In addition to learning appropriate modes of behaviour, it is possible also to learn bad habits, incorrect patterns of speech, unfavourable attitudes and inappropriate skills.[4]

Adults may thus have to unlearn some prejudices and habits, but will certainly resist doing so if their point of view and background are ignored. The point is that the tutor must be on the alert to use the learners' mature experience and help them to sift from it what is most valuable. At all times, **learning, to be effective, must be centred on experience**.

A second asset which many adults have, and which is partially the result of experience, is a developed power of *deductive reasoning*. They are very often better placed than the younger generation to draw inferences and follow a discussion through to a conclusion. This does not mean that they may not often be illogical or draw inferences which greater knowledge will show to be false; but their long habit of deduction is something of which an adult educator may make use. For one example, logic is a subject which can be very rewardingly taught to adults, as work in Tanzania and Zambia has shown; the title of such courses is usually a descriptive one and not just the forbidding word, logic. Most importantly, adult learning programmes should give every opportunity to learners to exercise their reasoning faculties and to be helped 'to see the point' for themselves; they should not be expected to learn mechanically or by rote. **Learning, to be effective, must be based on the adults' use of reasoning**.

Further, as we have already seen, adult learners have their own preoccupations. They come to adult education with all the responsibilities of their various social roles, as we have mentioned, and are concerned with specific problems encountered in these roles. They are not primarily interested in the academic's classification of aspects of life into disciplines, useful (indeed essential) as these are for the academic; they want solutions to dilemmas which may cut across these disciplines. In short, **learning, to be effective, must centre on problems**.

In any teaching–learning exercise, there comes a point at which the learners have to rely on *memory*. One disadvantage that older persons do have over younger ones is that their so-called 'short-term memory' is more easily disturbed. **Short-term memory** involves the receiving, retaining and using of information within a very short period of time; for instance a student at a lecture taking notes has to absorb the speaker's comment, hold it in logical order in his memory and then write it down in a digested form. Many people find that as they grow older, their short-term memory is less effectual, apparently because it is more subject to interference by other happenings in between receiving the information and making use of it. For instance, a young and an old policeman would both be able to remember and reel off a list of motor-car numbers, but if they are both asked to check someone's licence and then write down the list of numbers, the chances are that the older policeman will have a less accurate recollection of them (and even may have forgotten them entirely).

In providing for adult learning, we have to bear this difficulty in mind and reduce to as little as possible the amount of straight memorizing. It cannot be avoided altogether, particularly in some subjects (e.g. language learning), but it should always be supported with such memory-aids as instructional diagrams, charts or posters (see Chapter 7). In short, **learning, to be effective, must not be made dependent on large amounts of memorization.**

Conditions promoting adult learning

In studying the learner, we have already been led to some conclusions about suitable conditions for learning; let us now systematize these conclusions. A useful list of conditions has been made by Harry L. Miller;[5] although he was working from North American experience, his list is relevant to adult educational practices in West Africa.

The learner must be adequately motivated to change his behaviour. He must find interest, enjoyment, relevance and use in what he is learning, and at the end he must be himself convinced that what he has learned needs action (as the Americans say, he must 'internalize' it). In the first place, the tutor must stimulate and capture interest; he must then maintain it at such a pitch that the learners will accept the difficulties of a subject as well as its entertaining side. To do this, he must make an effort to meet the learners' need for security, recognition and self-respect, as well as for novel experience; this means working within their level of achievement and giving them a sense of progress.

We talk later about teacher/learner relations, but let us remind ourselves here that a friendly atmosphere and free exchange between tutor and students (and among students) is an important aid to motivation.

The learner must be aware of inadequacy in his present knowledge, skill or behaviour. Adult education is very often concerned with changing established habits and learners may become defensive when they are faced with this. Motivation must be harnessed to 'internalization', and learners must be guided to see any personal deficiency in combination with the means of remedying it. Self-righteous condemnation of beliefs or attitudes by counsellors or tutors will only stiffen learners' resistance.

The prospective adult learner may need guidance in choice of a course of study; at this stage he or she can be given a sense of the need for change. Later, when a course or programme has begun, learners must be given an early chance to express themselves freely about their own view of their present behaviour and whether they have any wish to change it.

The learner must have a clear picture of what gains in knowledge or skill or what changes in behaviour he will achieve. The captive docile pupil of primary school and the competitive, highly motivated secondary or university student can be induced to do a great deal of work at something whose outcome he may not immediately foresee. But an adult student wants a sense of direction. The tutor needs to plan a programme together with the learners, so that they have a joint view of its objectives, which should be spelled out as clearly and in as much detail as possible.

The learner must have opportunities to put his new knowledge, skill or behaviour into practice. Because adult students do not have a great deal of spare time, practical work is often neglected. And yet it is essential in all education, as we well know. Even if practice sessions are short, they should form part of every programme, and of each section of a programme.

The learner must have reinforcement of newly learned behaviour. Any adult following a systematic course of study needs to be kept aware of his own progress. It is useful to have recapitulation exercises, individual (but non-competitive) tests and general evaluation at each stage. These relate to the work of the tutor as well as the learner and should be used by him as an indicator of the relative adequacy or inadequacy of his goals and methods. Chapter 5 deals with the question of evaluation in depth.

The learner needs the support of a sequence of relevant and appropriate study materials. The comments we have made about adults' interest in problems and their background of experience of life make it plain that materials used in schools and universities are not appropriate to the adult learner. For instance, a school English reader may use a vocabulary about sport including such words as 'games-mistress', 'hockey', 'tennis'; for an adult post-literacy group learning English, we would need words like 'football', 'boxing', 'referee'.

Conditions for communication between persons

We have gradually, in this chapter, slipped into a view of learners as *students*, or persons undertaking a sustained programme of learning, and we have been assuming a *teacher/tutor* of some kind ready to help them learn. We must at this point remind ourselves that there are more and more opportunities today for the so-called **independent learner** and that not all learning is face-to-face. We will have more to say about the independent learner later in this chapter; Chapter 8 takes up the methods of distance teaching. But, while all learning is an independent act of the learner, he is brought to this act by some form of communication – whether with a tutor, a counsellor, a writer or a broadcaster. It is thus appropriate for us to look, not only at conditions for learning, but also at conditions for communication. We shall see that some of the latter are closely related to the former. Conditions for communication include:

An atmosphere of mutual trust and confidence. Mere transmission of information and ideas may not evoke any response unless there is a good human relationship. One of the principal tasks of a communicator is to build up a relationship of mutual respect and esteem with those to whom he desires to pass on his 'message'.

Familiarity with the ways of life of the recipients. Any communicator must make a deliberate effort to learn about the beliefs, value systems, customs and culture of the persons with whom he hopes to communicate. This will enable him to achieve that relevance to their own experience which we have already seen is necessary for learning. Even if a communicator comes from the same ethnic group as those with whom he is communicating, he may have a different viewpoint because he has more education or has travelled more or lives in a town and not a village; he thus has to make a conscious appraisal of the traditions and outlook of the learners.

A clear perception of the problem. We have said that for effective learning, the educational process must focus on the learners' problems. One barrier to effective communication is that the communicator may have a perception of the problem at variance with his listeners' or readers' perception. A public health communicator, for instance, may see a village's main problem as one of nutrition, whereas the villagers themselves may be preoccupied by the number of colds caught by their children. The communicator must share the villagers' worry over colds and use it to arouse understanding that a good and balanced diet can build up resistance to colds and allied ailments. A communicator will be most effective in changing attitudes when he represents a position not too different from that of the recipients.

An appropriate setting and appropriate methods. We have mentioned the need for comfortable physical conditions for learning. Comfort is not sufficient. The setting and methods must be appropriate. A former Community Development Officer in Ghana has reported that she felt much of her work was undermined because she had used a classroom: as a result the women with whom she was trying to communicate had a mental picture related to class, but not in any way to home.

Circumstances surrounding any demonstration in class very commonly made it much easier ... to use apparatus unlike that available in the home. For instance, if drinking water had to be boiled, a Mass Education Assistant was obliged to use a metal saucepan in class, because an earthenware vessel would have wasted time. Learners who did not possess a similar utensil were left to consider whether they could do the same thing (more slowly perhaps) without using a metal saucepan. But they did not usually consider that at all. More usual reactions were:

1 'I have no metal saucepan; I cannot boil drinking water at home.'
2 'I want a metal saucepan.' (*Not* 'I want to boil drinking water.')

Very often, women who react like that are blamed for stupidity. In fact, inappropriate use of class method must bear the blame.[6]

Problems of communication

The last quotation is a useful warning of the problems in communication. Something clear to us may be misunderstood or perceived quite differently by others. A British Council film about nursery schools was once shown in East Africa. One of the children in it was left-handed, and many persons who saw the film came away with the impression that nursery schools taught children to be left-handed (and must therefore be bad institutions).

Sometimes a means of communication successful with one group of people may fail lamentably with another. This is particularly true of visual communication. In New Zealand, a successful health education poster designed to encourage young adults to brush their teeth showed a whale jumping out of water in pursuit of a tube of toothpaste. The poster was later reproduced for use in Fiji, and the response was immediate and overwhelming – Fiji fishermen sent a rush call to New Zealand for large quantities of this wonderful fish-bait![7]

We must also remember that a message transmitted through several persons may end up distorted. There is an old exercise to test this, which may be tried by any group of trainee adult educators. A message is given to one person who whispers it to his neighbour and so on. The last person announces what he has heard and his message is compared with the original. A message which started: 'He lay in his bed till afternoon' has been known to end up as: 'She sat up straight and ate a bun.' This is a salutary lesson in some of the difficulties in verbal communication.

Some practical hints and suggestions to promote adult learning

We have seen that learning needs a suitable setting, that it should start from the learners' experience and the problems which worry them and that we have to take account of physiological and psychological changes in adults and the social roles they play. We have also seen that to communicate effectively with anyone, we have to establish mutual trust, and to start from a familiarity with their cultural background as well as a clear understanding of the problem as they perceive it.

The following hints are an attempt to translate these precepts into practice. Although we may be talking of a classroom setting, we must constantly remember that many adult educational activities are less formal (see Chapter 1).

1 It is essential that you as tutor/communicator have a good grasp of the subject. You aren't pretending to be a know-all, and can sensibly admit ignorance of some aspects, but unless you have some confidence in transmitting knowledge and ideas, you will not inspire confidence in others. *It is a fatal mistake to assume that less-educated persons can be taught from a background of limited knowledge*; they often ask more searching questions than the better educated person.

2 Be sure that you are aware of the barriers to communication which may be encountered and that you have equipped yourself with knowledge of various communication methods, including some proper training in audio-visual aids.

3 Avoid rigidity in content and method. With regard to content, plan your programme in such a way that you are not committed to a set time for each item, but can linger over subject-matter which the learners are particularly interested in or challenged by. Be ready to add to or alter the programme if the learners clearly need this.

With regard to method, remember that the lecture is only one means of communication and not always the most effective. By itself it may not be sufficient to stimulate learners' memories or change their behaviour.

4 Nobody learns much from a single experience and no two people learn in the same way. Use several different methods in combination to encourage learning.

5 Know your students. Learn as much as you can in advance about their community; and when you meet them find out something about their occupations, life-histories, etc. This not only helps to establish a friendly atmosphere; it also enables you to incorporate their experience into the learning exercise.

6 Ensure that the learners participate at all stages in the programme. Do not assume that you know what will be good for them to learn (this is what happened in colonial times!). Involve the

learners in planning your programme so that you work out together the main objectives and they have a clear idea of how much time they will need to achieve them. If you are committed to a course of study with a syllabus, consult them on it; if they are diffident, feeling they don't know enough about the possibilities, present them with several alternatives for discussion, so that there is some element of choice.

7 The learners' experience must be referred to and built on and its relevance shown. A group should learn from each other. If you are talking about keeping poultry, get a description of what happened from the person who has lost several birds from Newcastle disease. Then follow up with a discussion on the causes, prevention and cure of various diseases common in the area.

8 Many adults enter upon a course of study with a lack of confidence in their ability to make the grade. The slightest suggestion of failure may trigger off their retreat. You need to do all that is humanly possible to prove to the learner that he or she *can* learn.

9 Adults resent being treated like children and if they are treated like school pupils they cannot give of their best. Avoid admitting children to adult classes (this often happens with literacy classes and usually results in the older persons abandoning the class).

10 The learners must feel free to express themselves and must be encouraged to do so. It is not enough to give a lecture and say at the end, 'Any questions?' A dialogue must be established at the start.

11 Adult education is usually a voluntary activity. Adult learners are under no compulsion to participate in a programme and they come to a class or course (or listen to a radio series) at the expense of alternative uses for their leisure time (going to a pub or a football match or staying at home to chat with friends). Help the learner to see adult education as a good way of spending his or her time by making the course lively and entertaining as well as clearly useful. If a participant in a programme does decide to leave, he may not say so because he may not wish to cause offence; on the other hand, his absence may not be due to a decision to drop out. He may be ill or have had a quarrel with a fellow class member, or have taken time out to get married. An adult educator should try to make contact with any apparent drop-out to find out the cause.

12 As adult learners are usually workers with family and community commitments, it is not realistic to expect them to undertake lengthy assignments or 'home-work'. Such tasks should be given in short units.

13 Include plenty of practical sessions in your programme, so that learners may be convinced of what they have learnt.

Learner–teacher relationships

Trust between teacher and learner is crucial to the creation of a genuine learning experience. One can even suggest further that there should be the same kind of relationship of mutual respect and confidence among the learners themselves.

It is often remarked that in an adult class of twelve students and a tutor, there are thirteen learners in the class. This must be so, since no one can credibly encourage others to go on learning in adulthood unless he is obviously ready to do it himself. In a situation where the kind of rapport described above exists, the tutor has submerged his identity as a teacher and is identified with the learners, playing the role of a guide through the programme while at the same time learning from the experiences of all the participants.

By his training and discipline, the tutor is more capable of directing the educational activity towards the predetermined goals. To do this unobtrusively, he encourages the spirit of inquiry and independent initiative among the students. He must be prepared to listen with patience and understanding, to share learners' problems and sympathize with their perplexities, and to give them credit for any new ideas, techniques or information which emerge from discussion.

It will be seen that the roles of an adult educator in relation to the learners are many and varied. He is among other things a planner, a mediator, a compromiser, a counsellor, a social worker and a facilitator. He plans the curriculum, together with his students, and organizes their programme; he is expected to mediate and help to effect a compromise when there is disagreement or tension among a group of learners; students go to him with their educational and personal problems for advice; and he is deeply concerned with the problems of his and their environment. Lastly, as a facilitator of learning, he is the resource in the hands of the learners. He is expected to simplify complex matters and make the whole process of learning as painless and enjoyable as possible.

If this sounds as if he is to be superhuman, it is not meant to. But adult education is not just a matter of erudition; it requires certain human qualities. Above all, the adult educator needs to have a profound respect for human dignity and a faith in human capacity for learning. He needs to have patience and tolerance in the face of frustrations. He must have a capacity for leadership and at the same time be an exemplar of intellectual humility. He needs to be courteous; if, for instance, he is late for a class, he should offer an apology and explanation. He himself is at all times ready to continue to learn. Finally, he must have enthusiasm for learning as such and for the subjects he is helping others to master.

Notes and references

1. J. K. Nyerere, Address to the Tanzania National Assembly on the occasion of the five year development plan (Dar es Salaam: Government Printer, 1964)

2. R. J. Havighurst, 'Changing status and roles during life cycle: significance for adult education', in W. H. Burns (ed.), *Sociological Backgrounds of Adult Education*

3. *Ibid.*

4. Gary Dickinson, 'Learning processes in ABE', in W. M. Brooke (ed.), *Adult Basic Education* (Toronto: New Press, 1972)

5. H. L. Miller, *Teaching and Learning in Adult Education* (New York: Macmillan, 1966)

6. J. Gordon, 'Communicating with women: classes or other means?', *Community Development Journal*, no. 1 (January 1966)

7. P. Du Sautoy, 'Can we communicate?', *Community Development Journal*, no. 1 (January 1966)

Suggestions for further reading

Eisenson, J. *The Psychology of Communication*. Appleton-Century-Crofts, 1973

Kidd, J. R. *How Adults Learn*. revised ed. Association Press, New York, 1973

Knowles, M. S. *The Modern Practice of Adult Education: Andragogy vs. Pedagogy*. Association Press, New York, 1970

Kuhlen, R. G., ed. *Psychological Backgrounds of Adult Education*. CSLEA, Chicago, 1963

Rogers, Jennifer. *Adults Learning*. Penguin, Harmondsworth, 1971

3 Structures of adult education in West Africa

E. Kwasi Ampene

Introductory

To begin with, what are 'structures'? A working definition was
adopted by a Unesco-sponsored seminar in 1975, at Nairobi, on
'Structures of adult education in developing countries, with special
reference to Africa':

The term 'structures' embraces several facets. It refers to the various functions which together constitute the total framework within which the system of adult education operates. It thus includes the role of central government, and relationships between the various sectors of government, both horizontally and vertically. The term includes the place of local government in adult education, and also the position of the non-governmental organisations. Structures, however, embraces more than all these, for it also includes the essential services which are required to ensure that the purpose behind the framework is accomplished.[1]

This broad definition should remind us that some adult educational structures are inherited from the past. In West Africa especially, circumstances impel us to a study of *traditional structures*. Despite the signs of technological, social and economic change typical of the twentieth century, most people still live in a way not too different from that of their ancestors, respectful of tradition and with horizons in some measure limited by illiteracy. The villagers who use plastic buckets and over whose heads fly the great international aeroplanes, are still participants in social arrangements and institutions which have been built up and tested through many generations.

The success of agricultural extension and of development programmes in nutrition, health and literacy will depend largely on how effectively workers in these fields can make use of traditional institutions such as chieftaincy, age groups, youngmen's associations, etc., to communicate their ideas to the people. Indeed, no community development officer in West Africa worth his salt will ignore the importance of the traditional structures in his work with the people.

Furthermore, a study of traditional arrangements for adult education provides a useful background for understanding the failures or successes of modern structures of adult education, and the extent to which some of the non-indigenous structures have succeeded in adapting themselves to meet changing needs.

Also, in considering the various modern structural arrangements as they exist today in West Africa, one has to bear in mind the fact that adult education in the modern context has been moulded by complex factors of history such as Islam, Christianity, education and nationalist aspirations, and by the interaction or otherwise that has taken place between these major factors of social change and traditional structures of adult education.

Therefore, this chapter will first mention some features of the traditional arrangements, already outlined in Chapter 1, that West Africans had and still have for lifelong *socialization*; and by that is meant learning social norms for adjustment, earning a livelihood, preparing oneself for an important traditional office, knowing how to 'walk with the gods', etc. Second, attention will be given to the introduction and development of foreign structures of adult education and new institutional arrangements that have developed as a result of modernization. The support of these institutions and structures in terms of financing, research and staffing will also be discussed. Finally, there will be a section on cooperation with international agencies.

Traditional structures of adult education

Since adult education or socialization is part and parcel of the total social, political and economic framework of any society, one finds, in West Africa, traditional arrangements made for the education of the adult to prepare him for the different roles in society which he may play. It would be a time-consuming exercise to describe in detail the various educational procedures in traditional West African societies, and any reader wishing to acquaint himself with some of these customs is advised to consult anthropological books on West African cultures. From the brief outline already given in Chapter 1 one may make certain generalizations:

a) The concept of adult education, taken as meaning learning new skills and new ideas to be able to adjust to one's environment, is not new to West Africa, as indeed arrangements for lifelong learning exist and are still practised by many West African communities.

b) Generally, learning basic skills and *mores* is not organized in traditional West African societies and is therefore informal, and takes place within the family, lineage and other social groups.

c) More specific skills such as those of craftsmen and medicine-men, and also special knowledge pertaining to important traditional offices such as that of a chief, are learned in an organized manner or in a non-formal way of continuing study alongside the business of earning a livelihood.

d) It is important for the adult educator to know the existing structure or arrangements in his area of operation since the traditional culture is still a living entity and the majority of West African peoples can best be reached with adult education programmes that follow traditional channels or structures of communication.

The introduction and development of modern adult education structures

Structures for learning political adjustment for traditional authorities

The contact between West Africa and Western Europe through the firm establishment of colonial governments early in the nineteenth century meant that the people of West Africa, willy-nilly, had to learn new ways of doing things. The new political, social and economic order required new knowledge and types of behaviour for a successful adjustment to the situation. For instance, chiefs had to learn to cooperate with the colonial administration and to accept a central government authority which, in some cases, notably in French-speaking Africa, inter-fered drastically with the chiefs' traditional authority. Where powerful chiefs challenged or resisted the new political authority, they met the might of colonial forces which were technologically superior. For instance, the kingdoms of Ashanti and Dahomey were ruthlessly subdued by the British and French respectively. Thus, the lessons of accommodation were learned by traditional political authorities in West Africa when they came into contact with colonial systems. In French-speaking Africa, the chiefs and their people were compelled to accept a process of adaptation to French culture because a high premium was placed on the ability to speak and write the French language. English-speaking Africa had a pattern of indirect rule imposed on it, and the chiefs became the spokesmen of British colonial administration.

Learning to adjust to the new political order was both organized and informal. Houses of chiefs and legislative councils in English-speaking Africa were the classrooms, so to speak, where tradi-tional authorities received their lessons in the intricacies of colo-nial administration. Informally, too, they learned from observing how the colonial administration dealt with difficult chiefs and rewarded obedient ones.

Traditional authorities in French-speaking Africa were gener-ally discarded in the implementation of the policy of assimilation into French culture. The process of acculturation was carried to its logical conclusion for ambitious West Africans who acquired full citizenship and the right to sit in the French Assembly as representatives of their respective French overseas provinces.

The training of a colonial administrative cadre

The colonial administrative systems depended also on a cadre of African administrative assistants and clerks who had acquired their basic literary skills through formal schooling. The rest of their training consisted largely of informally acting as understudies to their bosses and, for a few promising ones, opportunities for further education and training in the metropolitan country were offered.

Training for agriculture, industry and commerce

The economic system introduced by colonial powers emphasized commerce, mining and the cultivation of crops such as cocoa, coffee and cotton, which were needed by the colonial administration for their home factories. Little or no interest was shown in the development of the staple foods of West Africa – maize, millet, yams, plantain, etc.; hence the structures of adult education which were developed to support the economic system were mainly for areas in which the colonial administration had an interest. It is therefore not surprising that extension services for the staple foods of West Africa are of very recent origin.

In support of commerce and industry, the early form of training which the commercial and industrial concerns (e.g. mining companies) developed was largely of the 'on-the-job training' type, which was carried out informally by understudying a superior officer, especially if the job was of administrative or marketing nature. Where specific skills had to be learned, e.g. motor mechanics or mining techniques, training was offered in apprentice schools. Employees earmarked for positions of responsibility were usually sent to the training institutions of the companies in their European countries of origin. It is true to say that in these programmes the companies provided training in a rather narrow sense of fitting a person to a particular job in the company.

As the colonial government hardly entered into the field of industry or commerce, there were generally no governmental institutions of training except the workshops of the railway systems, notably in Ghana and Nigeria. These workshops had training facilities for mechanics and middle-level skilled workmen. Workers in allied government-owned institutions such as the ports also received training in the railway workshops.

Structures for literacy and community development

Structures of adult education for literacy and of general adult education for community development in the early colonial period were created mostly by the churches and other voluntary organizations. Indeed, the missionaries in English-speaking Africa have the credit for introducing formal education on a comprehensive scale; they also instituted adult education classes in their churches to combat illiteracy and to teach elementary housecraft.

The efforts of missionaries to improve literacy were limited to their adult converts, and it must be pointed out that the high level of illiteracy in West Africa today is due to the fact that the colonial administrations showed little interest either in providing education for all children or in making illiterate adults literate. Nevertheless, the present efforts being made in West Africa to combat illiteracy are spearheaded by governments. The interest of governments in literacy was manifest in West Africa after the Second World War, in the early 1950s. In Ghana, the Department of Social Welfare and Community Development became the main government agency for combating illiteracy and educating rural adults generally. Similarly, in Nigeria, Sierra Leone and the Gambia, the British administration saw to it that a government department was assigned responsibility for literacy.

Literacy was not the only adult education activity that the government agencies charged with the responsibility for promoting rural development confined themselves to; they were even more active in general adult education for community development. For instance, in Ghana, the Department of Social Welfare and Community Development mobilized rural communities to undertake self-help projects such as the building of schools, community centres, feeder roads, improvements to water supply, and environmental sanitation. Women were organized into learning groups in such subjects as nutrition, baby-care, and health. The department also assisted various government departments, particularly ministries of health and agriculture, in their extension programmes. For instance, the success of the 'Swollen Shoot Campaign' in Ghana, in which cocoa farmers agreed to cut their diseased cocoa trees as the only means of arresting the spread of the swollen shoot disease, was due largely to the efforts of the Department of Social Welfare and Community Development. What has not been often emphasized in this success story is the close cooperation that existed between the modern structure of adult education, namely the Department of Social Welfare and

Community Development, and traditional institutions such as chieftaincy and *asafo* companies (traditional organization of the 'youngmen'). The women were usually reached through 'queen-mothers' and *'mmabaahene'* (leaders of the young women). It is worth emphasizing that no modern structure of adult education can reach the mass of people in West Africa, particularly in the rural areas where the majority of the people live, without seeking the cooperation and support of traditional institutions.

The development and emergence of adult education structures in the post-independence period

As might be expected, the independent states of West Africa have embarked on ambitious development programmes of economic and social reconstruction since they attained their independence. It is fair to say that it was not obvious to many governments in the beginning, as they formulated their development programmes of agricultural betterment, expansion in formal education, improvement in health facilities, extension of communications, etc., that they were in fact planning for human development and that, therefore, the most important factor in all their plans was the cultivation of the individual. However, there are now indications in almost all the West African countries that physical planning goes side by side with human development. For instance, Ghana's Five Year Development Programme (1975–80) recognizes the importance of the role of adult education agencies in training middle-level manpower. There are clearly stated expectations from agencies such as the National Vocational Training Institute, the Department of Social Welfare and Community Development, the Institute of Adult Education, etc., with regard to the development of the human resources. Again in Ghana, an integrated agricultural development programme for the Upper Region, financed by the World Bank and the British and Ghanaian governments to the tune of £25 million, has functional literacy and adult education as necessary components. The Mali Functional Literacy Project, which is part of a programme of rural development, shows the interest that is being taken in the cultivation of human resources in development.

Categories of adult education structure

Adult education structures which have emerged in West Africa to cope with development programmes may be classified into three main categories:

a) governmental organizations;
b) parastatal institutions;
c) voluntary agencies.

Governmental organizations

As development in West African countries is spearheaded by governments despite the fact that almost all West African economies are mixed, the majority of providing agencies in adult education are sponsored and fully funded by governments. The government-sponsored organizations may further be subdivided into two categories: a) those whose stated objectives are entirely educational and get funded primarily for that purpose, and b) those that are divisions within bigger organizations and are not funded directly by the government for adult education but get their funds as allocations from their parent-organizations.

Examples of the first category of governmental structures of adult education in West Africa are the usually well-identified departments of adult education in ministries of education (as in the case in Nigeria and Sierra Leone) or *Direction de l'Alphabétisation* in Senegal.

The second group of government-sponsored and funded organizations which provide adult education are departments within ministries or units within departments which have clearly stated goals of education that are subordinate or considered complementary to the main objectives of the parent ministry or department. For instance, ministries of agriculture are known to have extension units built into the programmes of the various departments in the ministry; thus a fisheries department or a cotton development board will have extension as part of its programme, but the amount of support it gets in terms of resources depends largely on what the director of the department thinks should go into extension. Although the importance of extension services to a successful implementation of agricultural programmes or effective health education is accepted, yet West African countries, as indeed most developing countries, do not allocate enough resources – trained personnel and supporting services such as transport – to their extension services to make them effective. Leaving the allocation of resources to a departmental head whose interests and sympathies may not be in extension or adult education is perhaps not the best approach. It must be recognized that extension services are as important as curative measures in the field of health, or the promotion of scientific agriculture.

Judging from the complaints of extension personnel and other adult education officers about lack of personnel and facilities, structures of adult education for extension in agriculture, health, etc., which are appendages to departments having education as a secondary objective, lack recognition and support for effective implementation of their work. What is regrettable is that their work is in areas of prime importance for development, notably agriculture and health.

Parastatal structures of adult education

These organizations also fall into two categories. The first includes those whose primary function is adult education, such as university departments/institutes/centres of extra-mural studies/adult education/continuing education, etc.

The university structures for adult education in English-speaking West Africa started in the British tradition of providing extra-mural opportunities for liberal education for adults who, for one reason or the other, would not be students in the university colleges established by Britain in her former colonies. The extra-mural classes provided a much-needed adult education service for the would-be leaders of the independent states. In Ghana, Nigeria and Sierra Leone, the university colleges made their impact on the general public through their extra-mural departments.

Now, these departments/institutes/centres of extra-mural studies/adult education/continuing education have added new programmes and adapted their approaches to meet the new challenges and tasks which they have had to undertake. For instance, the University of Lagos Centre for Continuing Education provides courses in skills such as management, accountancy and banking which are very much in demand in Lagos and its industrial environs. Similarly, the Institute of Adult Education of the University of Ghana has a variety of courses to meet the various needs of the educated adult population which is its main target clientèle. These courses include degrees of the University of Ghana; national seminars on topical issues, e.g. New Year Schools; General Certificate of Education courses (both by correspondence and face-to-face classes); short residential courses for particular interest groups, etc. Details on course offerings of the various university departments/institutes/centres responsible for adult education are generally available from the registrars of the universities.

The university departments have been criticized for concentrating on more formal types of courses – that is, undergraduate degree courses and even General Certificate of Education courses – and for providing them for the minority of students instead of exploring and researching into national issues of adult education. The major issue of adult education in West Africa is, of course, illiteracy. While generally university departments do not provide literacy classes as such, there are training programmes (short seminars, workshops) at places like the University of Nigeria, Nsukka; Ibadan University (which also runs full-time courses); Fourah Bay College (University of Sierra Leone); Institute of Adult Education, University of Ghana, etc., to support the work of the field officers in literacy. Certainly a lot more of university involvement in literacy problems should be encouraged; this might take the form of an interdisciplinary cooperation involving such departments as linguistics, languages and education.

The limitation of some university departments responsible for adult education is that arrangements for coordinating as many departments as possible in adult education do not exist in their universities. Thus, very often, there is no cooperation between the institute/department/centre responsible for adult education and extension, and other departments running their own extension programmes.

A second category of parastatal organizations includes those that make provision for adult education although that is not their primary objective. However, the organization may realize that it is necessary to provide an educational service if it is to achieve its declared objective. For instance, Social Security and National Insurance Trust of Ghana and the National Fire Service have education programmes as supplementary activities.

Funding of parastatal structures of adult education

A parastatal organization set up by an Act of Parliament or a decree usually gets its initial funding from the state, and if it is engaged in an occupation that brings in income, it is expected to be on its own financially as soon as possible. For instance, Ghana's Social Security and National Insurance Trust generates its own revenue and the allocation of resources for adult education depends largely on the discretion of its board. Some parastatal organizations that are hard pressed to generate enough revenue may not allocate enough resources to adult education, which is not their primary objective. Even training programmes for the personnel of these not-too-viable parastatal organizations may suffer from lack of adequate support.

Parastatal organizations such as university departments of extension or extra-mural studies may also fall into two categories as far as funding is concerned. First, there are those which are funded directly by the state through a kind of university grants committee. For instance, the Institute of Adult Education, University of Ghana, is funded directly by the Ghana government through the National Council for Higher Education. However, the institute is not the only university department enjoying this privilege; the National Council for Higher Education performs similar funding functions for about ten other institutes and schools in the university. Nevertheless, the advantage of this arrangement is that the Institute of Adult Education does not have to compete with other university departments for funding. But, if it should expect to continue receiving adequate support from the National Council for Higher Education, then there is the challenge of convincing the council members each year that it is doing a good job.

University departments of extension/extra-mural studies/adult education that have to compete with other departments for their allocation of a block grant given to the university have the problem of fighting the notion of marginality about adult education which still lingers in the minds of not an insignificant proportion of university dons. For instance, some professor of physics wishing to acquire an expensive item of equipment may not appreciate the request of the director of extra-mural studies for a substantial grant to buy books for his extra-mural library. 'Books for persons who are not students of the university?', the professor of physics might exclaim in bewilderment! Nevertheless, struggling with dons who may not yet be converts to the philosophy of adult education may not be unrewarding since there is the possibility that some day they may become supporters of the adult education movement.

Voluntary agencies

There is a wide range of purely voluntary organizations that provide adult education services to the people of West Africa. These agencies fall into two broad categories: first, those that provide an adult education service for profit; and second, those that provide the service for no monetary reward.

Voluntary agencies that provide adult education services for profit may be owned by indigenous people as well as by expatriate firms. The services provided range from vocational training for women in domestic science, especially sewing, to correspondence education for academic courses (General Certificate of Education and degree programmes) and professional studies in accountancy and secretaryship. Expatriate firms tend to offer the academic and professional courses while indigenous proprietors concentrate on vocational training.

Some of the vocational institutes, such as Mancell's Girls Vocational Institute in Ghana, specialize in preparing young women as modern home-makers, and provide literacy courses for illiterate students. Among the indigenous profit-making adult education structures are also numerous technical training places and workshops where fitters, carpenters, masons and other skilled persons are trained through a system of apprenticeship. This is a fascinating area for research with a view to improving the quality of instruction. Unfortunately, directories of adult education do not include information about these training places, but in the West African situation most skill-training takes place at these workshops. An attempt is being made in Ghana by the Institute of Adult Education and the Opportunities Industrialization Centre of Ghana (OIC) to organize the 'wayside fitters', as they are popularly called, into learning groups to improve upon their skills and methods.

The second broad category of voluntary agencies in West Africa embraces a multitude of non-profit-making institutions, both religious and secular, and also of indigenous and foreign origin. This group may be classified into *a*) those that have education as their primary objective, and *b*) agencies for whom education is a supplementary activity.

Among those that offer educational services as their primary function may be mentioned the Young Men's Christian Association and Young Women's Christian Association, and the Boy Scouts and Girl Guides movement, which are found in almost all West African countries. Even for such groups there is now emphasis on productive training and rural development.

An interesting agency in the category of voluntary non-profit-making organizations which have education as their primary objective is the People's Educational Association of Ghana (PEA). The main objectives of the PEA as stated in its constitution are:

a) to stimulate and satisfy the demand of the people for education in subjects they consider important for adult study; and particularly to provide opportunity for serious study and discussion for all those in Ghana who wish to understand the problems of their own society and to discuss these problems frankly and independently;

b) to work in association with other organizations for a system of education in Ghana that would provide for everyone opportunities for individual development, and thus fit all for the exercise of their social rights and responsibilities.

The PEA started as an association of extra-mural students and other persons interested in the work of the Department of Extramural Studies of the University of Ghana in 1948 when the University College of the Gold Coast was established. The PEA was conceived along the lines of the British Workers' Educational Association (WEA), but it has adapted itself to the challenges of a developing country.

Another unique effort in the field of adult education which has appeared in Ghana is the sponsoring of integrated rural development, comprising agricultural extension, health and nutrition education, literacy and cooperatives, by a group of volunteers known as the Ghana Rural Reconstruction Movement. The organization has as its objective the motivation of the rural folk through practical and scientific demonstrations in agriculture, health and nutrition to improve upon the quality of their living. Education for fruitful living may therefore be considered as the main objective of the association. The Ghana Rural Reconstruction Movement, which is affiliated to the International Rural Reconstruction Movement based in New York, has a centre known as the Mampong Valley Social Laboratory, about forty kilometres north-east of Accra, comprising twenty-two communities with a total population of about 3000. The results so far are encouraging. The Ghana Rural Reconstruction Movement has no religious affiliation and it obtains the bulk of its funding from its international affiliate and also from local contributions.

Funding of voluntary agencies in adult education

Most voluntary organizations in the field of adult education in West Africa, e.g. YMCA, YWCA, some of the churches, Ghana Rural Reconstruction Movement, have affiliations with foreign parent bodies and therefore receive part of their funding from the foreign organizations.

Hardly any of these voluntary organizations obtains enough funding, and what may have to be investigated is the most effective promotion procedure for obtaining funds. Because of lack of adequate funding, the voluntary agencies either do not have the necessary personnel or their personnel are not well enough trained to be effective.

National and international organizations in adult education

The need for national associations of adult education

As has been indicated in the preceding sections of this chapter, there exists in almost all West African countries, both Anglophone and Francophone, a variety of structures, some traditional, others modern, through which adult education services reach the people. Since, understandably, no one organized the emergence of the various structures and outlined for them their respective functions, no one knows the exact number of adult education institutions in a country or even what exactly each institution is supposed to be doing.

There is also the lack of exchange of information among the institutions of adult education which deprives the whole adult education movement of the opportunity of learning from each other's experience. For instance, it is fashionable now for various organizations to claim to be engaged in integrated rural development and give the impression that one institution alone can provide all the education needed by a person or a community for integrated living. The concept of integrated living implies the coordination of various services – agricultural extension, health, nutrition, education, etc. – with the agencies that already provide these services coming together to give integrated service to a community. There is the story of an illiterate farmer who had three extension officers from various government departments visiting him in one day. After listening to the pieces of advice from the extension officers, the farmer sent a message through the third one to the others that next time that they planned a visit, they could all discuss their ideas together and send only one person to him at his village to deliver the message. The story illustrates the bewilderment of some consumers of adult education services who are served by agencies that hardly seem to know each other.

Another reason for a national association of adult education is the fact, mentioned in Chapter 1, that governments in the past did not and many now still do not appreciate the importance of adult education to their development plans. There is therefore the need to educate policy-makers about the importance of developing the human resource, since development programmes can only be implemented by human beings who have the requisite education.

Even in the matter of providing clean water, where it may be assumed that every human being will appreciate its value, it has been found out that people have to be educated about the proper use of water in order to obtain the maximum benefit from it.

In view of the importance of education in development, particularly the education of adults on whose shoulders rests the responsibility for development, the importance of having a national body that has a consultative status with economic planners and policy makers cannot be over-emphasized. The Nigerian National Council for Adult Education (NNCAE) has achieved such a status with the Nigerian Federal Government. There are even plans to institute in Nigeria a National Commission for Adult Education which will presumably have executive powers and a budget to promote the development of adult education in all its forms throughout the federation.

Elsewhere in Africa, such as Tanzania and Somalia, there are national institutes of adult education which have responsibility for backing up field-work in adult education with research, publications and the training of personnel. In Ghana, the National Adult Education Council, and more particularly the Ghana National Party on Literacy, advise the main government agency responsible for adult education and rural development on literacy matters. It is to be hoped that efforts being made in Liberia and Sierra Leone to form national associations of adult education will develop into successful bodies that will provide advice to their governments and learning opportunities through conferences, seminars and workshops for their members.

International agencies of adult education and their functions

The importance that international agencies concerned with the developing countries attach to education in all its aspects, both formal and non-formal, was underlined by Mr Robert S. McNamara, president of the World Bank Group:

> In the five year period, 1974 to 1979, the World Bank and its affiliate, the International Development Association, intend to increase their support for educational development. They will do so with the conviction:
> – that every individual should receive a basic minimum education as soon as financial resources and the priorities of development permit;
> – that skills should be developed selectively in response to specific and urgent needs, by training the right people, both urban and rural, for the right jobs – both in the modern and traditional sectors;
> – that educational policies should be formulated to respond flexibly to the need to develop educational systems (non-formal, informal and formal),

so that the specific requirements of each society might be met; and
– that opportunities should be extended throughout an educational system
for those underprivileged groups who have been thwarted in their desire
to enter the main-stream of their country's economic and social life. This
must include more equitable access to education for the poor, the ill-fed,
women and rural dwellers, and must provide, as well, a better chance to
advance from the classroom to the place of work.[2]

The conviction that if there is to be purposeful development,
particularly in the poorer parts of the world, the opportunities for
education and training for all must be made available, has sustained and led to the emergence of many international agencies
concerned with adult education. The best known of these agencies
is the United Nations Educational Scientific and Cultural Organization (Unesco), based in Paris; its Africa regional office, known
as BREDA, is at Dakar in Senegal, and there is a Unesco Commission in each West African country. Appendix 1 gives the major
international agencies in the field of adult education that deal
directly with West Africa, and seek to exchange views among adult
educators the world over and offer assistance to programmes of
adult education. It also includes international organizations such as
the World Confederation of the Teaching Profession (WCOTP),
the International Labour Organization (ILO) and the Food and
Agriculture Organization (FAO), which are interested in adult
education relevant to their main objectives.

We very often hear people say that the world is increasingly
becoming smaller because of improvement in systems of communication. Similarly, the interdependence of nations and peoples
in the world is also becoming increasingly evident; therefore individual adult educators, agencies of adult education and national
associations of adult education everywhere must consider themselves as all having a common cause and must tackle problems of
adult education as a movement linked by the systems of communication available. A letter, a cable, a telephone call or, if need be, a
journey by jet, will link any adult educator in West Africa with an
international structure for mutually fruitful consultation.

Notes and references

1. Unesco and African Adult Education Association, Final report of
seminar on 'Structures of adult education in developing countries with
special reference to Africa', Nairobi, February 1975 (1975), p. 3
2. World Bank, *Education* (sector working paper), 1974

Suggestions for further reading

Unesco. *Directory of Adult Education Institutions in Nigeria*. Paris, 1971
Unesco. *Directory of Adult Education Institutions in Ghana*. Paris, 1975

Part Two
Tasks of the Adult Educator

4 Planning and administration of adult education activities

J. T. Okedara

Introductory

Most adult educators at the higher levels of our profession find themselves removed from direct contact with the learner and are expected to concentrate on programme design and administration of learning activities. This chapter highlights some of the main obligations of programmers. It distinguishes between learning activities focused on individuals and those focused on groups; and it discusses twelve main components of adult educational programming.

It stresses throughout the need to refer constantly to and to work with the learner or the group of learners, and points out the importance of cooperating with other agencies with an adult educational interest or with advice to offer.

Practical suggestions are made about syllabus preparation, meeting places and seating arrangements, record keeping, publicity and budgeting.

The concept of administration

One of the most important books of this decade on the planning and organization of adult education, Cyril Houle's *The Design of Education*,[1] does not use at all the words 'administration' or 'management', and prefers the word *design*. Because adult learning requires flexible conditions and because adult education has always stressed the participation of the learners in the planning and arranging of their own learning, some of the ideas and approaches used by the management scientists are foreign to adult educationists and adult educators. Nevertheless, it may be helpful to mention some terms used in administration, since much adult education in West Africa is a governmental responsibility and thus many persons concerned with adult education do find themselves in a government machine.

An *administrative system* can be defined for our purposes as composed of two aspects: **organization**, which is the static structure, and **management** which is the dynamic function. Each is necessary to the other, just as anatomy and physiology are intertwined. *Organization* is the structure of authority and personal relationships within, say, an adult educational system; it implies a distribution of power and a hierarchy. *Management* is action to achieve national cooperation in bringing about change or in promoting the smooth running of a system. Management also refers to the efficient use and control of power in an organization.

Administration is also related to **culture**, that is, the entire complex of *beliefs* and *ways of doing things*, so that an adult education administration in one country or part of a country may differ in its operation from one in another country or part of a country. The location, the environment, the people and the tasks will all affect administration. This means that we cannot lay down a set pattern for an adult education system; we can only lay down principles.

One principle is that administrators need to allow for, understand and respect the non-rational elements of human behaviour; as Sir Francis Bacon said, 'Nature, to be commanded, must be obeyed.'[2] An administrator of adult education programmes has in particular to take account of the characteristics, both rational and non-rational, of adult learners (see Chapter 2).

Adult educators must regard the administration of adult learning activities as both a science and an art. As a science, the administration of adult education must be approached systematically; as an art, the process of organization and management must be practised wisely, with regard to the importance of the learner, his behaviour and his culture.

The components of adult educational organization

Any adult educational organization will have two essential elements:

a) learning–teaching;
b) programming–administration.

In addition, somewhere in the structure, though not necessarily in the same organization, will be two other elements:

a) major policy-making;
b) professional training and research.

Learning and administration will both take place at various levels of a hierarchy. Major policy-making will be the responsibility of governments, at the top level of decision-making; but it is to be hoped that they will consult learners, teachers and administrators in the formulation of policy. Professional training is usually carried on by separate institutions (such as universities and polytechnics), which are outside the adult educational organization and hierarchy.

There are two main levels of operation: the **field level** and the **programming level.**

At the field level, the main persons involved are likely to be the learners and those directly engaged to help them to learn – discussion leaders, tutors, instructors, committee members, organizers, supervisors, local librarians and others. Among the helpers' functions are:

1 Helping learners diagnose their needs for particular learning within the scope of the given situation (diagnostic function);
2 planning with learners a course that will produce the desired learning (the planning function);

3 creating conditions that will cause the learners to want to learn (motivational function);
4 selecting the most effective methods and techniques for producing the desired learnings (the methodological function);
5 providing the human and material resources necessary to produce the desired learning (the resource function);
6 helping the learners to assess the outcomes of their learning experiences (the evaluative function).

At the programming level, there are the senior officials of any adult education agency – heads of divisions or departments in ministries concerned with literacy, agricultural extension, or continuing out-of-school education; training directors of companies; heads of university outreach programmes, etc. It is hoped that there will at this level be representatives of the learners and of those who assist them directly, since it is a principle of adult education work that learners should participate in planning their own learning. The whole group would be responsible for the planning and operation of broad programmes, consisting of a variety of courses and other learning experiences. Their functions include:

1 Assessing the individual, institutional and societal needs for adult learning activities that are relevant to their organizational setting (diagnostic function);
2 establishing and managing an organizational structure for the effective development and operation of an adult education programme (organizational function);
3 formulating objectives to meet the assessed needs and designing a programme of activities to achieve these objectives (planning function);
4 instituting and supervising those procedures that are required for effective operation of a programme, including recruiting and training of leaders and teachers, managing facilities and administrative processes, recruiting students, financing and interpreting (the administrative and training function);
5 assessing the effectiveness of the programme (the evaluative function).

Adult education, being a human-centred activity, should ideally be democratically organized, but some ladder of responsibility is usually essential. An adult educator, whatever his status in the organization, should be a **leader** and not a boss. A well-known formula says:

The boss drives his men. The leader inspires them.
The boss depends on authority. The leader depends on goodwill.
The boss evokes fear. The leader radiates love.
The boss says 'I'. The leader says 'we'.
The boss shows who is wrong. The leader shows what is wrong.
The boss knows how it is done. The leader shows how to do it.
The boss demands respect. The leader commands respect.

The idea of an adult education programme

The word programme implies **planning, arrangement** and **purposefulness**. We will be discussing planning and arrangement later. Let us talk here of *purpose*. In any educational programme, it is important to have clear objectives in mind and to work towards them consciously. Functional literacy for tobacco farmers aims to raise their productivity at the same time as teaching them to read; health education for slum-dwellers in Lagos, Abidjan, Lomé or Banjul aims to improve personal well-being and the cleanliness of the environment. These examples also carry a further lesson. An educational programme, to be effective, must be directed towards a specific learner or group of learners.

Programming may *originate* from an individual, a group or an adult education agency, any of whom may conclude that there is a need for some specific learning activity and may decide to supply that need, either directly or by calling on another individual or group or agency to assist.

Varieties of adult educational activity

The basic dictionary definition of an *activity* is an exertion of energy; but a closer description is given in *Webster's International Dictionary*: 'Any ... process ... that actually or potentially involves mental function'. In an adult education activity, people expend energy in a process that actually or potentially involves learning.

The line between what is an *activity* and what is a *method* is sometimes difficult to draw. As Professor Coolie Verner says:

> The method of education identifies the ways in which people are organised in order to conduct an educational activity. A method establishes a relationship between the learner and the institution or agency through which the educational task is accomplished.[3]

Methods of teaching adults are discussed in Chapter 6. Here it is only necessary to note that adult education activities may involve, as Verner says, isolated individuals, small or large aggregations or communities.

A whole range of adult educational activities is available for helping *individuals* to learn separately and at their own pace, depending on their unique objectives. Such activities have the advantage that they are very personal. Some can be undertaken, too, by geographically isolated learners and by persons unable to join in group education for many other reasons, including women in *purdah*, physically disabled persons and the elderly.

Individual adult educational activities include:

a) *Apprenticeship and internship* These both involve learning a skill while working in the job or profession. Apprenticeship is a contractual relationship between an employer and an employee, through which the latter is trained on the job under the guidance of a master-craftsman and with some formal instruction. Internship is also an arrangement whereby learning is encouraged through supervised practical experience, usually as a stage in qualification for a profession (e.g. housemanship for doctors).

b) *Tutorial* This involves personal face-to-face tuition, and may be for an individual or a small group.

c) *Distance teaching* Educators teach learners from whom they are separated by space, using writing and/or one or more of the channels of communication created by modern technology. This is discussed fully in Chapters 7 and 8.

d) *Programmed learning* The learner uses texts or simple machines, in which the materials to be learnt are presented in a series of carefully planned steps; at each step, the learner has to make a response, which tests his comprehension, and receives immediate feedback on its correctness or incorrectness.

e) *Counselling* This is another word for advice. Educational and vocational counselling involves advice on the individual learner's educational and career problems. He is provided with information on educational options available, personal reading programmes, study problems, etc. Sometimes counselling may have to be psychological, to help the individual to learn more about himself.

Group adult education activities may be planned for a small or large group, a loosely knit or a highly organized group, a group specifically formed for an educational purpose or a group formed for another purpose but with education as part of its aims. Activities for primarily educational groups (whether pre-existing or brought into existence by the activity itself) include: courses, demonstrations, lecture-meetings, discussion meetings and workshops. Activities for other groups include: conferences or conventions, clubs and action projects.

General principles of programming

Houle asserts that any design of education can best be understood as a complex of interacting elements, not as a sequence of events; and it is true that a variety of factors may influence the starting point of a programme. But for clarity we will try to list the steps involved in programming in a logical sequence.

1 Identification of need

The starting point of any educational programme ought to be the needs and interests of individuals or groups or of the masses. The people may express these themselves and demand or arrange for themselves an educational activity to suit them. But, very often, agencies of adult education have to assess needs and interests because they are not voiced out. Assessment may be done by observation, interviews, questionnaires, studying written evidence or by calling a meeting (in conjunction with the leaders in an area or organization).

After collecting information on individual and group preoccupations, it should be possible to frame objectives for a programme, which should be related wherever possible to any local, regional or national policies on development and on education, and also to institutional aims.

2 Enlisting learners: formation of a committee

It is necessary to keep continual watch on a programme to ensure that it meets the needs and objectives for which it was designed, and there must therefore be some mechanism for consultation within the learners' community. Further, adult education is non-compulsory in nature and therefore its programming demands democracy, cooperative endeavour and coordination. A useful device is a committee. This should be set up at a very early stage, unless there is one already in existence. An adult education agency may need to encourage the formation of specific programme-area committees, e.g. one for literacy education, another for health and family life education. Such committees would have the following responsibilities:

a) deciding on the needs of the community, the priorities of programmes to be run, the subject-matter that they wish to learn, and the time, frequency and place of meetings;
b) providing links with target populations, institutions and community agencies;
c) motivating adults to learn;
d) recommending resource specialists;
e) lending volunteer help in registering learners for the more formal programmes, in conducting orientation, in checking physical facilities, in performing miscellaneous administrative services and in periodic evaluation (their help in evaluation is very important, since they can give first-hand reports of administrative and educational strengths and weaknesses).

The committee should have the following three types of representation:

a) the various points of view within the participating group;
b) the types of experience in the community that are significant in relation to particular programme (e.g. business, labour, religion);
c) those with specialized skills or knowledge that are needed in the programming (e.g. librarians, audio-visual experts, artists).

The committee should be made up of people who are interested in the programme, who are willing to serve, who are competent to perform needed tasks, who are available for work, who are able to work with other people, and who are in a position of influence in the community. To be successful in its programmes, the committee should:

a) understand clearly what it is to do;
b) concern itself with real problems;
c) avoid rubber-stamp approval to policies;
d) base agenda of each meeting on matters important to the group;
e) continually interpret the outcome of its work;
f) serve as resource people in the programme;
g) handle administrative work smoothly, e.g. sending notices of meetings promptly;
h) evaluate its work periodically.

3 Deciding on subject-matter

The general subject-matter of a programme will be determined by the needs to be met. Except in adult education parallel to the school system, the most useful approach is to focus on problems, rather than to think in terms of traditional academic disciplines, and to work on subject-matter which arouses the learners' immediate interest.

Alan Holmes's experience in East Africa illustrates the latter point:

> Because of malnutrition in a certain area, the health educator may be anxious to teach the people something about the need for good food and its work in human body. He finds that they have not entirely discarded the idea that they eat only because they are hungry and that they are not in the least interested in the function of food; they are however interested in its taste, and the women are interested in learning new ways of cooking. The educator, instead of giving the people a series of talks on nutrition, would do much better to teach them cooking and impart his information on food in this way.[4]

It goes without saying that the educator of any such group must know his or her subject-matter, but he must also decide, in consultation with the learners, on main points of emphasis and must be aware of the underlying problems which his course is intended to help them to solve.

4 Designing a syllabus

In any adult education activity, it is helpful for learners and educator alike to have an idea of the direction in which they are moving. This means that it is important to have a programme plan or course outline, often known as a **syllabus**.

A syllabus should be duplicated and made available to literate learners and they should be encouraged to keep it with them whenever they come to the class or course or other learning activity. Illiterate learners should be made aware at the outset of what the syllabus contains and should be reminded of it from time to time, so that they can judge their progress.

A syllabus should be tailor-made for each group of learners and should start from a statement of the main objectives of the programme. For example, in the case of Alan Holmes's suggested cookery course, it might run:

> This is a course about food, and how to prepare it so that the family will enjoy it better. We will look at new ways of preparing our usual food and

also at ways of cooking food and vegetables which we grow but at present
don't use, e.g. soya bean, which we grow to send overseas, but which we
could be enjoying for ourselves. In learning these things, we shall also be
asking ourselves what makes different foods good and how we can cook
dishes which will be the best for our families.

A syllabus needs to be flexible, so that adult learners can move
at their own pace, spending longer on one particular topic which
interests them than on another. If one is planning a course for say,
ten weeks, it is good to identify three or four main problems *at
most* which can be tackled in the time. *It is contrary to all the basic
principles of adult learning* to draw up a plan like this (for a group
of trade unionists interested in wages and prices):

Lecture 1: What is economics?
Lecture 2: Demand and supply
Lecture 3: Money
Lecture 4: The price mechanism
Lecture 5: Theories of value
   (and so on).

In the first place, of course, no programme for adults should consist only of lectures, which do not allow for full participation and
discussion. In the second place, this sort of scheme is rigid and
gives a sense of rushing on without time for serious consideration.
A better plan would be one which consists of three or four paragraphs, each with a main heading and one of which might go like
this:

Price or value   The price offered by those who want to buy an article,
or the amount of sacrifice they are prepared to make for it, depends to
some extent on its *utility* (usefulness). But utility is not necessarily the
same as price or value. Air has more utility but a lower value than rice; so
has water compared with palmwine. Why? Buyers 'demand' and sellers
'supply' goods. The demand means the desire to buy coupled with the
ability to do so (the necessary money or object to offer in exchange). The
supply means the amount available for sale at any one time, and this also
may affect the price or value.
   Under free competition, price is fixed by the interplay of price and
demand. Competition means in effect trying to forestall others by buying
at a lower price or selling at a higher price. But this is not always possible:
other factors may influence prices. What are they?

It will be seen that another advantage of this type of syllabus is
that it sets the learners questions to think about. If there are literates in the group, the syllabus can also include a short reading list
to guide them towards information which will help them to find
their own answers.

5 Deciding on forms and methods to be used

What forms of adult education and what methods are best pro-grammed for the subjects and topics identified? The answer depends on the cultural, occupational and educational levels of the group.

In non-literate, rural environments, the adult educator may use discussion, demonstration, film shows, exhibitions, study tours, and broadcasting and narrowcasting, as available. If the learners are already literate, he can employ, in addition, all the resources of print material, e.g. newspapers, pamphlets, charts, books, corre-spondence (see pages 67–9, Chapters 6, 7 and 8).

6 Deciding on meeting places and class facilities

Depending on the nature and content of adult education pro-grammes, meeting places should be scheduled within easy reach of as many participants as possible. It is better that the adult educator travels five kilometres to reach the target group rather than that members of the group travel to meet him.

No doubt, there is a wide variation in the space requirements of different types of programmes. Certain criteria apply to all of them, especially those dealing with comfort, convenience, per-sonalization and maximization of interaction among participants. There must be space enough for everybody to see and hear what is going on, adequate light to avoid strained eyes, adequate shade to avoid a hot sun and adequate ventilation to ensure pleasant atmosphere. If participants are expected to learn how to write or must take notes, they must be provided with some kind of support for books and writing pads.

In setting up seating arrangements, it is ideal for all participants and resource people to be on one level, with nobody looking at the back of another and with maximum flexibility for chairs to be moved back and forth from a large circle to small circles. Figure 1 overleaf illustrates ideal small and large meeting arrangements. These ideal situations may have to be compromised sometimes, especially when numbers are too large or when visual aids must be used for everybody to see simultaneously.

It should be noted, however, that whenever possible learners should meet in an environment congenial to them. On the whole, a school is *not* a desirable place for adult education, as it is furnished for children and may also have an unfamiliar and even intimidating atmosphere, especially for non-literates.

SMALL MEETING ROOM ARRANGEMENTS

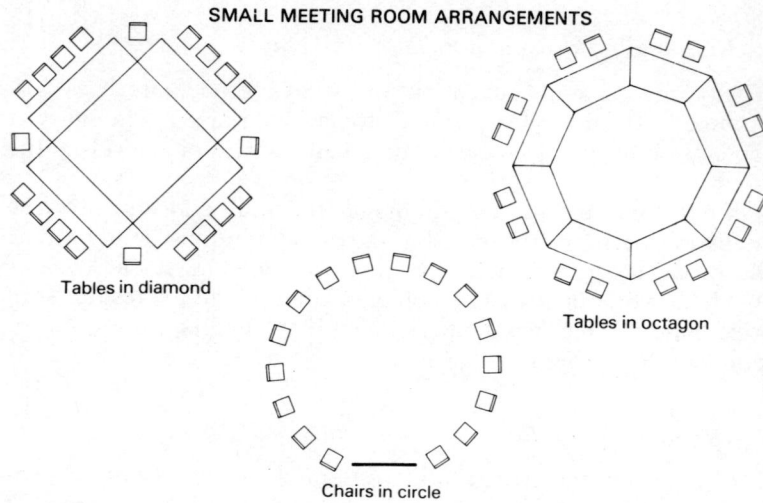

Tables in diamond

Tables in octagon

Chairs in circle

LARGE MEETING ROOM ARRANGEMENTS

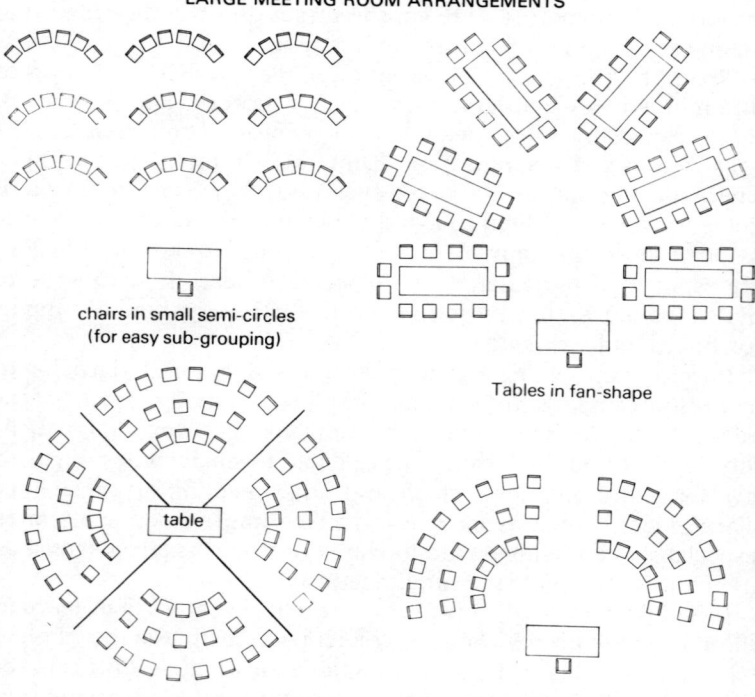

chairs in small semi-circles
(for easy sub-grouping)

Tables in fan-shape

Theatre in the round

Semi-circular theatre

Figure 1   *Ideal seating arrangements*

7 Deciding on timing and time-tabling

Taking participants, subjects, time and places into consideration, adult educators need to be cognisant of the following points in deciding and drawing up time-tables:

a) The *convenience* of the participants is a key to maximum success. Avoid scheduling a programme at busy periods, especially when people are holding celebrations and festivals, or at times of adverse weather.

b) *Availability* of teaching personnel must be ensured. For instance, in places where most of the adult teachers are school-teachers, adult education courses should be scheduled within the school terms when they are available.

c) Teaching *periods* should not be over-long in order to ensure effective learning. Periods where participants are expected to pick up a lot of new knowledge should be put at the beginning when minds are relatively fresh. Hours right after lunch and dinner should be avoided. In case of adult literacy courses, hours before dinner (e.g. 4–6 p.m.) or after dinner (8–10 p.m.) may be considered, depending on the culture and convenience of the participants.

d) *Prerequisite courses* that help understand other parts should come first in the time-table.

e) *Breaks* and *social evenings* need to be built into the time-table to guarantee adequate relaxation.

8 Keeping vital records

This is essential for the successful management of adult education programmes and also as a basis for any programme evaluation. Therefore, adult education personnel should be mandated to keep records properly. Essential for all programmes is a syllabus or course-plan (page 71), an attendance record and a report at the end. Where the learners are literate, an information card may be used and, if the programme is relatively formal, a record of learners' performance (grades) may be needed.

The syllabus or course-plan The syllabus should be made available to all learners who desire it. In addition, the tutor should supply to the director of the programme a plan of the forms and methods he intends to use and also a plan for evaluating the activity.

Attendance record or class register   This is necessary to indicate how far the level of interest is being maintained and can also help a tutor to identify absentees, follow them up and revive their interest. It is, of course, a prerequisite to the issue of any form of attendance certificate. It should be designed to include the following information:

Sponsor of programme
Description of programme (title of course)
Meeting place, day and time
Name and address of tutor/group leader
Students' names, addresses, occupation and sex.

Attendance certificate   This is one of the motivating factors, especially at the adult literacy level. It serves as evidence that efforts have been expended on an adult education programme. It is a good practice that those sponsoring formal adult education programmes issue simple attendance certificates, stating the level of achievement of participants. An attendance certificate is illustrated in Figure 2.

These certificates may be needed by learners for further educational progress, for promotion at work, etc. Some countries demand a basic literacy certificate before issuing a driving licence.

Beyond the basic literacy level, certificates may have to be associated with tests or examinations, so that they are accepted as equivalent to various educational qualifications in the formal system. For example, the government of Nigeria is planning a post-literacy curriculum which will lead to a level of achievement equivalent to that of the first school-leaving certificate.

Learners' information card   Literate learners may be asked to fill in an information card which will assist the tutor and the programme director in determining needs and interests and in assessing the effectiveness of their administration, e.g. over publicity. Besides the details required for the register, the card can include data on education, details of type of work, including previous adult learning activities, and such questions as:

What do you hope to gain from this course?
How did you hear about this course?

Tutor's report   This should include a summary of data on the register, as well as on the learners' information cards where available, and an evaluation.

REPUBLIC OF SONGHAI
MINISTRY OF RURAL DEVELOPMENT

Literacy for Farmers
(Programme)

CERTIFICATE OF COMPLETION

This is to certify that

_____

(name of learner)

has satisfactorily completed the
above programme, conducted at

_____

(place)

between _____ 19___   and _____ 19___

(date)   (date)

Signed _____   _____

Name in type _____   _____

Tutor   Director of Programme

_____

Date

Certificate No.: _____

Figure 2 *A sample certificate of completion (Republic of Songhai)*

9   *Publicizing a programme*

Educators are not always publicity-conscious, and sometimes even view publicity with distaste. But no matter how good an adult education programme is, it will fail, or be less effective, if people do not know about it, or if, hearing about it, they are unaware of how good or relevant it is. It therefore behoves a director of an adult education programme to spread a message to as many people as possible about what he has to offer. They must be informed about content, venue and time and must be motivated to attend.

The following steps have to be followed to ensure the success of publicity in any adult education programming:

Clientèle must be defined in order that promotion materials may be designed to appeal to them. The more precisely the clientèle is defined, the more effective the promotion campaign can be.

A publicity campaign must be planned   The director of the programme has to decide how much to earmark for each type of publicity device, such as newspapers, direct mailing, advertising and other media. However, the best guide is experience. The next step is to draw up specific schedules which show exactly when and how the general plan is to be accomplished through each medium.

The programme must be integrated into a theme   The theme may be a slogan, title or symbol. It may be expressed in words with a distinctive lettering or by a design. For example, Tanzania used the caption, 'Man is Health' in programming adult education for better health of the entire population.

Publicity materials must be prepared and distributed   As part of his training an adult educator should be familiarized with the basic principles of publicity media and be taught how to prepare a radio message, press handout, etc.

Types of publicity include personal contact, town-criers ('gong-gongmen'), public meetings, drumming, praise-singing, acrobatic displays, picture posters, mention in church sermons, radio and television announcements, notices in cinemas, etc.; these are all ways of reaching non-literates. For literates, it is also possible to use such means as printed posters, circular letters, leaflets, press advertisements and press articles. Personal contact and publicity methods embedded in our culture are likely to be the most effective.

When using mass media, it is useful to think of them not only as agencies which have to be paid for accepting advertisements, but as agencies which will be grateful for interesting news items. Any special achievement by an individual learner, a group excursion, an exhibition of learners' work, community service by an adult education group – all these are newsworthy and will help to keep the programme in the public eye.

10 Supervising a programme

The responsibility of the adult education supervisor is to see that planned adult education activities are carried out successfully. He should be a teacher, a facilitator and a resource person to his learners' continuing self-development, rather than a boss. The people who direct affairs of adult education at the central, regional and local adult education offices are **supervisors**. They include:

government staff who are responsible for directing national adult education programmes in health, agriculture, rural development and adult literacy; ·

regional or middle-level adult education executive officers;

directors of training in public and private agencies, e.g. principals of cooperative colleges and civil service training centres;

heads of university outreach departments, e.g. departments of extra-mural studies or continuing education;

chairmen of adult education committees in public and private agencies.

Regardless of the variation in their adult education activities, adult education programmers have to be familiar with the following supervision principles, as regards *the person to be supervised:*

a) He has to be motivated;

b) he should be informed fully about his responsibilities and the standards by which his work will be judged;

c) he should be trained to do his work satisfactorily;

d) he is expected to get information about how the programme is operating by looking over enrolment records, checking attendance registers, checking the records of fee payments, receiving reports of classes, talking to people (personnel, students and community leaders), and observing adult education activities.

As regards *the supervisor*:

a) He is expected to hold discussions with people whom he supervises on the difficulties that are noticed. His attitude to the person supervised should not be: 'This is the way it must be done; I am telling you to do it.' Rather, his approach should be: 'We all want to make this a success, let's discuss how it can be done better.'

b) He should follow up the results of his discussions with the programme personnel, to find out whether or not new methods and techniques discussed are introduced.

c) He should measure results in relation to aims in the planning stage; the process by which he can accomplish this evaluative task is discussed in the next chapter. At the same time, the supervisor can measure his *effectiveness* in relation to how well the people whom he supervises perform their tasks, and the contribution which each one makes to the total educational process.

11   *Financing a programme*

Finance here refers to *revenue* as related to adult education programming.

Financial requirements and practices vary widely according to the type of programme and sponsoring institution (see pages 50–8). There is no single formula for tackling financial problems. There is, however, a good chance of success if adult education sponsors and directors are cognizant of the following *general principles of financing*:[6]

A financial goal should be set, based on the consideration of estimated necessary expenses and possible income. When a financial goal is set high enough to provide a programme of high quality, the funds necessary to achieve the goal are more likely to be forthcoming. Correspondence education and vocational education classes (e.g. typing, accounting and secretariat subjects) fall into this category. The converse is the case in adult literacy education. None of the West African countries spends up to 1 per cent of its educational funds on adult literacy education. This practice contributes to slow progress of this aspect of education.

A detailed plan should be formulated for producing whatever income is required. The following possible *sources* are available to adult education programmers:

a) *charges to participants* in the form of tuition fees in organized classes, admission fees in lecture series and forums, membership dues or special assessments in clubs and on-going groups;

b) *appropriations* from the general funds of an organization or agency, be they private or public agencies;

c) *government grants*, either to the organization or to fund a particular programme;

d) *grants from other outside agencies*, e.g. foundations, philanthropists and community organizations such as town development associations or church groups;

e) *Industrial Training Funds* and other industrial monies, used to pay for programmes designed for their employees, to contribute to the general financing of programmes designed for a category of personnel which includes some of their own employees, e.g. woodworkers or drivers or managers, or to pay tuition charges for the enrolment of their employees;

f) *an appeal to the public*, such as is organized by the Red Cross from time to time (please note that in most countries, you need a police licence to organize such an appeal).

*A budget should be prepared to serve as a basis for financial planning and control.*The programming agency should formulate a reasonable estimate of income and expenditure, clearly broken down into specific items.

Expenses should be incurred only under proper authorization. The common practice is to permit an authorized individual to spend up to a fixed amount of funds without specific approval, but expenditures over this amount should be approved by the policy-making authority.

Adequate records of financial transactions should be kept as they occur and should be supported by vouchers and receipts. These records should be accurate, clear, simple and practical.

The accounts should be audited at least once a year by internal and external auditors.

A financial report should be published at least annually. This should consist of actual income and expenses, accompanied by interpretative or explanatory comments.

In *determining fees*, these factors should be taken into account:

a) amount of outside subsidy, whether from private funds or government grant;

b) the income-level of the clientèle being served;

c) the degree of motivation of the learners;

d) the cost of tuition (i.e. remuneration demanded by tutors);

e) standards set by a similar organization in the community.

Budgeting or resource allocation is an essential skill for an adult education administrator. It may, for instance, be argued that one reason why adult literacy is among the least-funded government programmes in West Africa is because those responsible for adult literacy have not learned how to do their budgeting convincingly.

In a government, there is a division of responsibility in budget matters. One agency in a ministry of finance will be the *budget department*, which produces guidelines for budget preparation and should also produce a budget manual and promote workshops and training sessions for other ministries. The ministry of finance will also be concerned with how to raise revenue and with matching income to proposed expenditure. In a smaller, non-governmental institution, by contrast, the senior adult education staff will be responsible for all phases of its budget.

In a government ministry, the first step towards **budget preparation** is a *call circular*, asking for proposals from each budgeting unit and giving guidelines and a target date for submission of estimates. Each unit then has to submit a draft, giving a clear statement of objectives and including feasibility reports, project studies and other relevant supporting papers in justification. All units in a ministry (including adult education) then meet to study all draft proposals and reconcile them. The final proposal should be within any limits set by the budget department.

Budget content includes a statement of proposed expenditure by function, a clear description of costs and benefits, and the implications of new activities for existing ones, a list of priorities and targets for the year, as well as indications of problems, prospects and foreign exchange requirements; justificatory data should be appended. A usual *format of presentation* is to put requirements in order of priority.

Budget implementation must be preceded by approval from the ministry of finance and the political authority. Major activities have to be phased and reported on at regular intervals. Implementation stages are:

a) Acquisition of resources – buildings, manpower requirements;
b) fund releases;
c) monitoring of performance;
d) revision and preparation of supplementary estimates if necessary;
e) budget evaluation, by examiners in each ministry and by an inter-ministerial committee.

The budgeting process described calls for *cost effectiveness and efficiency* of adult education programmes. Is the value of the result great enough to merit the cost of attaining that result? Could the same end-result be achieved in different ways at less cost? Or would there have been a greater value to participants, to the agency or to society if the same resources had been invested in a different programme? Answers to these questions can be provided by analysing adult education system through PERT (Programme Evaluation and Review Technique), PPBS (Programme Planning Budgeting System) and Cost-Benefit Analysis. In this context, adult education programmers should find the services of consultants or experts useful for their work.

12   Cooperating with other agencies

Houle stresses that adult education is a *cooperative art*.

More often than not, adult education agencies in West Africa design and administer programmes in isolation from other relevant bodies. Yet inter-agency cooperation is essential for the success of most programmes, especially in such areas as integrated functional literacy, while cooperation between the educators and any group representing the learners can greatly enhance the usefulness of any programme. The People's Republic of Congo uses the device of inter-ministerial committees for functional literacy, including representatives of the various technical ministries for advice on health, agriculture and nutrition. In Ghana there is a national organization of learners, the People's Educational Association (or PEA), which is consulted by agencies providing programmes. At local government level, it may be helpful to have a coordinating body made up of representatives of all agencies with an adult educational interest; this used to be the pattern in Nigeria in the 1950s.

Whatever the mechanism used, a successful adult educator will need to have his mind set on collaboration and must not be afraid of initial rebuff or of others claiming credit afterwards.

The importance of training

Central to the effective administration of any adult education programme are qualified educators and educationists at all levels, both full-time and part-time. Each needs relevant and if possible tailor-made training programmes.

This handbook is designed as an aid to such training.

Notes and references

1. Cyril Houle, *The Design of Education* (San Francisco: Jossey-Bass, 1972)

2. Quoted in Dwight Waldo, *The Study of Public Administration* (New York: Random House, 1964)

3. C. Verner and A. Booth, *Adult Education* (New York: Center for Applied Research in Education, 1964), pp. 68–9

4. A. C. Holmes, *Health Education in Developing Countries* (London: Nelson, 1964)

5. Malcolm S. Knowles, *The Modern Practice of Adult Education: Andragogy versus Pedagogy* (New York: Association Press, 1970)

6. *Ibid.*, pp. 211–12

5 Evaluation of progress in adult education
E. Odinakachuku Okeem

Introductory

This chapter starts with the fact that there are varieties of adult education programme – e.g. functional literacy, continuing, cultural, vocational and civic education – both for youths and adults, literate and illiterate. Because of this variety, we need to discover precisely the *what*, the *why* and the *how* in order to be able to assess *how well* it was done and the scope and level of such an assessment. Reasons are given for evaluation, including goal clarification and the need for efficiency in the pursuance of the current programme, in the design of future ones and in the teaching–learning process in general. Evaluation also helps to generate self-confidence among the practitioners.

It is suggested that instruments should be designed so as to measure not only what is measurable, but also what they are intended to measure. An adequate plan for evaluation should contain, among other things, a clear statement of the programme's goals, scope, duration and, if possible, of the assumptions made both now and for the future.

Different forms of assessment are distinguished, ranging from casual observation to laboratory experiment, as are different forms of objective, i.e. diagnostic, predictive or terminal. A comprehensive evaluation should cover the assessment of the tutors, of the participants and of the adequacy of the curriculum content. Constraints on evaluation are discussed, including non-clarity of goals; inadequate skill in social science techniques; over-reliance on the attendance register; and the fear of adult educators that their weaknesses may be exposed and their programme in consequence seriously modified or abandoned.

Finally, an individual self-evaluation scheme for tutors is discussed; this is essential if a tutor is to assess objectively his success in teaching or guiding adults.

The uses of evaluation

Because of varieties of adult educational programme, it is vital for evaluation purposes that we should discover, right from the very start of the programme or project, the following:

a) the *what* of the programme – the type or brand of the programme and its precise scope;

b) the *why* – the reasons for undertaking it and the goals that are intended to be achieved;

c) the *how* – the procedure for accomplishing the goals, e.g. the facilities or resources that would be required, the detailed stages or phases of the programme, the duration of each stage and the methods appropriate for each stage.

With this basic information one would be in a better position to determine the most appropriate criteria for assessing the *how well* – how effective a particular programme has been **Evaluation**, after all, **is simply the process of determining the degree to which the aims and objectives of an educational activity are achieved**. Answers to the above questions would enable us to determine the scope of the evaluation and *at what level* – whether the national, regional, community or group level, or even the family or individual level – it would be most appropriate. We would also be clearer about what precisely or primarily we are considering, whether it is a functional literacy class, a correspondence course, a GCE-oriented class, civic education or a continuing education programme. It may be necessary to note the relationship between evaluation and other forms of research. Both seek to discover facts, information or realities yet unknown to us; evaluation, however, is an inquiry specifically for purposes of improvement in planning and programming, while other forms of research tend to be more open-ended inquiries. As Suchman argues, evaluation connotes some judgement concerning the effects of planned change and represents a measurement of effectiveness in reaching some predetermined goal.[1] Evaluation has also been defined as the procedure used in determining the value or worth of a process or thing, whereas educational evaluation is the process in determining the effectiveness of teaching and/or the value of a learning experience in assisting students to achieve the goals of education.[2] I have suggested elsewhere that the evaluation of adult education programmes should be done in the context of the overall national development policy or plan.[3]

Education generally aims at some sort of modification of behaviour through the experience of the recipient or participant. Learning involves a sequence which implies that successive activities grow from, and build on, previous ones, and that earlier activities prepare for later ones. In the final analysis, the test of any programme is the character or nature of its products. Before that product emerges, however, it is useful to have an occasional glance at it to see how it is shaping up. In the case of an industrial product, there is usually supervision at the various crucial stages in the manufacturing or production process. This is to ensure quality control at the lower stages, an exercise which helps to guarantee the high quality of the finished product. This process of assessing how well we are doing, in the light of our objectives and also taking into account the resources employed, is what evaluation is. It enables us to answer more objectively the question: 'How well are you doing?'

Other reasons for evaluation would include:

The clarification of the goal of the programme.
The need for efficiency in the implementation of the programme.
Justification of the present programme in terms of the results achieved.
The desire for greater efficiency in future programme design and implementation.

The overall need for teaching/learning effectiveness.
The desire to generate professional self-confidence among the practitioners.

Measuring the measurable

Unless an appraisal or evaluation of any aspect of education is systematically planned and conducted, it may have little or no value. This is because it may not measure adequately what it set out to measure. It may give the impression that there is only one way of measuring or assessing the success of an adult educational experience when, in fact, the measurement is multi-dimensional. For example, a dictation test of fifteen minutes may not be the only way of testing the success or failure of a literacy educational experience for an individual. The test could have been more effective if the learner had more time. Moreover, the individual's assessment of the value of a programme may be quite different from that of the teacher. Although he may not have done well in the dictation test, yet he may have made some very good friends or may have developed greater self-confidence and courage to assess a situation and make up his own mind; he may have become more sociable. The same, or even more, could be said about the evaluation of an individual's participation in a community development project which may even be judged a 'failure'.

It is therefore necessary to have an adequate plan for appraisal or evaluation and it is essential that such a plan be adequately implemented. An adequate plan should, at least, include the following:

1 *A clear statement of the purposes* or the aims and objectives of the programme or project. It may even be useful to classify these into the principal aims and the subsidiary ones, if possible. The clearer and more precise the statement of goals the better, because to state them in a general, ambiguous, and vague way will only create confusion and make evaluation very difficult, if not impossible. The behavioural change sought from the programme should be stated. It would help evaluation if it were known that the expected behavioural outcome were, say, reading proficiency, or a change of attitude toward the authorities, or acquisition of some basic facts, or whatever.

As an illustration let us take a course on *civic responsibilities*. What behavioural changes can we expect from one who has undertaken the course in a West African country? There are certain examples of changed behaviour which might serve as the basis for evaluating such a course. Among them might be:

A greater interest in important matters concerning the citizens at the time.

A more active participation in the affairs of his community, e.g. through initiating, encouraging and implementing constructive action about its needs.

An ability to discover the sources of information about civic affairs and to assess the quality of such information in order to utilize it appropriately.

A capacity to formulate his own opinion and make up his own mind about issues involving him and his community.

An ability to weigh evidence in order to decide on alternative solutions or approaches to civic problems.

An understanding of the value judgements, vested interests, and of the consequent conflict of views involved in civic affairs, and furthermore, the possible limitations of any action owing to the complexity of the factors involved.

Ability to know one's rights and have the courage to express and defend them.

A second illustration could be a course on *national unity*. Some of the behaviour changes expected from the course could be:

An understanding of the concept or meaning of national unity.

An understanding of why it is important for the country, whether it is Nigeria, Ghana, Sierra Leone or any other.

An appreciation of the many consequences of disunity.

Personal efforts to implement unity, through 'bridge-building', e.g. learning the language of at least one of the other ethnic groups; choosing close friends from among them; spending holidays with them; inter-marrying with them; making continuous efforts to understand them, their culture, history, problems, etc.

Ability to speak up about unity and to defend it and also to encourage others to do so, etc.

If the intended behavioural outcome from the courses was formulated and stated at the beginning it would make evaluation easier later on as it would be a guide not only to the tutors and the participants, but also to the subsequent evaluators.

2 *A definition or delimitation of the scope of the project* as a whole together with the scope of its various stages or phases. This is important so that people would not judge, say, the first phase of

the project in terms of the final stage which is yet to be reached. It also helps the participants to assess their own progress stage by stage.

3 *A statement about the duration* of the programme.

4 *An indication of the essential resources* that would be needed and the techniques that would be used. The importance of this is that if, for any reason, these resources do not become available and the intended techniques are not employed, then due allowance can be made in the evaluation or appraisal of progress.

5 If possible, *a statement of the assumptions being made*, both at the beginning (e.g. about the background of the participants, the motivating factors for initiating the project and the dominant ideology of the organizers, etc.) and for the future. The relevance of this is that when people evaluate the project later on, they will be more able to appreciate and assess the progress made.

What may we assess?

What would be assessed would vary, of course, according to the actual policy or programme and its specific objectives. The following are some examples of what could be assessed.

The programme needs

To do this we need to ask such questions as:

Why was it necessary to embark on the programme in the first place? What overall needs or desires was it meant to satisfy, and for whom?

To what extent have these been achieved as originally intended?

How specifically or in what concrete ways have the lives of individuals been affected?

The design of the policy or programme

Take for instance, a mass education programme. How realistic was the design?

a) To what extent was it based on accurate statistics of the population to be covered?

b) Was the design for a limited area instead of the whole population?

c) Did the design take adequate account of the actually available resources (material and non-material) necessary for its successful completion?

Was the implementation broken down into manageable units, stages or phases?

Did each stage or phase have the requisite quantity of personnel and materials originally anticipated; if not, why was that the case?

How can any of the constraints be eliminated in the future?

Given the limited resources of finance, time and personnel, have the actually positive benefits of the policy to the individuals and the community justified it? Or, in other words, are there not better alternative ways of more profitably utilizing the same amount of resources?

Are the results likely to receive general moral approval?

To what extent have the masses themselves or their representatives participated in the planning and educational experience involved? Or, how democratic has the planning or policy formulation been?

The adult education process

This could be subdivided into two sections: first, the evaluation of the *curriculum*, taking as an example a literacy curriculum. It could be asked, for instance: How useful and practicable has the curriculum content been to the participants? In other words, how functional has it been? This will seek to test how immediately meaningful and applicable the vocabularies of concepts learnt are to the participants' everyday activities, whether they were those of 'petty traders', market women, blacksmiths, farmers, bricklayers or motor drivers.

Secondly, the *methods*. Evaluation of this section would seek to discover, among other things, how teacher-centred the process has been. To what extent have the participants contributed in the formulation and solution of the problems of illiteracy? Were they consulted at any stage? If so, what was the nature and duration of such a consultation? If adults are genuinely taken into confidence as mature, responsible people, then a more serious and continuous consultation ought to occur.

It is assumed here that increased participation would aid retention and that therefore activity is preferable to passivity. As we saw in Chapter 2, the tutor should guide but not dominate the class; an authoritarian tutor is more likely to be resented by adults than children.

The teaching/learning materials used

If we assume that the more senses (sight, hearing, smell, etc.) are involved, the more effective the learning experience, then we could ask, for example:

How effective was the audio-visual aid used?
Was it so technical that many of the participants did not get its message?
How relevant was it to their own specific local situation?
Was it so time-consuming that there was no time for useful discussion and effective learning?
Was there no more effective alternative material? Was the material easy enough to be learnt by a group with such a background and experience? Was the material sufficiently broken down into small digestible units? Or had the tutor merely reproduced materials designed for a different group with a different background (probably because of lack of time or experience, or both, in adapting it for the use of the present group)? For example, has foreign material (perhaps British, designed for a European audience) been used because of lack of local textbooks or local examples? How appropriate or ambiguous for the group's members was the meaning of the concepts used? (This is an important question because some European concepts have slightly different meanings or connotations in Africa. For example, the European sentimentality about cats and dogs could be irritating in some parts of Africa, especially to adults.) If so, how could the foreign material be made to be more relevant to the local situation in future?

Evaluation of learning gains

What did the learner know before he started the course? What does he know and understand now? Is there any appreciable increase in what he now knows and understands?

Also, what skills had he before and after the course? Under what conditions can we observe such skills demonstrated? Has he sufficiently benefited from the course or not? If not, what were the major constraints in the course responsible for this? How could the obstacles be removed; or, how could the benefit derived be substantially increased in future?

The overall behavioural change

Have there been any noticeable behavioural changes since the learners completed the course? If so, what are they? Under what specific situations can they be observed? If not noticeable, what are the possible areas in which benefits must have occurred, whether these were intended or unintended? (The assumption here, of course, is that the resulting behavioural change is attributable to the lessons received or to the exposure to an adult education process.)

An illustration here would be appropriate. The major objectives of a National Youth Service Corps could be the instilling of discipline and a sense of service to the nation through physical work. But an informal conversation with some of the participants in Nigeria would seem to indicate that some of the latent and probably unintended functions actually fulfilled include:

minimization of a previous deeply entrenched prejudice about the people from other parts of Nigeria;

a new emotional attachment (some have subsequently gone to work there);

inter-marriage, which could be very significant in promoting national integration; and

the enrichment from practical geographical lessons which people could not easily have had when they were at school.

Similar illustrations exist in other adult programmes or projects.

Forms of assessment

As had already been indicated the purpose of evaluation or assessment is mainly to ascertain the effectiveness with which the objectives of the programme is being achieved. It helps us to answer the question, 'How well are we doing in achieving the general and the more specific goals of the programme?' Such an assessment almost always takes place in one form or another. There are these major examples:

1   The **built-in evaluation component** in an ordinary classroom situation. In most adult education classes there should be a continuous dialogue or, at least, an occasional question from the tutor or leader to the class. The answer to such questions helps him to assess quite readily how well he is doing in putting across his materials or in achieving his basic objective. Ideally, the sort of answers he obtains should enable him to readjust or

modify his approach in the right direction. So this is the tutor's on-going evaluation as the class proceeds.

2   **One's casual observation**. This rough and impressionistic assessment is very often made by those who have some knowledge of what the course is about. One might hear them say, 'Your course is going very well, isn't it?' They may continue to explain the basis of their judgement thus: 'I passed there and I saw for myself what was going on.' This casual evaluation could lead to a more formal evaluation based on an interview administered by the teacher himself immediately after the course.

3   **The survey method**. In addition, more extensive information could be obtained through a more elaborate survey technique. By this method information would be obtained from the participants through an exploratory questionnaire. The questions would seek the learners' opinions about what they considered the strengths and weaknesses of the course, the merits and demerits, areas for improvement in the future, the overall degree of success or satisfaction, etc. They are often allowed to complete such a questionnaire anonymously in order to increase chances of objectivity.

4   **Field study**. This method permits an intensive investigation of the dynamics of the processes in a smaller group rather than surveying a larger population as could be done in a questionnaire.

5   **Field experiment**. This enables one to extend the field study and carry out a more detailed in-depth study of the dynamic social process, using a control group in an area where people have not yet been exposed to such a course.

6   **Laboratory experiment**. This is perhaps the most advanced of all. The technique is borrowed from the physical sciences and it seeks to reproduce as much as is possible the laboratory situation in the assessment or evaluation of programme.

Furthermore, particular types of assessment may be found more suitable for particular types of course, depending on what the objectives are. For example, we would not use the same method for evaluating both a lecture and a community development project, nor would we use the same method for assessing a basic literacy class without some modification.

At what period in the course should the evaluation occur? Here again it depends on what the objective of evaluation is. For example, it may be necessary to have a diagnostic evaluation *even before the course starts*. The purpose of this would be to have a rough assessment of the background and experience (socio-economic and educational) where such an information would be useful in the course. *Periodic tests* or assessment exercises, formal or informal, have also been found useful as the course progresses. This could be done inside or outside the class or the formal session. They may be predictive and so might help to direct the course of events. Terminal assessments are also useful as they give the overall picture as to how well the group or the individual participants have done. They are also useful because they could constitute the initial rung in a higher educational ladder. Where a certificate is to be awarded, an evaluation would normally be a terminal assessment. Most courses have some sort of *built-in* evaluation component.

It is not intended to cover all types of evaluation techniques here but only to indicate some of the major ones. Using the two variables of 'mode of assessment' and 'appraisal objective', diagrammatically we have:

Mode of assessment	Appraisal objective		
	Diagnostic	Predictive	Terminal
Built-in evaluation	pre-course test (to assess background)	first stage in a continuing project, e.g. OFN, OFY, UPE	Unit 1 in correspondence course
Periodic	occasional assessment of progress	mock exam	x
Terminal	x	end of term test	final literacy test

Long-term evaluation

Apart from the assessment of the degree of success undertaken immediately after a programme, there is also the need for a Participants' or Programme Revisited exercise after a long period of time. One purpose of this long-term assessment could be to counter-check the earlier result and thereby to ascertain the degree of retention of what was learnt and the durability of the skills acquired. Probably some other longer-term effect of behavioural change could be indicated.

However we need to be cautious in attributing all later successful changes to that particular earlier exposure. (It makes one wonder when a primary school headmaster of yesteryear sees one of his pupils in a prominent academic position and readily claims 'he is one of my products'.) A present prime minister or president may have benefited from an adult education programme several years ago but it would not be quite legitimate to attribute his present status to that particular experience because so many variables no doubt contributed to his present achievement.

Yet the long-term assessment, carefully designed, could be a useful method in ascertaining the extent of, say, permanent literacy achieved through a literacy campaign or the extent to which non-literates have reverted to illiteracy. In the latter example, the reasons for such a set-back could also be sought through the evaluation.

Such evaluation might sometimes reveal a total collapse of the original programme or project or an unexpected displacement of goals, where, for example, a community centre became a recreation centre for cattle, goats, and chicken, or a well became a refuse-dumping pit.

A comprehensive evaluation

In West Africa we tend to be so preoccupied with certificates or paper qualifications and, consequently, to be obsessed with students' performance that we need to remind ourselves that any educational experience involves the interaction of the *tutor*, the *students or participants* and the selected *curriculum content*, to produce new patterns of behaviour in the participants (all in accordance with the overall goals of the adult education programme). The most adequate or effective type of evaluation would be one which covered all three aspects. This is because any major weakness in any of these areas (i.e. ineffective teaching, irrelevant curriculum content, or poor unmotivated participants) could lead to failure of the programme to achieve its goals as was anticipated. As I have suggested elsewhere, such a comprehensive evaluation should be related to the overall national developmental policy.

Constraints in effective programme evaluation

The major difficulties in trying to achieve an effective overall evaluation of adult education programmes include the following:

Lack of clearly formulated aims and specific objectives of the programme. This results very often in the uncertainty of what to evaluate and how to set about it.

Inadequate training in the use of social science research techniques. This creates the problem of inability to formulate questions and tests which would effectively test the degree to which the aims have been or are being achieved.

Over-reliance on attendance register as almost the sole method of evaluating success. This leads to the fallacious argument that the course was successful because learners attended regularly or because the hall was full. This ignores the possibility that there might be other reasons for attending the course apart from its stated objectives.

The fear of exposing the weaknesses of the course and its organizers. Someone's reputation might be at stake.

The underlying fear of the organizers of the programme that evaluation results might lead to serious modifications of their plan, if not its abandonment.

From the above it is clear that for a successful evaluation exercise, cooperation is needed from all the parties involved. It is important for the organizers to plan carefully and be specific in what they hope to achieve at the end of the programme. Furthermore they should not be too secretive about assessing their programmes, because without assessment not much meaningful improvement can be made in future. Failure to cooperate with evaluators would normally suggest that one has something to hide. The danger of a lack of evaluation is that organizers might continue 'to do their own thing' years after the original needs had disappeared, or might continue to use tools and techniques that ought to have been abandoned long ago. It is also important that the individual tutor or organizer should have a self-evaluative scheme in terms of his own behaviour (attitudes, temperament, mannerisms, illustrations, etc.) and its effect on the participants as such an honest evaluation would help him to assess his success in teaching or leading adults. A continuous method of self-assessment is necessary if the tutor is to ensure an on-going improvement in his ability to perform his task.

Notes and references

1. E. A. Suchman, *Action for What? A Critique and Guide for the Evaluation of Action and Service Programmes*, quoted in R. N. Tobias, 'The theory of evaluation in adult education', *ICUAE Journal*, vol. 11, no. 3 (November 1972), p. 67

2. Ray C. Phillips, *Evaluation in Education* (Columbus, Ohio: Merrill, 1968), p. 2

3. E. O. Okeem, 'Adult education and national development in Africa', *ICUAE Journal*, vol. 11, no. 3 (November 1972), p. 57

Suggestions for further reading

Institute of Adult Education, Dar es Salaam. *Adult Education Handbook*. Tanzania Publishing House, 1973 (*See* Chapter 8)

NNCAE. *Adult Education in Nigeria: The Next Ten Years*. Kano Conference proceedings, 1972 (*See* especially pp. 76–90)

Ohuche, R. O., and Akejusa. *Testing and Evaluation in Education*. AER Nigeria Ltd, 1976

Okunrotifa, P. O. *Evaluation in Geography*. Oxford University Press, Ibadan, 1977

Popham, J. *Evaluation in Education: Current Applications*. McCutcheon, Berkeley, Calif., 1974

Unesco. *The Experimental World Literacy Programmes*. Paris, 1976

Worthen, R. B., and Sanders, J. R. *Educational Evaluation, Theory and Practice*. Jones Publishing, Worthington, Ohio, 1973

Part Three
Methodology of Adult Education and Ancillaries to It

6 Teaching adults: styles, methods and techniques

E. Kwasi Ampene

Introductory

The purpose of learning is to bring about a desired change in the behaviour of the learner: therefore, all who engage in a learning activity are concerned that the learning should be as effective as possible, so that the objectives of the learning efforts may be achieved. In this regard, what the teacher does or does not do is of crucial importance. Educators are therefore concerned with such questions as: how should a teacher or the leader of a learning activity conduct himself in order to promote learning in all its forms? And, which learning techniques are most effective in particular learning situations? The aim of this chapter is to examine these and other questions about face-to-face learning situations, where probably most organized learning in the African context takes place.

A teacher's behaviour can be altered by training; for instance, training can help those who tend to be authoritarian to consider the characteristics and interests of the learners, as described in Chapter 2. Training should inform teachers about how learners can best be helped to achieve their personal objectives which, one hopes, will not be in conflict with the collective or community needs, since adult education in Africa cannot ignore the collective interests; the teacher of adults cannot just promote student interests, especially when such interests are clearly against the common good.

Using Coolie Verner's definition, a distinction is made between **method** and **technique**, to help adult educators use these terms more accurately.

Various suggestions are given regarding the use of appropriate techniques. The guiding principle in selecting a technique, it is suggested, should be the extent to which it helps to make the learning task real and encourages the participation of learners. Appropriate African plays, songs, stories and proverbs convey ideas very clearly and can be useful teaching techniques.

Teaching behaviours or styles

Teaching behaviour or style may be defined as the way in which a teacher or a leader of learning activity consistently conducts himself so as to create a characteristic relationship between himself and his students. Learners may find that their teacher is either jovial or serious, a hard taskmaster or *vice versa*. The teacher's behaviour is a significant factor in shaping the atmosphere in which learners work. Thus a learning situation may be described as *a*) 'democratic' or 'student-centred', meaning that learners have the freedom to discuss among themselves and with the tutor their learning needs, to share in planning their learning programme and to participate actively in the learning process; *b*) 'authoritarian' or 'teacher-dominated', where the leader or teacher does not involve the learners adequately in identifying learning needs, the planning of learning activities and in the learning process.

Studies of teaching behaviour

An American pioneer in adult teaching, William S. Gray, in considering how best to teach adults, particularly European immigrants to the United States of America, noted in 1933:

> Most teachers of adults ... are engaged daily in teaching children in elementary and high schools; they need guidance in adapting instruction to the needs and interests of adults.[1]

Gray's comment applies very well to the situation in West Africa, and indeed in many parts of the world, where, whenever there is a need for teaching adults, it is to the primary and secondary school teachers that the authorities turn. There is a general, but erroneous, belief that all teaching is the same, and therefore that teachers trained for and accustomed to teaching children are good enough as the teachers of adults.

A survey of research into teaching behaviour shows that, taken as a whole, these studies have not led to conclusive evidence that either student-centred ('democratic') or teacher-dominated ('authoritarian') behaviour is better in all situations. In fact, some of the results within the same society even seem to conflct. An American study of college engineering students' appreciation of their teachers[2] concluded that whereas students rated highly a teacher's knowledge of the subject and ability to stimulate his students, they did not seem to care about such qualities as 'warmth' and 'sociability' of the teacher. On the other hand, other American studies involving adult students came to the conclusion that a tutor who was 'warm' and 'friendly', and also 'good at communicating' his ideas, got his students to understand problems well.[3]

A general criticism of such studies is that a learning situation involves so many variables that one variable – such as the type of leadership offered by the teacher – cannot be the sole cause for the outcome of the learning efforts. Some of these variables are:

a) Student characteristics such as age, sex, socio-economic circumstances, whether the learning is full-time or part-time and, in particular, the degree of his or her motivation.
b) Teacher characteristics, such as age, sex, level of education, training for teaching a particular group of students, and degree of enthusiasm for the subject and for adult education.
c) The nature of the learning task, be it the learning of manipulative skills, or ideas.

d) The objectives of the learning task, such as students being required to pass a public examination, as against non-credit liberal education or community development.

The interplay of these and many more factors in any learning situation makes it difficult, as we have already said, to attribute changes in students' behaviour to a pattern of teaching behaviour; it is also hard to determine whether the tutor's influence extends beyond students' cognitive achievements to other, psychological, changes which might occur.

Another criticism of the studies is that they have not been guided by theories of human behaviour. The 'Committee on Teaching Effectiveness of the American Educational Research Association' recommended nearly three decades ago that any investigation into teacher characteristics or behaviour should face the question, 'on what grounds in learning theory (or any other body of theory) can he justify hypothesizing that this or that characteristic is related to a given effect?'[4]

For my doctoral dissertation, I pursued the need for a theory of human behaviour to explain observed teacher characteristics.[5] I accepted the challenge from social scientists that teaching behaviour is part of human behaviour, and therefore that research into the characteristics of successful teachers cannot be conducted in a theoretical vacuum; it must take into account theories of human behaviour formulated by psychologists and sociologists.

My study tested a behavioural model developed by two American scholars which states that human behaviour is the result of the interplay between societal norms and regulations on the one hand and the person's own characteristics, such as his biological constitution and early experience, on the other. The interplay seems to lead to three types of behaviour:

1 **Normative or nomothetic,** which is close to the social norms. This is the behaviour of the law-abiding citizen, who subordinates his personal interests and inclinations to expected patterns of behaviour in his community.

2 **Idiographic,** which is the opposite. This describes the behaviour of a person who gives full expression to his personal interest and inclinations and considers societal norms and regulations as just a nuisance.

3 **Transactional,** which tries to marry personal interests with the desired behaviour in the society. In this case, a person does not disregard social norms and regulations, but pursues his personal interests as far as possible within their limitations.[6]

I was interested to find out whether these three types of behaviour could be found among teachers. Society has always required education for the young, and, in recent times, has accepted that if poverty and human misery are to be reduced or eliminated, poor and underprivileged adults should be educated to be self-reliant. Moreover, countries which have made the fastest economic progress have placed emphasis on education for *all*. I therefore decided to study teaching in Adult Basic Education (ABE) classes in an American city, Chicago. These classes are part of a programme aimed at the uneducated and unemployed; although the circumstances of the United States are not the same as those of West African countries, such classes share with some West African adult education programmes the objective of making the people self-confident and knowledgeable enough to contribute to economic growth.

I studied the teachers' own attitudes to the programme and to the students, as well as their ideas as professionals about handling problems in various learning situations. I also studied students' reactions to their teachers.

I found that there were indeed three types of teacher. The nomothetic one accepted, without question, the goals of the programme, did not make allowance for the expression of students' own interests and believed that there was no need to train teachers especially for the teaching of adults (the majority of the nomothetic teachers in the study had had no such special training). He permitted little or no humour in the classroom, kept at a distance from his students and strongly believed that formal examinations provided the best means of assessing students.

There were also teachers of the opposite type, the idiographic. They were sceptical of the formalism of the programme, and were more concerned about generating confidence in the students, who had been tossed around by life and had little self-respect. They encouraged students to feel as free as possible, joked with them and did not trust examinations as the fairest assessment of students' achievements. This type of teacher had usually been trained to teach adults and, supported by some years of experience, had worked out his own philosophy of teaching behaviour.

The third behavioural type – the transactional – also emerged clearly as a teacher with a well-considered course of teaching behaviour. He, like the idiographic, had had training for teaching adults and was also generally experienced in his work. He accepted the goals of the ABE programme as being realistic although he felt that there was the need to find out how best each student could be helped according to his ability and interests. He did not think that all the students needed the academic training required by the ABE programme, although he thought that with some encouragement and persuasion most of the students could pass their examinations. He permitted humour, but he never lost sight of the learning tasks; he accepted examinations as necessary until better ways of assessing achievement have been devised.

The students who were about to complete the ABE programme and due to take their final examinations in about six months (for most students the programme lasted for about two years) preferred the transactional teacher, and named the nomothetic teacher as a close second choice. These final-year students were not enthusiastic about the idiographic teacher. On the other hand, students who had just entered the programme and those who had not been doing well in it appreciated very much the help and sympathy that they received from the idiographic teacher whom they regarded as a friend.

One hesitates to generalize too much from this study. However, it appears that training teachers to teach disadvantaged adults reduces the nomothetic orientation which may be presumed in those who teach the young and adolescents, and who are usually recruited to teach adults in Africa. One may assume that training teachers for adults may minimize the traditional 'authoritarian' teacher image that predominates in many African schools. I was once approached by a delegation of angry extra-mural students who threatened to close the branch if their tutor was not changed: they objected to the tutor reading out students' examination marks in class and making disparaging comments here and there. This tutor showed typical nomothetic behaviour, which is quite common in many schools in Ghana. Needless to say, I granted the wish of the delegation, and proceeded in their presence to relieve the tutor of his assignment by telephone.

Obviously training alone does not explain why some teachers are 'transactional' while others are idiographic. Perhaps the explanation lies in the theory that I was testing, namely, that a person's behaviour is the result of the interplay between social norms and his own constitution and experience.

However, the students' reaction to the teacher may let him modify his behaviour to suit their interests. Thus, a nomothetic teacher might change when he finds that his students are deserting his class ('voting with their feet') or, even, that he is relieved of his assignment. Similarly, the idiographic teacher might be compelled to take notice of the task in hand; one such teacher in the study reported that his students were so anxious to learn the 'trash' (as he called the curriculum) that he had to 'dish it out' to them.

Recommended qualities for the tutor of adults

While there is no one 'ideal' set of characteristics for a tutor, my own study and others have led to a picture of what sort of person is *likely* to be successful in teaching adults. Recommendations from studies of teaching behaviour, as well as other well-considered pieces of advice on how to teach adults, are usually related to the characteristics of the adult learner. We have already studied these characteristics thoroughly in Chapter 2 and have already drawn some conclusions on learner–teacher relationships. Miller gave six conditions for adult learning (see pages 35–6); we should remember that trust between tutor and learner is the essential prerequisite of any learning experience.

A recent survey by Grabowski summarizes the desirable qualities which seem to be suggested by various studies of teacher behaviour. A successful teacher of adults, he says:

1 Understands and takes into account the motivational and participation patterns of adult learners.
2 Understands and provides for the needs of adults in learning.
3 Is versed in the theory and experienced in the practice of adult education.
4 Knows the community and its needs.
5 Knows how to use the various methods and techniques of instruction.
6 Possesses communication skills, including listening.
7 Knows where to locate and how to use educational materials.
8 Has an open mind and provides an atmosphere that allows adults to pursue their needs and interests.
9 Continues his own education.
10 Is able to appraise and evaluate programmes.[7]

In sum, research results and well-considered advice encourage the tutor to behave in a way which will lead learners to participate in the identification of learning needs and in the planning of adult learning activities, and to be totally involved in the learning process. If the learning process is dominated by the teacher, and the student is not given the freedom for participation and reflection, learning will become a bore, a useless activity geared only to examinations. Ghanaian students contemptuously refer to this sterile process of education as 'Chew, pour, pass and forget!' –

learn by rote (chew), reproduce for the examiner (pour) and forget as soon as possible because you do not need that kind of knowledge. What an epitaph for education! Let us hope that stimulating behaviour on the part of teachers of adults may make education a dynamic process which can liberate the learner to take charge of the course of his life.

Methods and techniques of teaching adults

It is assumed that a trained tutor will aim at arranging the learning activity so as to give the learner the fullest opportunity for participation and the best chance to use what he has learned to deal with his environment – for example, for making a gainful living and for maintaining harmonious relations with persons around him. In other words, for the learning experience to be useful in life, it should be made as realistic as possible; it must not be dull drudgery which leaves the learner no option but to 'chew, pour, pass (if lucky) and forget'.

Making the learning experience as realistic and as useful as possible requires that the tutor should apply methods, techniques and devices which will encourage the participation of the learner in the learning process.

In discussing educational techniques and devices, it is useful to define some of the terms that are often used. Coolie Verner has made a useful distinction between methods, techniques and devices – the three elements in the adult education process.[8] The **method** is 'the way in which people are organized in order to conduct an educational activity. A method establishes the relationship between the learner and the institution or agency through which the educational task is accomplished'. Methods may be **individual,** such as correspondence study or apprenticeship; **group-related,** such as classes, discussion-groups and seminars; or **community-related,** such as mass campaigns.

The **technique** is the way in which the tutor helps the learner to establish a relationship between himself and the learning task. Different techniques are effective for different learning tasks. For learners wanting information, such techniques as lectures, debates and written study-guides are appropriate. For learners wanting to acquire a skill, there are such techniques as process-demonstration and role-play. For learners wishing to apply knowledge gained (and it is a theme of this chapter that most adult learning requires this) there are such techniques as group discussion, project-work and field-work.

The term **device** 'is a convenient way of identifying the many instructional aids that extend or increase the effectiveness of methods and techniques, but which cannot themselves instruct. Items in this category range from instructional materials to communication media and from illustrations to the arrangement of furniture'. This chapter is less concerned with devices (which are treated full in Chapters 7 and 8) than with methods and techniques.

In considering both methods and techniques, the teacher and the learner should both look for the one that is most appropriate for the aims of the learning task and also most relevant to the condition of the learner. Thus, if the aim is to teach a manipulative skill such as weaving, the use of a master weaver to teach or coach a learner on a one-to-one basis, giving the learner as much opportunity as possible to practise the skill under the master's supervision, may be the most effective method of promoting learning. To make learning effective within the method of coaching or apprenticeship, various techniques may be employed – for example, a demonstration by a highly skilled weaver or the exhibition of his work.

A group of extra-mural students interested in studying the works of contemporary African writers may meet as a class and use group methods of learning, such as lectures from professors. In this regard, also, learning may be made effective by the use of such techniques as drama and discussion.

To sum up, it may be stated that face-to-face learning methods fall into two broad categories: *a*) learning methods which are suitable for **individual** learning situations, and *b*) methods appropriate for **group** learning. Group learning methods may be further classified into those suitable for small groups numbering up to about fifty, and those used for larger audiences and town meetings. What may be called a *method* for a particular learning relationship will be a *technique* in another learning situation.

For example, **discussion** is the suitable learning method for learners wishing to better understand the Bible, but in an extra-mural class, **lecturing** would be the learning method and discussion would be a technique. Techniques to make learning effective do not belong exclusively to any method or situation but depend on the ingenuity of the teacher and his determination to make learning possible. It is advisable that the guiding principle in the selection of a technique should be the extent to which it will help in making the learning experience as meaningful and as real as possible.

Individual learning techniques

Where individuals learn face-to-face (for instance when they want to acquire manipulative skills), it is best to employ the techniques which will give the learner the maximum opportunity for participation; in these cases the objective of the learning activity is to make the learner as perfect as possible in the skill. Indeed, in the learning of some skills, such as driving a motor car or practising medicine, the learner has to satisfy a licensing authority of the level of his competence before he may practise his skill. Therefore, techniques which will help the learner to achieve a high level of performance should be selected; these include *a*) observing the master craftsman at work; *b*) discussing with him how to manipulate some tools; *c*) demonstrations by masters; and *d*) the use of such devices as pictures and films to illustrate the required skills.

The teacher of cognitive subjects may find it necessary to teach only one person at a time because of some characteristic of the learner. The learner may either be physically handicapped and therefore unable to join a group of learners; or, as is usually the case in adult education, the learner may feel shy because he is threatened by the possibility of failure. I have often been approached by wealthy but illiterate persons to arrange private tuition for them because, ostensibly, they are too busy to keep regular class hours. It is important for the community good that everyone is equipped with functional education, and literacy and other adult education programme organizers should therefore make arrangements for the private tuition of persons who do not want to risk exposing themselves in a class of learners. The experience of Britain in assisting persons who are functionally illiterate is that some learners prefer to arrange privately by telephone for private tuition. Of course, a person asking for private tuition should be made to bear the cost of it.

Techniques to be employed with individual learners should include **counselling** (advising) with a view to letting the learner develop regular learning habits and gain confidence in his ability to learn. The learner should also be encouraged to practise his newly acquired skill, be it literacy or accountancy, in real-life situations, such as reading the newspaper or computing his own accounts. The emphasis in selecting appropriate techniques should be to enable the learner to practise as often as possible what he has learned so that his learning efforts are reinforced.

Small group learning techniques

We are used to the class or small group method of learning because it is the only method that the formal system of education employs. In this learning situation the method as well as the technique used for facilitating learning is lecturing and one may say without hesitation that lecturing is over-used if not abused. Lecturing is a method, because it is the established relationship between some adult educational institutions such as extra-mural departments and extension divisions and their students for learning, and a technique since it is employed by the teacher as the medium for facilitating learning.

Lecturing as a technique

It is quite natural to think that if a teacher has to impart knowledge, the most obvious way to do it is to lecture to a group of learners. Old-style university teaching is the use of the lecture technique in its absolute form: a university teacher may announce at the beginning of his lecture that he will not tolerate any interruptions (by that he means no questions from students during his lecture), and then proceed to read his lecture, including jokes, for a full hour. The justification for this kind of behaviour is that the professor is giving precious information and therefore the students should listen and take down notes; they will be given the opportunity to ask questions later during tutorials.

Where the tradition of **tutorials** is still observed perhaps the use of the lecture technique may be understandable. However, to encourage student participation, the tutor should require his students to do some reading about the subject on which the learning activity is based. The tutor may test the previous reading done by the students by either asking questions or requiring the members of the class to break up into smaller groups ('buzz groups') to discuss the questions. The tutor's lecture will then have to take another form; he may comment on important issues in the general subject area of the learning activity, and invite questions and comments from the students.

Obviously this tutorial approach or technique is useful for adults in all areas of learning where the teacher does not have to give hard facts. Reading material should be available to the students who, ideally, should be able to read reasonably well. I believe, however, that if teachers were under less pressure to 'prepare their students' for examinations, they would be less anxious to lecture to the students (give them facts for the examinations) than is the case now.

It is open to question whether a lecture is the only, or even the best, method of imparting facts, except to very 'experienced' students, such as university students. But lectures do have their use. A good lecture can inspire and thus motivate students. It can reinforce learning achieved in other ways. It can provide a background for learning. So, although more and more people are coming to distrust the lecture method and technique, one should know when to use it and should remember that a good lecture is a bridge of communication between learners and lecturer.

If lecturing appears unavoidable, the lecturer should convey to his students that he knows his subject, by talking to them instead of reading tediously through prepared notes. If the teacher is not tied down to a written lecture, he can draw his students into participation, with anecdotes, jokes, gestures and questions, both to and from them. The lecturer's ability to demonstrate his mastery of the knowledge he is imparting will generate confidence in his students and motivate them to learn. The joke is told of a professor who was reading his lecture as usual when he found that page ten was missing; he was so disabled by the missing page that he could not continue the lecture and so ended the class. The impression given by such a teacher is that what he teaches is not useful, and that it is only to be copied from books and reproduced in examinations.

The Socratic technique

As the name implies, this is an ancient technique of learning used by the Greek philosopher Socrates. It is particularly suitable with adult learners when studying subjects such as political science, psychology, philosophy and religion which are related to life experiences.

The objective of the Socratic method is to get away from the drudgery of lecturing, which can degenerate into talking down to adults, and to engage the adult learners actively in discovering for themselves truths and principles. The tutor makes challenging and controversial statements, to which learners respond; he questions the validity of the learners' responses further, and leads them gradually to the discovery of valid statements and principles. It might be helpful to read some of the works of Plato to find how the ancient Greeks studied philosophy and politics by questioning the validity of widely held views and assumptions.

The Socratic technique requires that the tutor should plan

thoroughly the line of his questioning and discussion. As student responses and questions cannot be fully anticipated, the tutor should prepare to concede his ignorance on some of the issues that may be raised. The 'all-knowing' traditional image given by some teachers has no place in a Socratic exercise. I have found that a tutor who genuinely accepts his ignorance improves his rapport with his students, who respect him more because they realize that he is in some ways like them, namely, still in the process of learning.

Obviously the Socratic technique cannot be used in all learning situations, but it is worth applying to the study of subjects related to adult learners' life experiences. A chance to test the validity of widely held assumptions is stimulating to learners. I have no doubt that in the changing circumstances of Africa, Socratic exercises on such topical issues as the status of women, polygamy, inheritance and the acquisition of wealth with a group of adult learners can be most rewarding to both the tutor and the student.

Contact with real problems

While it is impossible to let every learning experience enable the student to see, touch and feel, tutors cannot overlook the fact that seeing is believing for many people. Real life experiences which can be built into learning activities, through such techniques as demonstrations, planned visits and entering into someone else's way of life, are very powerful in changing behaviour patterns and attitudes. As adults are capable of altering situations, the exposure of adult learners to problems can lead to corrective action very quickly. I have known adult learners either to take action themselves to improve a situation, or to face out the authorities who have responsibility for the situation.

Approaches to tribalism provide an example. I believe that the problem of tribalism should not be tackled only with slogans and lectures but that opportunities should be provided for citizens, especially young persons, to live in as many areas of the country as possible with a view to learning about the cultures of various ethnic groups. This would be a more powerful way of breaking down tribal prejudices than exhortations by political leaders for cooperation among people of various ethnic origins. The following episode will illustrate the point better.

I read a letter in a Nigerian newspaper telling of the change in attitude and behaviour of a young Ibo man who lived and worked among the Hausas of northern Nigeria. The young Ibo university graduate served the period of his national service, which is one year compulsory community work for all Nigerian university graduates, at Kano city in Hausaland. There he fell in love with a pretty Hausa girl, but he felt the need to appeal to the newspaper's adviser on social problems for help in telling his parents about her. The young man wanted to devise a strategy for making his Ibo parents, who had not had his experience of living and working among Hausas, first to accept his fiancée, and second, to accept that Hausas were wonderful and nice people.

In view of the possibility of changing behaviour and attitudes through contact with real life situations and problems, adult educators (both tutors and administrators) need to plan visits so that adult students can be involved in surveys of specific community problems and in the planning and executing of some community development projects with community members.

Simulation

It is not always possible or convenient to let learners experience 'the real thing', at least at early stages in a programme. For instance, it is not wise to let someone who wants to learn to drive a lorry climb into the cab and drive off alone into traffic. It is often necessary to simulate real life conditions, so that the learner can experience the result of his mistakes (and learn to avoid them) without damaging himself or others. For professions like driving, or piloting an aeroplane, it is possible to use 'simulators' – mock lorries or aeroplanes which are actually bolted to the floor, but give a feeling of movement and record the effects of the learner's steering and manoeuvring. Such simulators may be seen at the Nigerian Driving School in Lagos and at the Civil Aviation Training School in Zaria.

Elaborate mechanical devices are not necessary in most cases, but there are several simulation techniques which can make problems vivid to learners, and help them to weigh up consequences and understand other people's views and reactions. Below are some useful simulation techniques which adult educators use.

Role-playing

The usual purpose of role-playing is to put learners in a simulated social relationship, with a view to widening their understanding of a particular problem or predicament and possibly changing their own attitudes. The tutor or group leader presents a situation, which he has either thought out himself or discussed with the group: for instance, a messenger wanting permission to go to a family funeral, but frightened of annoying the boss and losing his job. Roles are then allocated – the boss, the boss's girlfriend, the chief clerk, the messenger. Each of them then acts the assigned part. To add realism and entertainment, each person may be given a sketch of the individual characters, either verbally or in writing: 'You are a self-made businessman, very conceited and anxious to impress everyone with your importance', or 'You are a twenty-year-old who left primary school seven years ago, became bored with the village, came to the city and have lived by begging, borrowing and stealing. This is your first genuine job and you have been in it now for four months.'

The learners may, by contrasting role-play, see a subordinate person reacting rebelliously to bullying by a senior; or they may see respect and cordiality from a junior in response to respectful behaviour by another senior person. Such an experience is more likely to change attitudes and behaviour than a cold lecture on how to treat one's subordinates.

Since the objective of role-playing is not expert acting, as many learners as possible in a class should be given the opportunity to go through this kind of learning experience. It is always helpful to follow up a role-playing exercise with *discussion* to explain and thus provide reinforcement to experience gained in the role-playing exercise.

Drama

Role-playing is spontaneous, in that each player reacts as he thinks fit and there is no prepared story. A drama is rehearsed in advance and has a prepared story or 'plot', even though not all the dialogue is necessarily learnt by heart. The aim of drama may be to expose a social problem, or to reinforce cognitive learning, or to provide information and ideas in a stimulating way. An example of social-problem drama is Botswana's *Laedza Batanani*, in which some professional actors join with villagers to stage a play about, say, cattle-stealing, or the absence of the able-bodied men in the South African mines. An example of reinforcement may be when an adult class, which has been studying literature, put on one of the plays the learners have been reading.

An example of using drama to educate is the Ghana television serial *Osofo Dadzie* (the Rev. Mr Dadzie). This weekly programme conveys ideas through amusing morality plays. It has been on television since 1972 and, judging from its popularity, it may go on for years to come. Here television is being used as a device to make a technique of drama reach a wider audience. It also exemplifies the important point that a good play will be remembered and go more deeply into the audience's mind than any classroom activity. Very often the message is helped if the play is amusing and makes audiences roar with laughter.

Games

Resourceful adult teachers can invent or adapt local games to facilitate learning. Games can be used to simulate problems and their solutions as well as to reinforce cognitive learning. For instance, the game of 'Monopoly' can be adapted to play a health game. Players who get into patches marked 'unhealthy', such as allowing standing pools of water or drinking unboiled water from a shallow well, are penalized, while players who get into 'healthy' patches, such as eating a balanced diet or exercising regularly get a bonus. I have found games effective in motivating new literates to practise their new skills. Competing either as individuals or teams to construct words and sentences with blocks of letters is a popular game with new literates.

Stories, proverbs and songs

These are well known in traditional African societies as learning techniques for teaching social values. For instance, among the Akans of Ghana, 'Ananse' (spiderman) stories are popular for teaching morality.

A research task which every adult educator should undertake is the collection of local stories, songs and proverbs which have educational value. African proverbs express ideas more succinctly than many an adult educator can, and therefore a search should be made for local proverbs which can be used to facilitate learning. For instance, this Ghanaian proverb expresses the idea that learning has no end and that no one person can acquire much knowledge: *Knowledge is like a baobab tree; no one person can encircle it with his two arms*. A couple of Ghanaian proverbs also give an insight into the political upheavals taking place in many parts of Africa in recent years, and of which Ghana has had her ample share. Proverb number one says: *If power is on sale you will be well advised to sell your mother to get the money to buy it, because when you have gained power you can claim back your mother at no cost.*

This proverb sums up neatly the lengths to which some people are prepared to go to obtain political power, since they know that once they have been enthroned over the political kingdom there is nothing else they cannot do. There is, however, another proverb which warns those who have acquired political power: *Power is like holding an egg; if you hold it too tightly it breaks; if you are careless in holding the egg it falls out of your hands and breaks*. The message is quite clear, and many a Ghanaian political leader should have heeded it.

Large group learning techniques

A common learning situation which adult educators may create is of the **town meeting, public lecture** or **rally** type. In this kind of situation there may be hundreds of learners, and one lecturer or a number of speakers to lead the learning activity.

The first matter of importance, which may appear to have nothing to do with learning or teaching, yet requires skill and considerable effort, is to accommodate the crowd of learners as comfortably as possible. In the African circumstances, this means providing tolerable seating arrangements in a well-ventilated hall, if the meeting is to be held indoors, or protection from rain and excessive sunshine if it is to be held outside. It is also necessary to ensure that every member of the audience hears clearly what will be said, and this may require the provision of a public address system that works. If the learning activity is to extend for a whole day or more, as is the case with conferences, then board and lodging arrangements should be made.

These physical arrangements and services are so important that failure to provide them adequately is never forgotten by the audience and may be remembered better than whatever was supposed to have been learned. And yet it is in these areas that many lectures and conferences have not been successful. Evaluation reports sometimes speak of good programmes but poor arrangements. Adult educators should not forget that their subject is both academic and practical, and that the end results of their learning activities are judged by the extent to which these activities lead to changes in behaviour. Therefore, physical arrangements and provision of services should be considered as part of the educational experience and should be planned and executed with as much care and attention as the academic programme.

For public lectures, town meetings and rallies, a chairman is also necessary. A chairman should be able to supervise the meeting independently. I have often seen prominent but illiterate persons being made chairmen at public functions where English was the medium of learning. Usually an assistant is appointed to translate the proceedings for the chairman. This arrangement is unsatisfactory since it is usually embarrassing and detracts from the effectiveness of the meeting. Important as it is to draw prominent citizens in the community into public learning activities, I do not think it is fair to put them in positions which will embarrass them.

Question-time should always be provided for, since it is absolutely important that the members of the audience get the opportunity to participate. The speaker should allow at least half an hour for audience questions and comments.

Seminars and workshops

The large group of learners at a conference may be broken into smaller units called seminars or workshops. These are small groups of learners under a leader, who might be an expert or someone elected by his fellow learners. The group may select its own topic or the organizers of the seminar/workshop may do so for the learners.

The atmosphere in a seminar or workshop is usually informal since the objective is to provide all the members in the group the opportunity of learning from each other. The leader, however, is responsible for arranging for supporting services and equipment. Some of the techniques mentioned earlier as being suitable for small group or class learning – lecturing, discussion, and role-playing – may also be employed in a seminar/workshop.

A *report* from the group is usually required, as it makes it possible for the entire conference group to share in the learning activities of each seminar/workshop as well as providing reinforcement for the groups concerned.

Panel discussion, symposium and debate

A **panel discussion** is a conversation between three or four persons chosen for their knowledge and interest in a particular subject. They carry on the discussion in front of an audience.

A **symposium** is a number of short speeches from two or four speakers, who are chosen because of their knowledge about a subject. They make their contributions before an audience.

In a **debate**, the pros and cons of an issue, which is put in a controversial statement, are offered by two groups of speakers –

one group for and the other against the statement or motion. Points are awarded by judges for such things as eloquence, logic and the truth of statements.

All these techniques may be used 'live' – face-to-face with the learners – or through the media, particularly radio or television. When used 'live', all three techniques allow for audience participation by way of questions, comments and contributions. As these techniques permit as many people as possible to participate, conference organizers are well advised to employ them in addition to the usual ones of lectures and seminars/workshops.

Colloquy

This is the discussion of an issue by a panel consisting both of persons with expert knowledge and of learners. Usually this technique is used at the end of a conference, to enable the learners to bring up some outstanding issues for open discussion with the resource persons at the conference.

Colloquy as a technique is useful, in the sense that it builds up confidence in the learners by encouraging them to put their questions and comments publicly to the experts. The learners who are to be on the panel should be chosen for their ability and confidence to speak in public. They should also consult with other learners to gather points from among themselves, while the chairman should permit contributions from the floor so as to involve as many learners as possible in the discussion.

Notes and references

1. William S. Gray, *Manual for Teachers of Adult Illiterates* (Chicago: National Advisory Committee on Adult Illiteracy/Chicago University Press, 1933)
2. A. S. Deshpande, C. Webb, and Marks, 'Student perceptions of engineering instructors' behaviours and their relationships to the evaluation of instructors and courses', *American Educational Research Journal*, vol. 7, no. 3 (December 1970), pp. 289–306
3. D. Solomon and H. L. Miller, *Exploration in Teaching Styles* (Chicago: Centre for the Study of Liberal Education for Adults, 1961); and D. Solomon, W. E. Bezdeck and L. Rosenberg, *Teaching Styles and Learning* (Chicago: Centre for the Study of Liberal Education for Adults, 1963)
4. *Journal of American Educational Research Association*, vol. 3 (1952), p. 255

5. E. K. Ampene, 'Teaching styles in basic adult education' (Unpublished PhD thesis, University of Chicago, 1972); and E. K. Ampene, 'Teaching styles in basic adult education', *Literacy Discussion* (Teheran), vol. 4, no. 3 (1973)

6. Three types of behaviour were described by J. W. Getzels and H. A. Thelen, 'The classroom room group as a unique social system', in N. B. Henry (ed.), *The 59th Yearbook of the National Society for the Study of Education* (Chicago: University of Chicago Press, 1960), pp. 53–8. See also N. Gage, *Handbook of Research on Teaching* (Chicago: Rand McNally, 1963)

7. S. M. Grabowski, *Training Teachers of Adults: Models of Innovative Programmes* (Syracuse University Publications in Continuing Education, 1976), pp. 10–11

8. Coolie Verner, 'The definition of terms', in G. Jensen, A. A. Liveright, and W. Hallenbeck (eds), *Adult Education: Outlines of an Emerging Field of University Study* (Chicago: Adult Education Association of the USA, 1964). See also Coolie Verner and Alan Booth, *Adult Education* (Washington: Centre for Applied Research in Education, 1964), ch. 5.The quotations that follow are from Verner and Booth

7 Teaching and learning aids in adult education

E. A. Haizel

Introductory

This chapter tries to group teaching aids at the disposal of the adult educator. The aids are divided into *a*) non-projected aids, where the emphasis is on the chalkboard and its derivatives; *b*) projected aids, divided into still and moving pictures; *c*) the use of recorded sound, where the tape recorder is discussed; and finally *d*) written aids and how they could be used in teaching.

Teaching aids are placed in a hierarchical order, and the point is made that as we move up the scale, aids become more expensive, more complicated and also less flexible and less specific in content. The choice of what aid to use therefore should be a matter of rational decision. The purpose of using aids is to help the tutor to communicate better, prepare a more effective learning environment, and, altogether, to do a better job.

The point is also made that aids require time in preparation and practice in instrumentation. Where aids come in to support subject matter, then they are being used **intrinsically**. Where they are used to motivate or reward, they are being used **extrinsically**. Since aids are to help the tutor do his work, they should not take over from the tutor. The tutor must know what he is doing, and choose that aid which will make him achieve the objectives of the teaching–learning situation.

The conceptual setting

In Chapter 1 we saw that an adult educator may have teaching functions, facilitating functions, and planning and organizing functions. In this chapter we are primarily interested in the adult educator whose main job is 'to teach', whatever else he may do.

We start with the proposition that every teacher's role is to prepare a learning environment. This is why we now refer to a 'teaching–learning situation'. The teacher provides the stimuli and the student does the learning. Ideally, the adult educator does less direct teaching of the traditional type and takes on the role of planner and organizer of learning situations, coach and gadfly. In other words, he gradually shifts the responsibility for the direction of learning to the student and helps the student to become his own teacher. The main purpose is to help the student *learn how to learn* and thereby develop the desire for continued learning. The adult educator must of necessity know the difference between the 'acquiring mind' and the 'inquiring mind'.

Broad strategies of instruction

When we have a group of learners to teach, we could adopt a number of strategies:

a) We could use 'direct face-to-face instruction'. This is when we stand before the class and talk to or with them. Where we have a chalkboard in support, we speak of 'chalk and talk'. Methods of direct face-to-face teaching/learning have been discussed in Chapter 6.

b) Where we have the necessary infrastructure and resources, we may use instruction mediated by print, recordings, television, teletape and pictures. Many multi-media correspondence instructional methods use a combination of these modes. Such approaches are treated in Chapter 8.

c) We could also, in direct face-to-face instructional situations, provide ourselves with other support materials in the form of chalkboard, flip charts, pictures, posters, models, films and recorded sound.

Some considerations in using aids

We are no longer satisfied with just providing a picture or a chart or a recording in the teaching–learning situation. To use a tool of communication effectively, we now realize, as C. J. Duncan puts it, that:

there is a constantly shifting interaction between the equipment on a technical level and the materials and methodology applied at the professional teaching level. The methodology of the design, selection, and utilization of communications with these media involve both technical expertise, the realisation and exploitation of the current technological capabilities, and the exercise of professional pedagogic principles. What at first sight seems a relatively simple decision to use an 'aid' to assist a learning situation turns out to be vastly more complex if realised in all its fruitfulness.[1]

The complexity of the use of aids does not only emanate from the particular aid. We have also to think of the **perception** of those for whom an aid is intended. Briefly stated, perception depends on 'figure and ground'. When parts of a field stand out, this becomes the **figure**, differentiated from the rest of the **field**, which forms the background to the figure. It is the figure that stands out and is readily perceived. These **figural experiences**, as they are called, are vital in the choice and use of an aid. The first reason is that they need not necessarily be visual; any pattern of sound, touch, taste or smell which is consciously perceived as such must first become 'figural'. The second reason is that people tend to perceive what is meaningful to them; where 'figure and ground' do not form a conceptual whole, people will try to make sense out of chaos and make a deliberate effort to avoid confusion.

Further, since we integrate new knowledge and experiences with what we already have, adult educators have to know the culture of their students. For instance, some people prefer bright colours and others soft colours, but particular colours also may give rise to certain emotional reactions, which are all culturally based; in most Ghanaian cultures, for example, red is a sign of danger, state of tension or preparation for a fight. White normally represents victory.

In our use of aids, therefore, we have to think about the *equipment*, our *method* and the *perception* of our students, including seemingly minor things like colour. The software of one's tools of communication, their arrangement in time and space must match the perceptual experiences of our students.

Why do we use aids?

We can say that we should use aids because they communicate better and they provide a multi-channel appeal. An action picture will describe the working of a machine far better than words. As a summary, this may be satisfactory. It is however necessary to go into the question a bit more.

The student learns through active interaction with his environment, with people, things and ideas. The adult educator's role is to arrange a learning environment that will encourage productive interaction which will in turn provide a learning experience. In this quest, the adult educator has to solve a complex equation, which means juggling with:

a) subject matter;
b) types of learning;
c) diagnosis of learning styles of students;
d) his own teaching style;
e) teaching strategies and learning;
f) stimulus modes and presentation media.

This process is crucial because we have to determine the individual strengths of our students, and begin to instruct, using media which will capitalize on these strengths. Our interest is not, and should not be, in fall-out rates and failures. We are required to produce a pattern which will not only satisfy a class of students but also satisfy each individual. Nobody is suggesting that this is easy to attain. It is just that it is a challenge which we must face and face squarely.

Getting a message before looking for a medium

The first step in our attack on the problem is to define objectives, describing as precisely as necessary what the student will be able to do, as a result of the teaching, that he was unable to do before. The definition of objectives is important, because it is after that that we can look for a medium capable of carrying the message. We must decide *what* must be learnt before deciding on *how* it should be learnt.

Parameters in the use of aids

Before we decide to use any aid we have to ask ourselves five questions. Is the aid:

necessary?
apt?
suitable for the teacher?
suitable for the requirements of the subject matter?
suitable for the needs of the learner

All these five questions have to be answered in the affirmative if the aid used is to achieve any worthwhile purposes. This warning is necessary because audience-centred communication has its drawbacks, if communication is not thought of as a process involving more parameters than the listener.

Intrinsic and extrinsic use of aids

As a rough guide in determining use of aids, we can start from the premise that the educative process is directed towards developing certain knowledge, skills and attitudes. It deals with people and it deals with subject matter.

Where an aid helps to achieve the goals of the process, it is regarded as intrinsic to the process. If, however, aids are used primarily to arouse interest, or to reward the learner, then their use is extrinsic. The aids will then not be directly linked with the goals of the learning process or with the subject-matter. Aids could be used, in specific terms, intrinsically to provide work, to allow learners to engage in self-instruction and to illustrate. Or they would be used extrinsically to arouse and maintain interest, to entertain or to pass time.

Extrinsic motivation is part of the trade, but it must be used judiciously. We may not be sure that the student so motivated will come to grips with the subject-matter. There is a danger that he may not only develop a superficial relation to the subject-matter in question, but may also think of learning in general in terms of extrinsic motivation. 'It is important that audio-visual aids should not become merely a means of entertainment, of developing superficial familiarity with the subject matter. They can be vital instruments to elucidate and clarify ideas and concepts, and to bring about a search for insight into structural relationships of the skills and concepts taught.'[2] That is, the learner's intelligence must be respected. In the words of Luchins, 'apart from appealing to an individual's likes, status or appetite [aids] should also appeal to his need for cognitive clarity and meaning, and should challenge his curiosity and decision-making ability'.[3]

Stimulus modes

An adult educator has a number of stimulus modes at his disposal in support of his 'living voice'. If we define a stimulus mode as any kind of stimulus presented to the learner, we can list **human interaction**; **direct observation of things**; **pictorial representation**; **recorded sound** and **written symbols**.

Yet we tend to put all aids under the title 'audio-visual'. This is probably because the two main channels in the teaching–learning situation are sound and vision. We have to remember that the other senses of smell, taste and touch could come in; indeed, when we want to get the 'feel' of a situation, we have to go beyond our supposed five senses. In using the term 'audio-visual', we must remember to give it the wider interpretation. This is why I have called this sub-section 'stimulus modes'.

Deciding to use aids

An essential element in any instructional plan is the choice of appropriate media. We are, however, very glib when we tell people: 'Now choose the best or most appropriate medium to serve your instructional ends.' How does one decide which is the best or most appropriate medium?

Often, there is no real decision. An aid may conveniently be available or the tutor may just have a liking for a particular aid. At times, novelty may be the basis of choice. To decide which aid to use demands that we know something definite about the media at our disposal, and also have a rational system of decision-making. We have already referred to the complexity of the use of aids. We can now go a step further.

Hierarchical order of aids

We can order aids from the simplest to the most complex, e.g. from the conventional chalkboard to computer-assisted instruction. As we move from simple to complex, we find that both unit costs and generality increase whilst the ease of use, flexibility and economy decrease. The reason for this situation is simple. The simpler and cheaper the aid, the more specific it is for selected audiences and tasks. We use the chalkboard for a specific class, but if we want to use TV the audience becomes larger and more diffuse. Mainly for economic reasons, complex and costly systems will have to have a broader base and appeal to a more general audience.

Figure 3 (page 128), taken from C. J. Duncan's article in *Media and Methods*, illustrates this situation. The diagram shows the perfect negative correlation of the two arrows.

Figure 4 (page 129) is a flow chart which could be of help as you grapple with the problem of which aid to use. It is a model for rational decision-making on choice of aid, culled from Jerrold E. Kemp's article, 'Which medium?'[4]

As you go through this model, remember that aids are no substitute for the adult educator. They will not do this work for him, nor will they make his task of preparation any easier. What we postulate is that aids correctly used will make the adult educator's work more effective.

Non-projected aids in use

We can now go ahead to look at some of the aids, their advantages and disadvantages and how we could use them effectively to aid our teaching.

The conventional chalkboard

'If only one method of presenting instructional aids could be selected, most experienced instructors probably would choose the

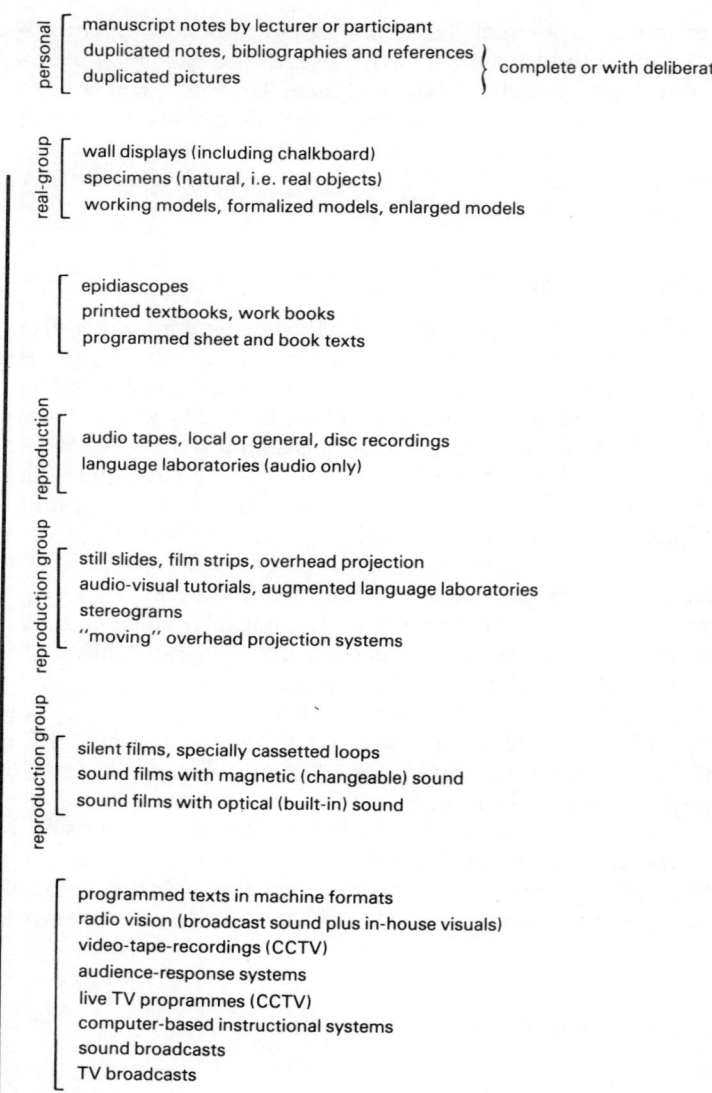

personal
- manuscript notes by lecturer or participant
- duplicated notes, bibliographies and references } complete or with deliberate gaps
- duplicated pictures

real-group
- wall displays (including chalkboard)
- specimens (natural, i.e. real objects)
- working models, formalized models, enlarged models

- epidiascopes
- printed textbooks, work books
- programmed sheet and book texts

reproduction
- audio tapes, local or general, disc recordings
- language laboratories (audio only)

reproduction group
- still slides, film strips, overhead projection
- audio-visual tutorials, augmented language laboratories
- stereograms
- "moving" overhead projection systems

reproduction group
- silent films, specially cassetted loops
- sound films with magnetic (changeable) sound
- sound films with optical (built-in) sound

- programmed texts in machine formats
- radio vision (broadcast sound plus in-house visuals)
- video-tape-recordings (CCTV)
- audience-response systems
- live TV proprammes (CCTV)
- computer-based instructional systems
- sound broadcasts
- TV broadcasts

Increasing prime cost — difficulty of provision — generality — potential size of audience

Figure 3 *A hierarchical order of selected audio-visual instrumental media*
In a single dimensional array, considerable overlap will occur between simple examples of one type and complicated examples of another. This makes the order at the bottom of the table extremely tentative.)

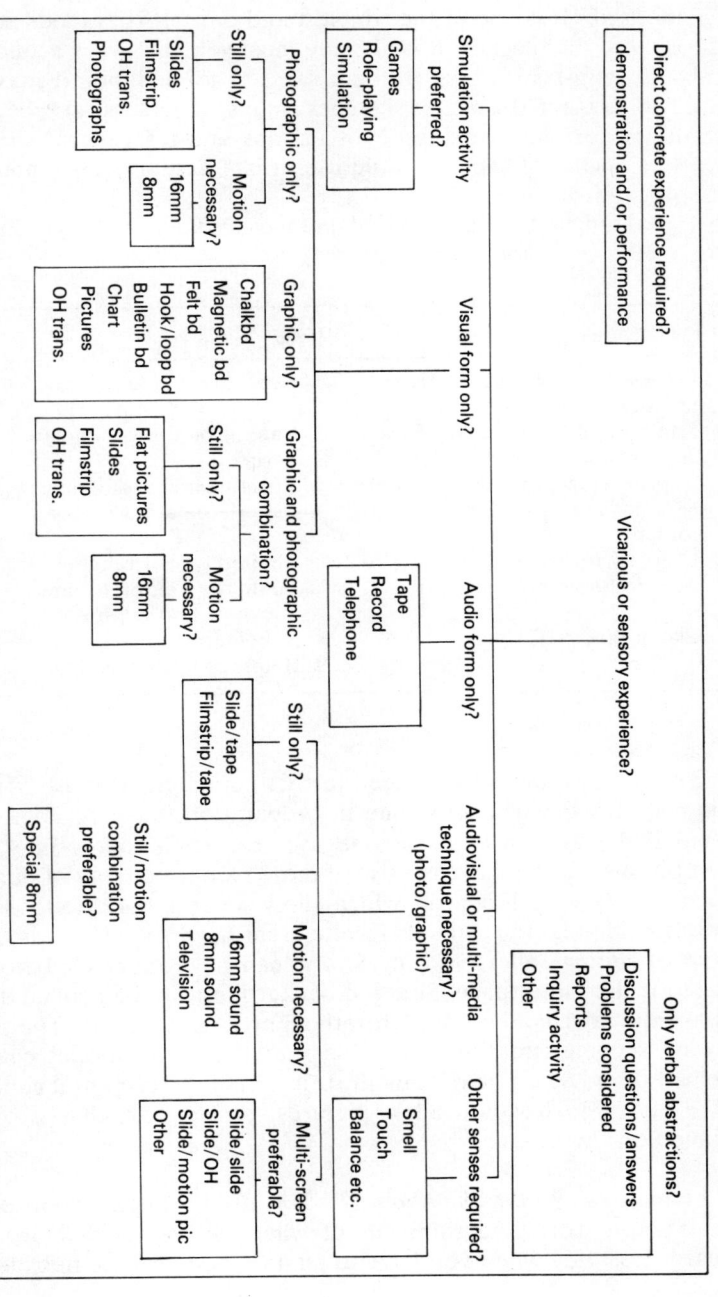

Figure 4   *Small group interaction*

chalkboard.' It is one of the simplest and most efficient aids at the disposal of the teacher. It is also the most versatile, very economical and long-lasting. As Botham says: 'The chalkboard may be used to present drawings, sketches, maps, diagrams, graphs and statistics: for summarising of discussions and for general written work. Capable of such versatile use, it is a natural supplement to all other forms of aids.'[5]

C. J. Duncan tabulates the advantages and disadvantages in the use of the chalkboard in this way:[6]

Advantages	Disadvantages
1 Freedom, to prepare when and to what extent desired	1 Need to be able to draw
2 Can be built up in sight of class	2 Cannot be too complicated
3 Spontaneous action possible	3 Dirty
4 Repeat, erase, redraw if possible	4 Visual contact sometimes poor
5 Familiarity to lecturer and students	5 Need large areas of board
6 Unlikely to become stereotyped	6 Limited colour range
7 No additional help needed	7 Limited variation in line thickness and texture
8 Cheap material	8 Ephemeral
	9 Requires lecturer's time

The disadvantages listed need further comment. The use of any aid requires the teacher's time in preparation, but one does not have to be an artist before one uses the chalkboard. In some institutions we may have the use of more elaborate types of board, such as rotary chalkboards, which allow squared backgrounds for graphs and diagrams, and also white areas for projection. Also, by help of sliding rollers or hinges, one can have more chalkboard area for the same space. Squared background can be provided on conventional chalkboards if forethought is given to it. The one strong recommendation would be that the conventional chalkboard should never be of cement. If it is made of cement it cannot take pins, which would allow pictures, posters and charts to be pinned on the board.

How may we use the chalkboard?   It is always necessary to plan chalkboard work and think about what will be needed on the board. It is only when you have to plan that you can be flexible in the use of your board and still retain presentation in a logical order. Neat work on the board attracts attention, and arrangement should be 'legible, simple, clear and interesting'. Drawings should be simple and bold, writing should be straight across the board, and letters should be not less than 5 centimetres in height for good effect.

When you decide to use coloured chalk for greater effect (and you must if it is available), you have to remember that:

a) Coloured chalks differ in quality and colour density;
b) some colours are easier to see than others;
c) the board provides a mat, or non-shining, background.

Generally speaking, pale colours are more effective than deep ones, and you have to select colours for their clarity. A useful guide, following Botham, is to use white and yellow chalk on green and black backgrounds. Red and light blue chalk are effective in underlining key words or phrases. Avoid brown, purple and dark blue chalks because they are rather difficult to see. Whatever colour of chalk you use, you have to select the best quality available. You do not require so much pressure when using good quality chalk and you avoid the unpleasant squeaks which make you grit your teeth.

Cleaning the board is not as simple as it looks. The habit of cleaning words with the fingers is both untidy and unhealthy. Use a felt block eraser if you can get hold of one, remembering to beat out the chalk dust frequently. When this imported product is not available, you can make a cleaner from pieces of cloth sewn into a bag. Practice has shown that cleaning the chalkboard with vertical strokes give the best results. You may, however, prefer horizontal strokes. What you have to avoid is irregular circular movements which leave the board dirtier than it should be.

But we do not only write on the chalkboard. We also have to draw and rule lines. When you have a chalkboard compass, the drawing of circles becomes easy; but there should be no problem if you have no compass. What you have to do is to get a string loop stretched between a finger in contact with the board and the chalk. Your finger becomes the centre of the circle, drawn with the chalk at the other end of the string. A flat piece of wood about 75 centimetres long will make a very satisfactory ruler, especially when a small handle is attached to give a firmer and better hold.

When it is necessary to produce a series of simple outline drawings of maps, human figures and other sketches, it is very useful to make templates. Sometimes when the composite picture you want on the chalkboard is complicated, you can prepare a 'dot-dusting' outline. You first have to make a full size drawing of the material to be presented on a sheet of paper. You then make a series of perforations at close intervals along the lines of the drawing. A compass point, a large needle or the sharp point of a pair of scissors will do the job. In class, you hold the perforated outline against the surface of the board and then pat gently with a chalk-filled board eraser.

One may ask, why all this trouble? Why not have the picture already drawn on the board? The fact is that the presentation of material on the board is crucial. If all visual material is on view before the start of the lesson you will lose spontaneity and the attention of students. The stimulus given as each new item is presented would be absent, and student expectation would have been frustrated. The build-up of a lesson as a joint effort of teacher and learner would also not be achieved.

It is also advisable that you go occasionally to the back of the class to view your chalkboard work. Is the writing legible? Is there a glare? If you can get a seat at the back, do sit down so that you can see the chalkboard in the same way as learners at the back see it. You may find that your beautiful work at the bottom of the board is actually out of view to those at the back.

Finally, before we leave what I regard as the most effective and easily available aid at our disposal, a word about maintenance and care. We must thoroughly wash our chalkboard from time to time. This is to remove accumulated chalk dust. We should try and get a thin type of chalkboard paint, called renovator. Where we apply the renovator, we can restore our board to its original condition.

Derivatives of the chalkboard

When we examine the disadvantages of the chalkboard as listed by C. J. Duncan – for instance, limited colour range, the board being dirty, the need to draw every picture – we see the basis for the various derivatives of the chalkboard. We will now look at these.

Posters and charts

It is customary, in the literature, to put posters and charts together. This is because posters have much in common with charts. But as a matter of fact, there are also some distinctive differences between the two, especially in purpose, content and use.

A good poster should be able to stand on its own and communicate its message very effectively without support from any external source. The adult educator may want to start a campaign or may want to remind members of his audience of a theme and persuade them to change in the direction of the theme. This is when the poster comes in as a useful visual aid with an instant and direct psychological appeal.

When you decide to use a poster, remember the following points:

a) *Your poster must make a positive approach*. 'Save Water: It's Precious' is preferable to 'Don't Waste Water'.

b) *The content of your poster must be limited*. Make only one point, since the poster has to achieve a lot in a short time.

c) *Use very bold lettering*, and if you add an illustration, it must reinforce the words.

d) *A short but catchy phrase, making use of alliteration or rhyme, is a very good way of conveying your message*. The commercial advertisers seem to have beaten us to it. 'Go Well, Go Shell.' In general, a poster must be attractive and memorable, but however attractive your poster is, do not leave it on display for too long. It will lose its appeal that way.

A **teaching chart** is essentially an aid to formal education. It can, however, be used to create talking points and stimulate discussions in non-formal education. Teaching charts are light in weight, easy to present and can be as effective as any sophisticated medium. When you use a teaching chart, you cut out time on repetitive chalkboard work, and are in a position to make better use of colour and contact.

When you decide to add lettering to your chart, keep it to a minimum. Too much printed matter, according to Botham, 'detracts from the spontaneous detail'. It is better to use the chart in conjunction with the chalkboard, writing your summary up point by point. The chart, unlike the poster, does not normally stand on its own. This is not the only difference between teaching charts and posters that can be noted here. Teaching charts have also more content than posters. But as you prepare your teaching chart, avoid small work and superfluous detail. The aim is to try and 'create' a clear overall impression of the subject-matter. And since the chart is for use in class, and must be seen from the back of the classroom, some thought must be given to its size. Anything less than 55 by 38 centimetres will be of doubtful value.

Flip charts

When you have a collection of charts arranged in a predetermined order and fastened together at the top edge, you have a 'turnover' or a flip chart. When one point and one picture have been presented, the first chart is turned up and over to reveal the next. You are then in a position to build up a composite visual image stage by stage. What you have to be careful about is the quality of basic material used. The paper should be good quality, and capable of withstanding a considerable amount of handling.

Flip charts encourage audience participation, create anticipation that something else is coming up and thus sustain interest. They can also be conveniently used with radio, especially when you are running a campaign on a wide scale and you require a lot of monitors who cannot be expected to run their classes unaided.

Picture cards

When you work with a small class, you may use picture cards in place of flip charts. You have a series of picture cards which you can hold in your hand or place on a small stand on a table as you go on with your lesson. Picture cards retain all the advantages of sequence presentation, and are also easy to carry from one place to another. They are also known as **flash cards** and come in very useful where viewing distances are not great.

Wall charts

Where you have a permanent place for your classes, you could use wall charts as a convenient way of following up your formal sessions. A wall chart can be described as a wall newspaper. In it you can supply additional information and get learners to participate in the preparation. What you have to watch out for is that the wall chart should be attractive and should have an aim and a conclusion.

You can produce a number of different types of wall charts. You could have a 'flow chart', starting with a known concept and going through a series of logical steps until the final result is reached. Or you could have a 'story-telling chart', employing a strip cartoon method but following the flow chart method. Where you have taught hard facts, you could produce a 'factual chart' presenting your material in visual form. Such a chart will always require careful explanation as it is not usually capable of standing on its own

Finally, you could produce a 'comparative chart' type of presentation. Export and import figures can be well represented this way.

Whichever type of wall chart you choose to produce, you have to be sure that it attracts attention, has a clear message represented in a persuasive and stimulating manner, and that the message is not only logical but within the comprehension of viewers.

Adhesive aids

Where it is possible for picture, illustrations, captions, and other symbols to be slapped on to a surface and adhere (stick) for at least a while, then we have adhesive aids. The two types of adhesive aids at our disposal as adult educators are the flannelgraph and the magnetic board.

Flannelgraph   To use the flannelgraph, you have to get a flannel board. If you glue material – a blanket, for instance – lightly over a hardboard or plywood surface you will get a permanent flannel board. You can improvise a temporary board by securing your blanket on a portable chalkboard. Next, you have to back your visual aids with blanket or other fluffy material. Blotting paper could be used as backing. You are then ready to use your flannel-graph, by sticking the various items at will on to the main blanket board. You can build up your composite picture step by step, adding and rearranging components at will.

But a caution. The colour of the flannelgraph background is of importance. It must be of 'receding' colour to provide adequate contrast with the teaching materials. The background must not lay emphasis on perspective or depth, otherwise items will look awk-ward when moved from one point to the other. Finally, flannel boards are more efficient when they are set at a slight angle to the vertical.

Magnetic board   Where you have to work in the open air, you will find the magnetic board resistant to even moderate gusts of wind. The magnetic board preserves the flexibility of the flannelgraph and adds the advantage of the fact that ordinary chalk can be used on it as well.

The board is a bit more difficult to make since ferrous material, tinplate or galvanized iron, has to be glued to a piece of wood. Besides, the aids have to be backed with small magnets secured with strips of sellotape. But once you produce these, you have an aid with the flexibility of the flannelgraph plus the facility for chalk use.

We have spent some time on the chalkboard and its derivatives because this range of aids combines easily available resources, versatility and facility of use. In the texts, these aids are referred to as 'non-projected aids'. A quotation from C. J. Duncan will conclude this section best.

The critical factor in the use of this large group of relatively non-instrumental aids lies in their proper integration with the personality of the teacher. They become, in the best example, merely an extension of his personality, sensitive to every nuance of class reaction and the variations of his performance. Thus they preserve much of the merit of true face-to-face teaching even with classes up to 350. . . .[7]

Projected aids

Projected aids are of two kinds. One series of devices provides still pictures and the other moving pictures. What is technically common to both is that they depend on the science of optics and on electronics. When it comes to actual use, they differ in instrumentation and in degree of preparation and flexibility of use. It is therefore necessary for the adult educator at least to ask for technical advice before any of these devices is bought.

Still pictures

The commonest type of device providing still projected pictures is the slide or filmstrip projector.There are many makes on the market and they differ in their individual features, size and light output. But the fundamental principles of operation are constant to all: light from behind passing through condenser lenses, through a transparency, taking the picture through a projection lens assembly on to a screen. Since the picture on the screen is the one on the transparency upside-down, it is necessary to turn the transparency upside-down in the gate in order to get a correct picture on the screen. This law of inversion requires that one takes care in loading a projector. It is better to turn a slide or filmstrip through 180 degrees so that the title is inverted. This is the way to ensure that the slide or filmstrip fits in the carrier for correct projection. Turning over the slide or filmstrip is an exercise in futility.

The technical operations of a projector are better demonstrated than talked about. Practice alone will make you master the use of equipment. Projectors may come equipped with stack-loading for up to 120 slides. They may have remote slide changing, both forward and backward. They can have remote adjustment of focus. All these are technical details. But your aim is to improve your teaching with the aid of the device. You therefore have to look also at the pedagogic aspects in the use of the device. The most important is the role of *commentary*. Commentary must be stimulating, and should be directed towards the important features contained in each picture. Sincerity and enjoyment of role will help you attain greater effect. And this is true whether you are using the more flexible slides or the less flexible filmstrip.

Slides can be arranged as you prefer, but filmstrips come to you in a pre-arranged sequence. Even where filmstrips are reversible or can be jumped, no audience likes this type of 'confused presentation' which is the result of jumping frames. The still picture remains a mode which you can control, and where there is the electric current or a car battery available use the projector whenever you can. But watch out! A car battery will give you direct current. A projector equipped for alternating current will collapse before your very eyes if connected to a battery. Your enthusiasm may land you in frustration before your class. Checking that you are using the correct voltage is fundamental to the use of all electrical equipment. It is therefore necessary to touch briefly on projector management.

You must set up and check the equipment before the arrival of the viewers. The title frame must be in the gate ready for projection. Then make sure that the screen is correctly aligned, and that every part of the picture is in focus. Arrange the power cable so that it won't be damaged by people or equipment to trip people as they find their seats. Finally, in your preparation before the 'show', be certain that the beam from the projector will clear the heads of the viewers.

If the cooling blower motor fails, you have to switch off the lamp immediately. This is rare, but your lamp may blow. Therefore it is best always to have a spare lamp with you. If you have a change in lamp, always remember to switch off the projector and disconnect from the power supply. You may not live to regret if you fail to disconnect the power supply. Generally, you must guard against dust and dirt, but do not touch or handle lenses with your fingers. In our conditions, screening in daylight can create some problems. In such conditions, screens are more effective when they are shielded from direct light. You must therefore find a way to mask the light. The easy answer is not total blackout. The exclusion of light may mean the exclusion of air and may result in a sleepy, inattentive audience. Blinds may help if you have a permanent classroom, but most probably a half-darkened room is the best you can manage. And finally, when not in use, your projector should be kept in its case or under cover. But do not be in a hurry to stow away. Wait until cooling has taken place.

Overhead projector

Before leaving stills, we should spend sometime on the overhead projector, leaving out the episcope and epidiascope, except for a brief mention. The episcope is the only piece of equipment capable of projecting non-transparent material. The epidiascope is an episcope fitted with an additional lens and a carrier system to be used for the projection of slides and filmstrips. C. J. Duncan has described them as 'expensive and inefficient'. It is no wonder that only a few models are manufactured now.

The overhead projector is so called because it projects over the head or shoulder of the teacher using it onto a screen behind and above him. Generally speaking, all makes of overhead projectors have a writing area of 25.5 by 25.5 centimetres. Using the special type of transparent writing paper and pens which go with it, one can do a lot of things with the overhead projector.

Once the technique of use has been learnt, the overhead projector offers a number of advantages:

a) The instructor faces the class as he uses the gadget. There is thus no contact lost between teacher and class – and since attention is controlled and directed the student rarely gets lost.

b) It is possible to use an 'overlay' system with the overhead projector. One transparency can be placed over another to allow a composite image to be built up step by step. It is also possible to insert tables and diagrams at will.

c) When not required, parts of the transparency can be masked off so that attention can be drawn to one special area. The tutor has the advantage of spontaneity even though he has to prepare beforehand. The overhead projector is clean and neat, can be used in a well-lighted room so that students can take down notes, and unlike the chalkboard, permanent record of what is projected may be kept.

This projector costs more than the chalkboard, requires electricity and produces a glare which can be troublesome. But it is worth possessing because, in the hands of a skilled teacher, lessons can, with its help, become dramatic and lively.

Cine film

Figure 3 showed us that as the complexity of aids increased, so their flexibility and the tutor's control of them decreased. Cine film comes under the category of aids of increased complexity. When we use films for the purposes of instruction, the film in effect takes over from the tutor; as Botham says, 'it is the producer of the film who decides exactly what material is to be presented, and who further determines the rate and mode of presentation'.[8] Films are expensive, and it is usual to aim at economy. The tendency is therefore to present as much material as is practically possible in a short space of time. Not only is there a cloud of information, but certain parts of the information may not be relevant for our immediate purposes, that is, if we are using the film intrinsically and not extrinsically.

We know that when we want to arouse interest in a group of people in our villages we show films as a means of attraction. We are then in possession of a captive audience for our real message. This is an example of the extrinsic use of the cine film. Here, however, we are interested in the film as a direct teaching medium. It is agreed that a film is generally very informative; but we are not usually in search of this type of information. We are interested in details of a specific nature. This is what should determine our pedagogic use of the film. The question is how to achieve this, knowing the nature of films.

The audience must be prepared with care. They must know what to look for. This means that **you must have previewed the film**. One showing will definitely not do the trick. This is why there is a strong case for review and a second showing. It is only after this that a full discussion of the film will become meaningful.

But to show the film at all, you must go through certain steps. You must see to it that the projector and screen are properly aligned. The film title, not the run-in numbers, should be in the gate. The film should be properly focused. If it is a sound film, the amplifier should be switched on. All these preparations are better completed before the audience arrives. Waiting can be irksome for viewers, and you may find yourself making mistakes because of the pressure on you. Also, see to it that your loudspeaker is by the side of the screen and points to the centre of the audience. Stand by, ready to adjust the volume level of sound, and never start with a loud burst of sound. It is unpleasant. Turn down the volume level of the amplifier at the beginning, bringing it up as quickly and as smoothly as possible. And one last point: when you use a portable screen in the open air, see to it that it is really secure. Otherwise, a gust of wind may prove a disaster. You will normally be working in the night, and a breakdown of this nature may stop you from continuing the show until the next day.

Tape recorders

Earlier in this essay, we said sound can be captured on tape, edited and played where, when and as often as we like. The advent of the transistorized tape recorder has brought this possibility within the scope of every adult educator. For both history and current affairs, the voices of people, living and dead, can be brought into a class to add perspective and interest to a discussion. Different viewpoints, expressed by different people always adds depth to a discussion. Where a new change is planned, messages from notable persons help to show personal concern and could play a considerable part in the development of good attitudes towards new ideas. The tape recorder can also be used in conjunction with film strips and slides. But note that, with this combined approach, logical representation will be gained at the expense of spontaneity and flexibility. Besides, this mode requires some degree of technical sophistication in preparation.

One would, however, say that the most fruitful use of tape recorders is in training sessions. Where you have to teach people roles in leadership, a recorded discussion or role play will provide an invaluable feedback to participants. Playback provides immediate feedback on performance. Where you have to prepare people for live broadcasts, for instance, the difference between a written message and a spoken message is best taught by using the tape recorder and seeing how fast or how slowly listeners shut off.

Where your class has to engage in a survey, you'll find that the use of the tape recorder will help you retain factual information as well as the nuances of tone and stress which a precoded questionnaire always misses; and you will find that when members of a sample population hear themselves speak you set up a rapport which makes them willing respondents.

As with any other aid, you will have to learn the language of your tape recorder. You have to check your batteries and always carry spare ones. You will have to keep your eye on the programme level meter as you record so that you get the correct tone during playback. And you always have to be on your guard not to wipe off valuable recordings just by recording over parts of the recorded tape.

Written aids

To be really literate, your class should develop a proper reading style. This means that learners should not only know what they should read but also why. They should be able to challenge, analyse and criticize what they read, and should not use the written word as an excuse to escape from their own ideas. This habit and this attitude are not things that happen by chance. You, as an adult educator, must foster them in your students at the same time as you guide them to gather information in the form of written symbols.

I have had a number of occasions to ask adult students how they would tackle a book which is not a storybook. The answers have been very interesting. Some students had replied that they would start from the preface, others from the list of contents, and some bright ones had said they would read a commentary on the book first. When I say I always start at the back, from the index, I sound very strange. The fact that one might pick only what one required from a book at any particular time was not readily appreciated. This is a skill we have to teach as adult educators. Where you recommend a book to be read, please give the appropriate references, chapter and pages. Tell the students about the general stand of the author and direct what they should attempt to do with the literature. When you ask students to read a book, you should not be asking them to undergo an endurance test.

Sometimes, the books are not readily available. You then have to provide handouts. This is easier said than done, however. A handout is not another book. Where you provide a handout as a final summary, it should be brief and restricted to one theme, e.g. types of organizations, models of communications systems, barriers to effective communication or non-projected aids. If you give such a handout to the class before you start your teaching, you will be deliberately creating competition for yourself and for your students. They would be torn between listening to you and reading the handout. You must therefore build up your lesson, have your discussion and distribute your handout after the lesson is over.

It is also possible to provide your class with an 'incomplete' handout. This then becomes a teaching aid and a learning resource since you and your class will be using it to develop subject-matter and theme. Students should be able to fill in details as the lesson proceeds, so you must leave gaps enough for them to be able to do so.

One final use of written materials as a teaching aid. We do not normally think of written assignments and tests, whether objective type or essay type, as teaching aids; but they are. A test should function to diagnose, motivate and direct. Tests provide 'practice of performance' for students to clarify their thoughts and to check on their command of facts, knowledge of subject-matter and the opinions which they hold. If you therefore have a literate class, it pays to give them essays, check-lists and objective tests. But follow everything up with a discussion, otherwise the exercise will remain a quiz and not a teaching device.

Notes and references

1. C. J. Duncan, 'A survey of audio-visual equipment and methods', in D. Unwin (ed.), *Media and Methods: Instructional Technology in Higher Education* (New York: McGraw Hill, 1969)
2. Abraham Luchins, 'Implications of Gestalt psychology for AV learning', in *Audio-Visual Processes in Education* (Chicago: Johnson Reprint Corporation, 1971), p. 14
3. *Ibid.*
4. Jerrold E. Kemp, 'Which medium?', in Howard Hutchins (ed.), *Selecting Media for Learning* (Washington: Association for Educational Communication and Technology)
5. C. N. Botham, *Audio-Visual Aids for Cooperative Education and Training*, FAO publication no. 86 (Rome: FAO, 1967; reprinted 1969), p. 8
6. Duncan, p. 17
7. Duncan, p. 28
8. Botham, p. 66

Suggestions for further reading

Coppen, Helen, *Visual Perception: A review of the literature relating to studies relevant to the development of teaching materials*. Commonwealth Secretariat, London, 1970
Edstrom, Lars-Olof, Renee Erdos and Roy Prosser. *Mass Education in Africa*. Dag Hammarskjöld Foundation, Stockholm, 1970
Holmes, A. C. *Visual Aids in Nutrition Education*. FAO, Rome, 1968
Saunders, Denys J. *Visual Communication Handbook*. Lutterworth Press, London and Guildford, 1974

8 The mass media, distance teaching and the individual learner

Madu G. Mailafiya

Introductory

This chapter is concerned with how the mass media could be utilized in meeting the challenge of expanding opportunities that accompany mass mobilization for development – the major task facing West African countries in the 1970s and 1980s. It starts from the view that since it is morally wrong and politically dangerous to impose changes on the people, it may be useful to look for alternatives, which can create *awareness* and *motivation* among the majority of the people who will come forward when it is demonstrated to them that education will have direct relevance to them.

In traditional societies such as ours, the *word-of-mouth* is still an important vehicle of education and culture. New ideas and practices can therefore have a desired impact when disseminated through those channels of communication nearest to those understood by the majority of the people. Whilst the mass media are foreign to the culture, many of the components, particularly radio and television, have unique advantages for the education of adults since they are the language medium. When considered in these terms, the major advantages of the mass media include their ability to:

1 Effectively maintain contact between the government and the people in both the urban and rural areas;
2 provide a national forum for continuing dialogue/education;
3 break barriers of literacy requirements, since with the spoken language as the main vehicle for interpersonal communication even groups without written languages can be reached and helped;
4 encourage imagination and participation in public affairs, more especially if the educators/communicators have a credibility base, i.e. if they can speak the language beautifully and give the people the opportunity to participate in discussing the messages. In traditional Africa, we usually want to participate in activities e.g. if there is a dance, it's open to all, and for a radio/television series to be effective, it must have a forum for audience participation.

Even the restrictive print media can be effective on a wider scale if properly applied.

In this chapter, we shall therefore ask ourselves what we mean by mass media and discuss some of the issues raised in this introduction. We shall discuss various strategies for using the broadcast media and stress the advantages of a multi-media approach, giving two important examples – one of a campaign in Tanzania, the other of an ongoing programme in Senegal. After some practical hints on broadcasting, we shall look at two uses of the written word, stressing the significance for modern Africa of correspondence education. The peculiar circumstances of the individual learner must not be forgotten. *Distance teaching* must not be allowed to become impersonal, and some combination of mass media and face-to-face activity in adult education is urged.

Mass media – a definition

Essentially, the term 'mass media' means the technological services used or extended to share information and ideas with many people in many places. In other words, it involves the use of machines and human talent to produce such things as books, magazines, newspapers, films and radio and television programmes for the consumption of large numbers of people across vast distances. The communicator and the audience are usually separated in space and/or in time.

A careful analysis indicates that the media belong to two main categories. These are:

Mass media   These consist of radio, television and newspapers. They are regular and available on a large scale.

Supplementary media   They are things like books, magazines and films. We cannot count on their regularity and accessibility.

The importance of the mass media

One of the most useful things about the various mass media components is their ability to channel information to many people across vast distances. Except in the case of books, the information they carry can be easily kept up-to-date, especially through radio and television. These two media have an added advantage. They can cut across the literacy barrier since they do not presume the possession of formal education to be effective.

It can therefore be argued that the mass media have a particular importance to Africa at this point in history when all Black governments are so desirous of communicating so much so quickly to so many people. But this is not all. As noted at the Lagos Festac Colloquium:

the mass media put on our people psychological pressures and are likely to profoundly modify our behaviour and the entire orientation of our destiny.[1]

Since the main challenges facing decision-makers in the attempt to awaken awareness is effecting attitude changes and providing the necessary motivation for change, the strongest weapons can be found in the mass media.

But one must lodge a caveat. In postulating greater and more efficient use of the mass media for the education of adults, it is necessary to add that success will depend to a large extent on how much such provision is related to the structural aspect of society. Any provision that threatens a people's culture will be resisted. Our adult education provision through the mass media must be system-supporting. Further, adult educators need to appreciate where the mass media can accomplish developmental goals by themselves and where they act as supports to human interaction and interpersonal communication.

The reason why we should assess the strength and weaknesses of the mass media before we use them is that the adult education task may be unified but not unitary. We have to do at least three things:

a) Spread information about development to the masses of the people, in particular, focusing attention on the need for change, the opportunities inviting change and the methods of change, and raising aspirations among individuals and their communities.

b) Provide an opportunity for the masses to participate intelligently in the decision-making process. We have to help broaden the dialogue to include all those who must decide to change.

c) Finally, teach the needed skills. Wholesale new skills are needed in the task of transformation of our societies. We need to develop new mental skills, new sensori-motor skills and new attitudinal skills.

We can argue that because of vast distances, small and scattered communities, poor transport and communication networks, all constituting impediments to opening up of educational opportunities in Africa, the mass media are our hope of effecting the changes we require. But the mass media are not therefore a panacea. It is the strategies of use adopted which will determine their effectiveness. We now have to turn to these strategies.

Strategies of use: the broadcast media

The two broadcast media at our disposal are radio and television. Television is at present very costly and its networks in Africa are limited. Lack of rural electrification makes its utilization still more limited. Radio, however, is relatively cheap and can reach millions of people across vast distances instantly.

Where we have television, we should try to use it, especially where facts and skills taught are demonstrable. For the present, however, we should exploit all the potential that radio has. Following McAnany,[2] we shall discuss five utilization strategies of radio.

Open broadcasting

These are broadcast programmes beamed to the 'unorganized audience'. Since we are not sure whether they are really listening or are benefiting from listening, we try to beam broadcasts to specific groups – farmers, housewives, fishermen or teachers – at specific times when we think they are likely to listen in. The members of our target group listen in as individuals. Here the parable of the Sower is very apt. He sowed by the broadcast method, scattering the seeds. Some of the seeds fell among thorns, some on rocky soil and some on good soil. This fact determined the final outcome of the enterprise. So it is with the use of the broadcast media in adult education, when beamed to the 'unorganized audience'.

It has been suggested that this strategy is best when the media come in as part of a genuine change effort by government or other change-oriented group. We can cite as examples the role the broadcast media have played in the change-over from left-hand to right-hand driving in anglophone West Africa; in the *Dissoo* programme of Senegal's 'Radio Educative Rurale'; and in the cocoa cutting-out campaign in Ghana.

Instructional radio/TV

Programmes using this strategy are beamed to 'organized learning groups': They can be used for both formal and non-formal adult education. Such programmes go according to a pre-prepared curriculum and require a definite structure. They normally require support materials, as well as monitors or teachers and some kind of definite feedback.

Instructional radio or TV are really multi-media systems of adult education where the broadcast media play a central role, giving information, pacing learners, reporting feedback to learners and generally being the prime motivator. The other media are supplementary to the main broadcast medium, which has the double advantage of wide coverage and instant communication.

Radio rural forums

These types of broadcast are meant for the 'decision group'. Normally, they are regular weekly programmes, with segments devoted to rural news, answers for listeners' questions, and the presentation of discussion, dramatization, demonstration or lecture on a topic. The aim is to induce a dialogue about the topic, expected to lead to group or personal action. The use of fertilizer, the formation of a local cooperative, the adoption of family planning techniques could all be covered in such a programme. Here again, the broadcast media are the main source of initiative.

Radio schools

Programmes broadcast under this strategy are beamed to the 'non-formal learning group'. The broadcasts are meant, here, 'to combat ignorance', by helping the audience to know about what is happening both in their little world and in the larger society. It is more of an information-giving programme. Intra-group discussion is expected to supplement the information, but everything depends upon the structure used and the culture of the group members.

Radio and animation

Using this strategy means that the programmes are beamed to the 'participating group'. It is an offshoot of the group dynamics approach. The broadcast media come in to support a dialogue in which members of the group participate in defining their own problems, putting them in a larger social context, and working out ways of mobilizing people to take common action to overcome these problems.

The basic assumptions underlying this strategy are that the solutions to problems are not imposed from above, and that they are within the capacity of group members to achieve.

We have listed five strategies of radio use. In actual practice, however, the boundary lines are blurred. We could start with one mode but modify it in the course of programming. There is nothing to be gained in trying to be a purist. It is the ultimate objectives which should determine our strategy. In our work of dealing with adults, we have to be pragmatic, since there are finite ways to reach the infinite. These strategies have been listed as a way of helping to define our objectives and seeing what the broadcast media can do on their own and in conjunction with other modes and media. We will find that when we come to the nuts and bolts, we need other structures to support the broadcast media, and, sometimes, the broadcast media have to come in to support or to supplement other principal modes. There is no question of any medium playing second fiddle. In a systems approach to adult education, each medium should make its distinct contribution at the correct time. But let us have a brief look at what to do when we use the broadcast media.

Guiding principles in the use of broadcast media

A leading factor in the use of broadcast media is the *objective*. We have to decide what we are trying to achieve. Otherwise the whole exercise will be defeated.

Next, we have to look at the crucial question of the *target group*. The adult educator must be clear about his clientèle. Broadcast programmes must aim at specific audiences to be effective. It is only by being specific that we shall be able to determine how effectively we can exploit the culture of the audience, their language and its use, and how best they can learn from our programmes.

Our third problem area is the *conditions in which the adult learner has to study*. If the learner is 'a solitary reaper' we need to motivate him and keep up his motivation. We will not succeed if we try to lecture and talk down to him. We may realize that dramatization, discussion or the voice of fellow-learners on the air keep our individual learner going. The *Open University* in Britain had a system whereby students discussed their problems as part of the broadcast programmes. The individual learner then knew that he was not the only person with peculiar problems. He was no dunce, and he knew there were people prepared to listen and to help.

The multi-media approach

It is not only variation in broadcast programme format that is required. Because of the problems surrounding the adult learner as he listens at home, perhaps at the end of a hard day's work, we need a multi-media approach. Study centres and viewing groups to provide interpersonal relations keep motivation going. Where the clientèle is literate, written materials can be used to supplement broadcasts, and the occasional face-to-face meetings can go a long way to raise flagging spirits.

We can now turn to look at two specific examples which have employed variation in programme format plus the support of other media to enhance learning through the radio.

Tanzania: Mtu ni Afya *(Man is Health)*[3]

This campaign, launched by the Republic of Tanzania in 1973, had as its aims:

a) the provision of information about the symptoms and effects of certain diseases;
b) the encouragement of groups and individuals to take positive action to prevent those diseases;
c) the encouragement and maintenance of reading skills among literates and neo-literates.

In a vast country like Tanzania, radio became the obvious medium through which to reach the people. But this was not all. The target was to reach one million adults, gathered in 65,000 to 70,000 radio study groups. Eighteen months of preparation was required to write, print and distribute textbooks and to get an organization going. It was necessary to get groups organized and group leaders trained. Thus, before the campaign started, the three components of the communication system had been effectively established: the radio programmes were ready, the textbooks and other printed material prepared, and the groups for face-to-face meetings formed.

Radio had the added role of getting the people prepared before the campaign started. Publicity by radio began very early. It was carefully staged and week-by-week items were broadcast so that by the time the recruitment of study group members and leaders was started, the whole country knew what the campaign was about and how it should work. *Mtu ni Afya*, the campaign title, soon became a household phrase. The publicity received support from newspapers and government publications. A specially designed campaign cloth was manufactured and made into dresses and shirts.

The broadcast programmes came on the air twice a week, and they complemented what was in the written texts. The results of the twelve-week campaign were overwhelming. The target enrolment figure of one million was nearly doubled. The drop-out rate was 35 per cent over the period; interest was therefore maintained. What is more, 700,000 new latrines were provided through voluntary labour.

How do we explain this success? For our immediate purposes, we could say that the multi-media appeal through the spoken and written word accounted for this. But there was more to it. There was audience participation followed by action. The organization had been near-perfect, and this was because this was a nationally directed campaign assisted by radio, written texts and study groups. It was a genuine effort for change by government and, fortunately, for Tanzania the multiplicity of languages which besets West African countries was absent. Swahili is the common language. Then radio broadcasts were beamed specifically to organized groups.

Senegal: RER's Dissoo[4]

Our second example is from Senegal in West Africa. Radio Educative Rurale (RER) began broadcasting its *Dissoo* (Wolof, meaning dialogue) on 18 December 1968. This was not a campaign but a regular broadcast programme. But it has one thing in common with the Tanzanian experiment. An inter-ministerial organization was set up to ensure coordination.

The programme did not cover the whole country. It was restricted to an area whose major occupation was the production of groundnuts, and whose people were mainly Wolof-speaking. Radio was to be the major medium of communication, but it was to be supplemented with fifty radio clubs, embracing 800,000 people. *Dissoo*'s purpose was to teach new farming methods, the diversification of agriculture and the administration of co-operatives. Though these result were eventually achieved, the handing over of the microphone to the peasants at first caused a stir. There was to be feedback from the clubs in the form of letters which were read over RER, and the peasants took up the dialogue in earnest. This was to ensure the participation of those who had to change in the change process. RER sent field officers to record the views of listeners at the beginning of the programme and continued to read their letters regularly. And the peasants did talk. The free expression of peasants embarrassed officials, so much so that an attempt was made to stifle their freedom of speech and of expression. The situation had to be saved by the president of the republic himself. He stated: 'My only choice is between dictatorship and dialogue, and I have chosen dialogue.' Government ministers had to go round the villages explaining policy. Their discussions were broadcast live.

Dissoo was not only a learning experience for the peasants. The government also learnt from the dialogue. For the first time the difficulties of the peasants were made known directly to the government. The president recognized the *malaise paysan* (peasants' discomfort), and as a result of *Dissoo*, certain definite changes were effected. The peasants complained that they were sprayed with insecticide when they could not pay their debts, but top officials who embezzled huge government funds were let off the hook. They also complained of the bad behaviour of the leaders of the cooperatives, who in collusion with officials sold equipment and fertilizers to them at a huge profit to themselves. Government on its side realized the multiplicity, complexity and the dishonesty of the administrative institutions. The cooperative movement was reformed, and debts of peasants incurred for seeds and agricultural equipment were cancelled. Further, the sifting of information on its upward way in the bureaucracy stopped. Lower cadres were satisfied that what they could not report was now openly on the air. The slow grinding bureaucracy had the added fillip of urgent matters being directly taken up because of radio. The poorly staffed extension officers found out that they had no need to travel to all villages. Radio had become a powerful tool of information.

Throughout the tumultuous programme, certain positive effects were achieved. Radio combined with listening groups, and with proper and regular feedback, had joined the governing and the governed in a mutual task of development. But one has to be careful in analysing the results. The central organization was there. The multi-media approach was present. But *Dissoo* was successful because there was political tolerance for free speech and expression. This tolerance is a crucial factor in the use of the mass media in adult education for development. Any government that fears criticism and indulges a sycophant press, radio and television will not have the necessary feedback on how people feel. If the dialogue is to be extended, and people become free agents in the developmental process, then the mass media should have the freedom to publish the truth, and those who control the mass media should be of the calibre to meet the challenge of democracy and free speech.

Some hints on using the broadcast media

Before we move to the print medium, it is necessary to add a few words on how to use the broadcast media effectively.

Always remember to use *everyday language*. Even though your broadcast message is intended for many people, you must aim at person-to-person communication. The radio or TV listener is not as captive as we may think. Even where there is a single channel station, the listener can refuse to listen further by switching off. The surest way to keep your audience listening to you is to be not only informative, but also engaging, precise and, above all, honest. Your sincerity must show. As Bernard Shaw has put it, 'the radio is a great betrayer'. What you say on radio or TV must portray your personality and your attitude towards your message and your audience.

It is essential to script your message. Scripting helps you to clear your mind and gives you the opportunity to rethink what you want to say. But you will notice that the most interesting broadcasts are those in which the broadcaster seems to be conversing with his audience. You should learn, through practice, not to read your script, but to *talk from it*; doing this is a skill which may take time to acquire, but it is worth the effort, since any direct reading always has a flavour of artificiality.

It is also necessary that you make on-the-spot checks on selected catchment areas to get a feedback on broadcasts. Listening panels may be set up, but one has to be careful to ensure that panels really represent the target groups. The best thing is to send people from the broadcasting house to meet listeners and to report back.

Where it is necessary to use supplementary written media, see to it that the messages from broadcast and written media supplement each other.

The medium of the written word

We can now turn to look at the written medium, which is used on a wide scale. We shall concentrate on rural newspapers and correspondence courses.

Rural newspapers

It has been said that: 'it is the fear of a return to illiteracy which has started the first attempts at an African rural press'.[5] In Niger, the Central Bureau of Literacy publishes a trilingual monthly to coincide with the annual literacy campaign. Other attempts at a rural press, however, go beyond literacy. In Mali, *Kibaru*, which has a circulation of 8000, is published in Bambara and is really part of general adult education. Meetings are organized for communal reading. In Ghana, the *Densu Times* and *Akora New Era* are published in English weekly and provide news and information for people who have been to school or are in school. They are not part of the literacy drive as such.

An interesting Ghanaian venture is *Kpodoga*, a rural newspaper published monthly by the Institute of Adult Education as a community newspaper and as an integral part of the 'Awudome Project'; the institute has a residential adult college at Tsito in the Awudome district of the Volta Region, which is a focus for various adult education and community development projects, including a demonstration farm to serve the farmers of the area. *Kpodoga* is the most recent addition to the adult education complex the institute is trying to establish. The paper is to help develop literacy, but the main idea is to publish news about and views from 'small people' who never get mention in the national papers. It is envisaged that success stories of rural people, written in their own dialect, will encourage awareness and promote general rural development. The intention of the institute is that the experiment will catch on and that district councils will take up the running of such community newspapers. This is deemed necessary not only because of the multiplicity of languages, but to ensure that news will be relevant to people in the catchment area.

Correspondence education

So far, it would seem that the emphasis has been on the use of the mass media for non-formal adult education. This is really what the actual situation is in West Africa. Our outstanding exception however is the use of correspondence education.

For some time now, ambitious individuals, young and old, have turned to external correspondence institutions like Rapid Results and School of Careers in order to get further education denied them at home. Of late, however, local institutions also have started providing education by correspondence. The new African effort includes programmes by universities, notably the Universities of Ahmadu Bello (Zaria, Nigeria), Ghana, Kenya, Lagos, Zambia; by governments, such as the Malawi Correspondence College; and by indigenous commercial enterprises (there are more than fifty at present in Nigeria, including the outstandingly well-run Exam Success Correspondence College).

Justification for correspondence education

The most common reasons advanced for the use of correspondence education are, first, the lack of qualified teachers and teaching facilities, and second, the social, political or economic restrictions which govern the intake of students into regular schools. We cannot ignore these reasons, but we have to look

further for a more fundamental explanation for using correspondence education, especially in adult education.

We are in a rapidly changing world. The old school system was
based on the notion that education is to give the youth knowledge
and skills sufficient for life, but this static outlook no longer holds.
Further, conventional education has tended to create an isolated
group of individuals 'who by the very process of their education
have lost touch with the community they once belonged to'. The
need to associate education more closely with the life of our
societies cannot be overstressed.

The adult has therefore to continue learning, but at the same
time he has obligations as a member of a family, a citizen and a
worker, and so he needs a more flexible means of gaining new
knowledge and skills. He requires a means 'which will allow him to
study at a time and place of his own choosing, without breaking off
his other activities for any length of time'.[6] Herein lies the
justification for using correspondence education.

Forms of correspondence education

Correspondence education can take many forms, determined by
the type of subject, the scholastic level, the student group, the level
of educational technology and the ecology of a particular area.
However, we can distinguish three forms which can be combined
and adapted to suit particular situations in the West African context.

Individual study by correspondence This is where the student
works on his own without contact with other students. His contacts
are with the correspondence organization and its teachers, mainly
through the written word. The purpose of this contact is to make
instruction possible and to provide an opportunity for advice, help
and encouragement.

The greatest problem that faces the autonomous learner is one
of isolation. He has no horizontal communication with other students, and for long periods he may be out of touch with the correspondence organization itself, except for the study material. The
strain can be great and possibly accounts for the high drop-out rate
in individual correspondence study. This form of correspondence
study will remain 'a survival of the fittest' contest if means are not
found to break the isolation. Occasional face-to-face meetings and
a regular newsletter have been found to help keep students going.
But it is of the utmost importance that students' letters and queries

are answered promptly and without any prevarication. This requires a counselling section staffed by people who are not only qualified but also have empathy with the students. When counselling services are of a high standard, the marking of assignments by tutors is bound to be effective.

Most of the time, marking of assignment has been 'attainment marking' – ticking of correct parts and crossing out of wrong parts, with a grade mark at the end. *Remedial marking* is what personalizes the communication between tutor and student. It is necessary for the tutor to show the student why he has marked a section as good. Where a student scores 90 per cent, it is necessary to explain why he missed 10 per cent. Where the student scores low, it is necessary to explain where he went wrong and show him how he could improve on his performance. A terse 'very good', 'satisfactory' or 'poor' does not help the student at all.

Nobody is suggesting that remedial marking is easy. To get tutors to mark in this way is not easy either. It means monitoring marked assignments and telling tutors about the way they mark. The confrontation is not normally a pleasant encounter. But if a correspondence organization is not just a mercenary unit, counting its students only as paid-up members, everything that goes to maintain student motivation and increase completion rates will have to be done.

Group study by correspondence   This is another format in correspondence education which could be used in our setting; it can be particularly useful in non-formal adult education.

A group is formed, and it elects its own leader. This leader is not a tutor, the teaching being done by the correspondence material. Each member of the group is expected to study the material on his own before the group meets. At the meeting, the members discuss the material. The group therefore serves as a clearing-house for ideas, opinions and solutions to problems. It also serves as a therapeutic horizontal communication channel.

At this point, two things can happen. Either each member of the group sends in an individual answer to assignments for marking and comments or the group submits a collective answer. It is the leader's duty to collect and send answers to the correspondence organization. When the marked assignments are returned, the group discusses them together.

We have a semblance of this format in the radio listening group or the farm forum and in the readers' clubs or rural newspapers. It is therefore not too novel. The major caution is to see to it that the leader does not become a controller or, without sufficient know-ledge, usurp the role of a tutor.

Supervised correspondence study This can be used where an edu-cational organization or institute already has face-to-face formal evening classes going.

The students attend classes normally but instead of having a tutor lecturing to them, they study the correspondence material. A greater amount of the instruction is left to the correspondence text and the tutor, when present, is left to give individual attention and provide immediate feedback. What makes this type of corre-spondence study worth trying in our situation is the shortage of textbooks. But the system is rather new and will require a lot of organizational support to make it work successfully.

Multi-media systems based on correspondence study

Whatever form of correspondence education we adopt, it is poss-ible to add other formats to the basic correspondence texts. Face-to-face, audio-visual aids, laboratory work, the use of radio and television could all come in to support the written text. Where we adopt such a multi-media system in part or fully, we must ensure that the parts complement each other, and that the failure of one mode does not lead to the collapse of the system.

This is a first caution. The second is that we must not rush into a multi-media system just because the other media are available. Perhaps in our situation, correspondence texts, face-to-face meet-ings and the use of radio to pace and to reply to questions which affect a large number of students will do for the time-being.

Conclusion

We have the mass media components. We have an educational programme of some magnitude on our hands. Already, there have been some very successful attempts in the use of the mass media for adult education. We are now certain that we can use the mass media to help provide flexible forms of education for adults, whether in the formal or non-formal setting.

However, we have to be sure about what we want to do. We have to watch the political climate in which we operate. This is a major constraint. Then we have to know the people we want to educate since we can only help them to learn. Lastly, we must know the strengths and weaknesses of the media to which we have access. It is only then that we can select the correct medium to carry our message.

Notes and references

1. 'Festac colloquium general report on black civilization and the mass media', *New Nigerian* supplement, Kaduna (17 February 1976), p. iv
2. Emile G. McAnany, *Radio's Role in Development: Five Strategies of Use*, Information Centre on Instructional Technology (Washington, DC), Information bulletin no. 4 (September 1973)
3. Based on Hugh Barrett, 'Radio campaign in Tanzania – the concrete results', *Development Forum* (Geneva), vol. 3, no. 4 (May 1975), p. 5
4. Unesco, *Mass Media in an African Context*, Reports and papers on mass communication no. 69 (Paris, 1974)
5. *African Communications Educator*, University of Minnesota, Minneapolis, vol. 2, no. 2 (March/April 1976)
6. Lars-Olof Edstrom (ed.), *Mass Education* (Uppsala: Dag Hammarskjöld Foundation, 1970). See especially his own article, 'What is correspondence education?'

Suggestions for further reading

Burke, Richard C. *The Use of Radio in Adult Literacy Education*. International Institute for Adult Literacy Methods, Teheran, 1976
Dodds, Tony. *Multi-Media Approaches to Rural Education*. International Extension College, Cambridge, 1972
Kabwasa, A., and Kaunda, M. M. *Correspondence Education in Africa*. London, 1973.
Perraton, Hilary. *The Techniques of Writing Correspondence Courses*. International Extension College, Cambridge, 1973
Schramm, Wilbur. *Mass Media and National Development: The Role of Information in Developing Countries*. Stanford University Press, 1964
Waniewicz, Ignacy. *Broadcasting for Adult Education: A Guide Book to World-Wide Experience*. Unesco, Paris, 1972

9 Supporting institutions: libraries, museums, exhibitions, fairs, shows and festivals

Michael Omolewa

The man who tells another man
    the title of a volume
which will enlarge his outlook on life
    has done a better service
        than he would
who might present him with a gift.

H. M. TIPPETT

Introductory

As shown in some of the earlier chapters, the processes of learning and the acquisition of knowledge are assisted considerably by the use of various aids and skills. Memory is assisted by a continuous access to literature; and extensive *reading* promotes knowledge; hence the relevance of libraries. The use of *sight* breaks the monotony of reading and presents images in a more real manner; hence the pertinence of museums. Individuals are brought in more actively through *performance and physical involvement*, which is the object of festivals. Attention is drawn to events and/or objects through advertisement which is the concern of trade fairs. And lastly, through *demonstration and shows*, man can be helped to a greater awareness of things around him and his knowledge increased. Perhaps this has been the most important function of exhibitions throughout history.

Adult education practitioners and policy-makers in the Western world seem to have appreciated these various aids to learning processes relatively early. Most established adult units are served by libraries and exhibitions.

The purpose of this chapter is to examine some of the supporting institutions for adult education. The importance and use of libraries is discussed, and attention is focused on the organization of adult education libraries. We then describe the place of festivals and trade fairs and exhibitions. Although most of the examples and illustrations given in the chapter are taken from Nigeria (partly because of the nature of sources available to the writer and partly because many of Nigeria's experiences are characteristic of most West African countries), an attempt is also made to discuss the subject broadly and to apply generally the deductions and conclusions reached. It is sincerely hoped that readers will find the survey interesting and the suggestions helpful in the prosecution of virile and dynamic adult education work.

Libraries

It seems incontrovertible that of all the supporting institutions in adult education, libraries are the most important.

Libraries are defined here as institutions providing library services. This excludes private collections of books belonging to individuals. In modern times libraries have become stores of knowledge where all forms of publications, books, periodicals, manuscripts, newspapers, diaries and other forms of works in print are kept and documented. More sophisticated libraries have gramophone records, tape and cassette recordings, filmstrips, slides, overhead transparencies and samples of agricultural and mineral productions among their holdings.

The development of libraries in West Africa[1]

The importance of libraries was recognized in literate societies even before the invention of printing, at a time when men collected written scripts, scrolls and paintings. The importance of libraries was also recognized very early by many of the literate adults in West Africa. For example, as early as 1879 in Nigeria, a Lagos Town Library Club was founded:

> For the purpose of establishing and maintaining a library of books, maps, etc., for reference; a reading-room to be supplied with the leading English journals and other periodicals; and for providing a selection of works of history, biography, travel, fiction, etc., to be lent out to the members, under such rules and conditions as may be approved by the committee.[2]

Christian missionaries who pioneered formal Western education in West Africa invested some funds in school libraries. And when the colonial administration began to interest itself in educational development, it gave notices of books and periodicals that were required for school libraries.

In Nigeria, the first public library, the Lagos Library, was opened in 1932 as a subscription library. The Lagos public library, sponsored by both the British Council and the Lagos Town Council, was opened in 1946. The British Council also helped to establish public libraries at Ibadan, Kano and Enugu as from 1943. By 1952 regional libraries were founded in the three regions of Nigeria.

Library development began in Ghana (then the Gold Coast) as early as 1928. During that year, the Lord Bishop of Accra, the Rev. John Aglionby, opened a library of some 6000 volumes in the Bishop's Boys' School. But it was not until 1933 that the question of public libraries was brought to the Executive Council by the Lord Bishop, who wished to know whether provision should be made for the annual upkeep, i.e. maintenance of buildings, salary of clerk, cost of periodicals and of replacements, etc. The bishop also set up a small lending library in his own home in 1935. The first public library in Ghana was founded in 1938, as part of the King George V Memorial Hall.

In 1939, the Carnegie Corporation of New York appointed two people long associated with literature services in Africa, Hans Vischer and Miss Margaret Wrong, to report on the expansion of library facilities on the west coast of Africa. They recommended, among other things, grants for developing a national circulating library and the possible provision of library vans, grants to town libraries and departments of education for strengthening the libraries in training centres and secondary schools. Miss Ethel Regan was subsequently appointed in 1940 by the Carnegie Corporation to report again on library needs in British West Africa. Miss Regan planned an elaborate training programme for West African countries but this was suspended due to war conditions. The British Council came in to fill the vacuum created by the discontinuance of the work by the Carnegie Corporation. Both the British Council and the Carnegie Corporation have assisted several African students to have their training in librarianship in England, and in the acquisition of literature for the public, university and school libraries. The British Council was also of much help in library development and the supply of literature.

In 1949 the Gold Coast Library Board Ordinance was passed by the Legislative Council. The Ordinance established a library board mandated 'to establish, equip, manage and maintain libraries in the Gold Coast, and to take all such steps as may be necessary to carry out such duty'. The board first met on 17 January 1950 to plan its work. In 1956 the Accra Central Library was opened and regional and branch libraries were opened in many parts of Ghana.

The British Council has been of tremendous help in the establishment of library services in Sierra Leone and the Gambia. The council had by 1957 a centre in Freetown and a branch in Bo, in the interior of Sierra Leone and a centre in Bathurst (now Banjul). The Town Council in Freetown supports a small public library in the town.

A seminar was hosted by Unesco at Ibadan in 1953 on public libraries in Africa. And on 25 September 1954, the West African Library Association was inaugurated.

On the attainment of independence, the various African governments began to give active consideration to the building of libraries. Thus in 1962 the West Regional Government of Nigeria in a policy statement declared that:

the provision of library services which will measure up to the new programmes for educational development presents a problem which must be dealt with urgently. In recent plans for greater expansion of education little has been said about library development. Yet books and other reading materials are the essential tools of the student, the professionals and the workers without which progress will be quite slow.[3]

And on the recommendation of the Lagos City Council, Irving Lieberman, Director of the School of Librarianship, University of Washington in the United States, was requested in 1963 to make a survey of the Lagos City Library and give advice on its improvement and development.[4] Since this date, library development has been a permanent feature in university education and national programmes.

In the foreword to a work on library development of Ghana, the first President of Ghana, Kwame Nkrumah, described 'the provision of library facilities for everybody throughout the length and breadth of the country' as 'an essential element in this national scheme of educational advancement'.[5]

The use of libraries

Libraries all over the world form an integral part of the community's social and political development. Thus in Britain libraries were founded:

a) to relieve the tedium of idle hours, quite irrespective of intellectual profit or educational gain. It is sufficient to satisfy this purpose that the rural inhabitant should be rendered a happier (and not necessarily a more learned) man by the provision which is made for him;

b) to ensure that the taste for good English, which should be acquired in the elementary school, is kept alive and developed by a provision of good literature after school years have ended;

c) to enable the rural inhabitant to acquire, without difficulty, that general knowledge which alone can enable him to appreciate to the full what he sees and hears;

d) to impart that knowledge of public affairs and of the history of his own neighbourhood which a citizen must possess as a member of the community ultimately responsible for the government of the parish, rural district, county and country;

e) to provide facilities for the study of the arts, trades, and professions which constitute the occupation of the inhabitants;

f) to remove as far as possible all obstacles from the path of the serious student of any subject.[6]

Perhaps to these uses of libraries could be added the encouragement through publication of the African mother tongues, and

African literature, history and politics. West African adults must be made aware of available texts which deal with issues of everyday experience. For example, works such as *How to Mend Your Bicycle*, *How to Improve Tobacco-Growing* and *New Techniques in Soap Making* could prove rewarding to the users of public libraries. Furthermore, the uses of the library have, since 1927, 'gone beyond the mere provision of books'. Libraries now add to their functions:

the provision of documentation, bibliographical data and other relevant information, needed to carry out research, preparation of seminars and examinations;

the publication of abstracts, titles of works and annotated bibliographies;

and in some of the advanced countries, the provision of lectures and concerts.

Good libraries have the unique advantage of acquiring more books than any single individual can buy and therefore making a variety of works accessible to the interested borrower and reader. They also have personnel to assist in locating materials either as classification or reference librarians. And assistance is given through information on new acquisitions. In this way libraries spread an awareness of literature of all kinds among the people. Books, magazines, scientific and learned journals all have the marks of leading thinkers and scholars. These scholars, contends a library user, 'listen to my doubts and perplexities and then in the kindest way tell me their convictions. No knowing looks, no prying questions, no snitching.'[7] Through the pages of books authors 'speak to us, amuse, vivify us, teach us, comfort us, open their hearts to us as brothers'. And in the libraries one can conjure the dead. As the lonely monk, Poictiers, testifies:

I call 'Plato' and he answers 'Here' – a noble and sturdy Soldier. 'Aristotle', 'Here' – a host in himself. 'Desmothenes', 'Cicero', 'Tacitus', 'Pliny' – 'Here', they answer, and they smile at me in their immortality of youth. . . . All the world is around me, all that ever stirred human hearts or fired the imagination is harmlessly here. My library shelves are the avenues of time.[8]

Summarizing the objectives for the institution of libraries in a developing country, a team of experts who worked in Nigeria under the Special Commonwealth African Assistance plan between November 1962 and February 1963 submitted that library development is needed 'to contribute to the supply of skilled manpower, to further the educational development programme, to help those who are studying privately and to encourage all who wish to read for a useful purpose'. The team also forcefully argued that libraries are repositories of records, 'all that is best in human thought, all that has stood the test of time ...', and that they contribute to the development of the community and speed it up. Libraries are thus considered useful investments.

Organization of adult education libraries

The organization of adult education libraries must follow the general pattern of organization of modern libraries. This means that a mere collection of books can never be described as a library. As Richard Le Gallienne warns:

> A library is not to be deliberately made. You cannot plan it out on paper and then buy it *en bloc*. Of course, you can make a collection of books in that way, but a collection of books is not a library. A library is an organism developing side by side with the mind and character of its owner. It is the house of his spirit and is thus furnished progressively in accordance with the progress of his mental life.[9]

There must be, therefore, a **core of well-trained librarians**. Indeed, the training and retraining of librarians is most important. For the exercise would produce seasoned and well-motivated personnel to do various kinds of work such as the provision of an information index and keeping it up-to-date and taking major decisions on the acquisition of materials or policy decisions on 'the extension of services to a particular group of readers'.

Trained librarians would also assess the needs of the library user and select suitable works for them. **Selection** is most necessary in equipping adult libraries for West Africans. First, there is the limitation of funds for the acquisition of relevant books. This makes it imperative for the librarian to obtain 'the best buy' from his limited financial resources. But perhaps of equal importance is the need to assess books and pick out those which are most relevant in the book markets throughout the world. There is a pressing need to provide books that will not repel the reader. And as an observer writes 'no book is readable unless it means something to us here and now – unless it piques our curiosity and awakens a fellow feeling'.[10]

It is also necessary to take into account the varied tastes of the adult reader. Some readers only wish to be entertained. Short, simple storybooks, paintings and cartoons could well satisfy a particular group. But there are the more discerning adults searching for works written by seasoned writers. And inbetween the two extreme categories are those in search of facts, information; and for whom textbooks, encyclopaedias, quick reference materials, directories and newspapers would be appropriate.

Because of the differing levels of literacy and preferences among the African adults, library collections should cater for a variety of tastes and interests. Modern libraries in self-professed democratic societies must provide a social service to all, without discrimination or preferences. The librarians must therefore be versed in history and sociology and capable of understanding the demands of the society being served. Primers should be provided for the newly literate adults, as well as simple writings on religion, history, politics, economics, agriculture. Works on recreations, games, sports, handicrafts; work on 'fundamental adult education', e.g. hygiene, sanitation and general health; and textbooks on advanced studies on philosophy, jurisprudence, etc. could also be provided. In serving the newly literate, Hiatt and Drennan advise that 'it is the responsibility of those directing the government's educational agencies, of which the public library is one, to work aggressively and creatively to increase the opportunities for people of limited reading ability to reduce their ignorance and to include them among those who are reading'. The writers further advise librarians 'reaching the under-educated' to 'call for different service policies and a differently trained staff from those which have become traditional'.[11]

Another aspect of library organization is **classification**. Even when some substandard works are presented as gifts to the libraries they must be classified. Selection and classification are possibly of equal importance to the librarian. It is only by classification and selection that the keen reader could profit from the use of library resources.

The organization of libraries cannot be complete without the traditional duty of **providing information** on the rules and regulations governing users. Admission criteria must be determined by the governing body of the library: and efforts must be made to ensure that only approved members are allowed in. The Lagos Town Library Club in 1879 excluded those 'convicted of any criminal offence' and those 'officially declared a bankrupt or outlaw'; and empowered its committee to exclude any of its members whose conduct 'either in or out of the Club-house shall in the opinion of the committee, be injurious to the character and interest of the Club'. The hours of opening and closing must be stated and the form of admission should also be decided. Entry cards or printed admission cards should be issued with or without identity photographs. And further regulations barring food or drinks should be introduced. Again, the Library Club in Lagos insisted that:

> No game of hazard or cards shall be on any account played in the Club; no member shall take a dog into the house; and no smoking shall be allowed, unless sanctioned by the committee.

The Club finally stated that:

> These rules and regulations shall be printed, and a copy of them, together with a list of the committee and members shall be delivered to every member, or transmitted to his address, but no member shall be absolved from the effect of these rules on any allegation of not having received them.[12]

In modern times, *suggestion boxes* are provided for comments, criticisms and administration of libraries from the users. These views could be helpful in further planning of the library services.

Each library must have a wide airy space for reading room, a smaller more relaxed room for reading newspapers and periodicals and rooms for reference works and manuscripts. A well-equipped auditorium, a tea or coffee (or palmwine) room, good toilets and washrooms are also recommended as vital areas in planning modern libraries. It is essential also that lending facilities are available. But equally important is the provision of make-shift libraries in the neglected and rural areas not served by the major public libraries. These emergency libraries should be stocked.Under this arrangement, mobile library units could provide book-boxes which would be made available to these 'bush' areas. The important point is to get library services to all the parts of West Africa as part of an elaborate adult education programme.

Libraries must launch massive campaign efforts to interest all categories of adults in available library collections. Perhaps the educationally advanced adults could be reached through the publication of information bulletins, bibliographies and notes on new acquisitions. But the observation made by some workers among newly literate people in the United States is equally valid for West Africans:

> Our big problem with the adult functionally illiterate is that of devising ways in which to reach them and bring them into the public library, inducing them to avail themselves of library services and materials, and helping them to understand their application to themselves.[13]

It must be admitted, however, that organizers of adult libraries in West Africa also face peculiar problems. In a region so vast, served with poor infrastructure and inequitable distribution of basic amenities, library organization must be carefully worked out to meet the basic needs of the society being served. Ologbonsaiye, like his colleagues, has advised that libraries be distributed and planned to cover all the regions in a given country. Major libraries could be established in the state capitals; town, district and community libraries should also be established to serve the urban and rural areas of the given country. It has further been advised that a mobile library service scheme be introduced to serve the districts which are starved of a supply of literature and other library services.

A national library board was established in Nigeria by the National Library Act of 1964, revised by the National Library Decree of 1970, 'to establish and maintain a branch of the library in each of the twelve states in the Federation'. The importance of the coordination of the various services in the country by a national body cannot be over-emphasized in African countries which are currently inculcating national and patriotic values into citizens of diverse regions that have been previously exposed to the centrifugal forces of disintegration, sectionalism and ethnic chauvinism.

The role of the adult educator

The adult educator has been likened to a manager who deals with his personnel as well as with a wide variety of adult population. He must be conscious of the services provided by the library. He must recognize, for example, that by using the works in the available libraries he will improve his own knowledge and understanding, keep himself well-informed, and thus (hopefully) 'eradicate his ignorance ... and kill the germ of blind arguments and unintelligent, shallow reasoning'.[14] The team which advised on library development in Northern Nigeria in 1963 contended that the library 'implants ideas, it opens up minds, it fires the imagination, it releases the brakes of ignorance and reinforces the dynamics of progress. It inspires young men to see visions and when they grow old it helps them to dream peaceful dreams'. The team further added that 'it is in the mind that progress originates and the library feeds the mind'. This exercise will most likely earn him a greater respect in his institution as well as among the general public with whom he is in regular contact.

The adult educator, by using the library himself, will not only, by learning more, render himself more competent to teach, he will also set an example to his students and will, by becoming familiar with the working of the library, be able to guide them in its use. He can also recommend suitable books for the library to acquire.

Some guidelines for a model adult education library

1 *Hours of Opening*: 8 a.m.–10 p.m.
This will make room for the use of the library by adult learners on full-time study; workers who leave their places of work about 3.30 p.m. and those who wish to return to libraries for works of leisure, fiction and recreation.

2 *Admission*
Free to all adult members of the public except those previously disqualified by the library management for doubtful integrity, noise-making or disrespect for the established rules of the libraries. The age could, sometimes, be relaxed.

3 *Facilities*
Full-time, trained librarians
Comfortable reading-room/lounge
Lending desk
Book stacks
Games
Auditorium

4 *Literature*
The emphasis should be on writings by African writers in all fields of learning, followed by useful publications on science and technology by African and non-African writers. Works by non-Africanists and general philosophers should also be kept, so that libraries do not exclude valuable works from the reach of Africans. The stock must include collections in African mother tongues, European and Arabic languages.

a) **Dictionaries** should inform us of the meanings of words in various languages, European, and Asian and African.

b) **Maps** would give readers ideas of places discussed; assist in the definition of time and space; and, through these, the promotion of a better understanding of other subjects. Among the current good maps is the *Atlas of Africa* published by Freeman-Grenville.

c) **Religious works**, such as the Bible, Qu'ran and other works on religion would be held, in view of the place of religion in West Africa; as Idowu comments in his book on *African Traditional Religion*, the African is 'in all things religious'.

d) **Newspapers and journals**, with the emphasis again on local publications, African publications and the reputable non-African papers and journals.

5 *Personnel*

Board of Management or Governing Board
Librarian or chief librarian
Heads of sections or heads of departments
Intermediate staff – secretaries, stenographers, executive officers, technicians
Junior staff – typists, porters, security men, cleaners, messengers

Museums

The development of museums in West Africa

Museums are traditionally places where old relics and antiquities are kept. Long before the coming of the Europeans, Africans stored their old relics and antiquities. Museums in West Africa thus preserve art forms created by our highly imaginative fore-fathers. Some collections include sculpture, carvings and images which portray the various head-dresses, ornaments and accoutrements; men eating, drinking, dancing or playing some form of musical instrument; kings and queens; priests and soldiers. For, to the African, the past is as important as the present and the future. Thus the possessions of the ancestors were greatly treasured; and it was considered a gift of the gods to hand over such possessions to subsequent generations.

There was, for example, a 'curator' for the 'museum' at Esie in pre-colonial Nigeria. This 'curator' was a priest who was charged with watching over the images. He acted as guide to visitors, addressed the images quite naturally and told them that the visitor wished to salute them. Such museums also had visitors who were not lovers of art but barren women who came 'to persuade the spirits to give them children'. But these relics were not arranged in any intelligible sense. If there was any reason for the state in which the Europeans found them, there was no means of explaining it. Nothing was written as a guide, quite understandably in areas where everyone was unlettered. And the Europeans who were ignorant of local languages and customs found no solution to their many questions. A European observer reports that one of his colleagues who accompanied him to the site of the images complained: 'Fancy all those little people sitting there still, out in the rain and the sun.' And these were the 'prized possession' of '450 little figures of white stone – about 2ft 6in high – jumbled together without any order in a semi-circle, surrounded by leafy trees which splashed the sunlight on to the images so that they appeared to be dancing and talking to one another'. He also observes that many of the collections 'are now broken, and the whole congregation of them looks as if it had been collected together by a people in a hurry, and who had thrown each figure down to the ground without any attempt to arrange or preserve it'.[15]

Europeans assisted in the introduction of modern museums in Africa, in the meticulous preservation, housing and arrangement of artefacts, and in the keeping of visitors' registers and general administration. The colonial administration also invested funds in the establishment of museums. Perhaps they were curious to find the relics in regions about which they had known nothing. Perhaps they were anxious to introduce their traditional approach to museums in their colonies. The few modern museums however took over: for as J. D. Clarke states, 'coated with the blood of fowls and goats they are disgusting, and in so far as African carving is inseparable from the old religion there is no doubt that it can only be preserved in museums'.[16]

Museums in adult education

Museums could become centres of adult education where adults would be reminded of the greatness of their forefathers and inspired to think about art works of the past. They could also be shown the various collections for enjoyment and entertainment. Seeing the various collections may also provoke the new generation to imitate their ancestors, whose interest in art work is proverbial. For as Kenneth Murray testifies: 'throughout, the African artist has had a genius for turning what he has derived from other civilisations to his own creative ends, giving it an unmistakable African character'.[17]

A National Antiquities Commission has been set up by the Nigerian Government and museums are actively developed. Among the major museums are those at Jos, Jebba, Kano, Owo, Ife, Lagos, Benin, and Oron. But parts of the palaces of Obas could be converted into museums. Similarly King Toffa's palace at Porto-Novo and the ancient trading forts of Ouidah in the Republic of Bénin could be fully converted into museums. Already, the Ethnographic Museum at Porto-Novo, the Historical Museum at Ouidah and the Historical Museum at Abomey – 'unique in Africa' and 'the centre of the remains of many royal souvenirs and vestiges' – are tourist attractions in the Republic of

Bénin. Ibadan in Nigeria has the Temple of Shango and there are shrines all over West Africa that could be made into museums. Old walls surrounding the ancient cities, 'large carved doorways ... on which are depicted scenes from the African way of living', pottery centres and old mosques could also be converted into museum collections.

These museums could attract visitors from other lands and promote the tourist industry in the various West African countries. These tourists would then learn about the great heritage that is the lot of West Africans. For a modern museum is certainly more than a place in which old relics are preserved. It has become a centre for the advancement of education. As Renee Marcouse explains, 'education in museums is becoming a key word in countries in all parts of the world'.[18] Guided tours of museums in all the West African countries must therefore be encouraged. Contending that developing countries have had their own civilizations and contributed much to man's knowledge, Mahmoud Hassan advises that 'the young should know this bright history and accept the challenge to emulate it'. Hassan further counsels: 'Nothing can help more than museums, which now are living institutions that can offer invaluable educational services to the new public.'[19]

Museums could be used by developing countries to promote much-needed scientific and technological education. Renée Marcouse contends that:

It is understandable that, in their present stage of development, museums of science and technology in developing countries should play a greater part in general education, and that the contribution of the art museum should appear less immediate.[20]

Many of the museums in the advanced countries establish adult centres designed to meet the needs of a particular group or interest and some run 'a variety of workshops where members receive instruction and can pursue their own interests'.

It is the duty of the adult educator, extension worker and community leader to use the services provided by the museologists. But he should do more than this. He should take the initiative. For West African countries have very few museologists and invest very little on museums in the region, which are mostly located in the big towns. Even then these are not usually big enough and their programmes are severely restricted. The adult educator needs to see the educational work of the museum as an extension of out-of-school education and thus an integral part of adult education. He should advise on the museum's programmes and suggest the inclusion of items such as concerts, lectures, discussion groups and film shows. Alternatively he could request the museums to draw the attention of their visitors to such programmes if they are run by the adult educator in other centres.

The adult educator himself must develop a keen interest in the museum, or encourage a member of his staff to train as a museologist, while still remaining primarily an adult educator. This special breed of adult educator would guide his adult students to museums and encourage them to develop their critical faculties. In some countries, such as Uganda, adult students have been encouraged to build up their own small local museums; this can give very valuable opportunities to them for learning about the past, the arts, the social organization and the technology of their own area, and enlist them in the task of preserving interesting objects.

It is the duty of the adult educator to draw the attention of government to the importance of museums and museum education. For in most developing countries the importance of museums is not yet recognized. And in a period when the emphasis is on other priorities and economic development, and when the museum has to compete with, say, the hospital for funds from limited national resources, the adult educator needs to draw attention to the invaluable services provided by museums.

But before he has 'sufficient' funds at his disposal, the adult educator could work with his students to convert some of the local shrines into museums, which of course would not be similar to the ideal, 'Western' model of museums. The idea is to promote adult education through traditional objects even when funds are not readily forthcoming.

Exhibitions

Exhibitions are usually shows or displays of materials. In modern times these may include drawings, paintings, pictures and other works of art, texts and handwritings, books and handicrafts.

The use of exhibitions

Exhibitions are as old as adult education. The display of past accomplishments encourages new generations of adults, inspires and fires them with new ideas. Exhibitions are indisputably a means of disseminating knowledge. D. V. Proctor aptly remarks:

... Nothing has replaced and nothing will replace the impact of the real object, the experience of seeing, or better still of handling, the actual piece made by a great artist or used by someone many years ago. Expres-

sion of the thrill that this experience gives is seen in the wonderful and
varied work produced by children and by students, in their willingness to
come back and find out more or to go on elsewhere to discover further
worlds of learning. Adults enjoy an enrichment of living and a broadening
of horizons.[21]

These real objects assist a learner 'to recognise, visually, characteristics which differentiate centuries or countries, or the work of
individual artists. This visual approach to learning thus effectively
replaces the system in which the emphasis was on listing names and
dates'. Olofsson has pointed out that the influence of an exhibition
on knowledge and attitudes has been studied in connection with
The Camera and other exhibitions; and that when television was
used in conjunction with an exhibition, it was found that the group
who were shown the television programmes before they saw the
exhibition learned most from it. Furthermore, exhibitions assist in
bringing about meetings of different persons working on related
subjects. And during such meetings, ideas are exchanged and new
knowledge is possibly acquired. But more importantly, exhibitions
are known to promote a keen sense of competition among participants, who will have put much hard work and enthusiasm into
the preparation of their display.

The colonial administration encouraged exhibitions in West
Africa. One of the earliest ones was organized by the Department
of Education in Warri Province on 22 July 1933.[22] It was an exhibition of school work and participants included all government
schools, the Catholic schools at Warri and Sapele, the Catholic
convent at Warri, the CMS (Church Missionary Society) schools at
Ozoro, Sapele, Uweru and Warri, the Baptist school at Sapele and
the New Zion school at Warri. Some of the participants in the
exhibition had to make a bush journey of about sixty miles each
way and to cross by three fairly expensive ferries on each trip. The
schools displayed their exhibits of basketwork, woodwork, weaving, sewing and farm crops. Among the visitors to the exhibition
site were the Resident and some of the workers from Warri.

Organization of exhibitions

The organization of exhibitions requires thorough preparation.
First, the use of a *suitable site* must be arranged. This can vary
from a 'fair-sized classroom' to a large strip of land. For example,
the famous Crystal Palace exhibition site, near London, completed
in 1851, 'was built to accommodate various exhibits' and visited by
more than six million people. Similar international exhibitions

were later organized in Paris (1889), Chicago (1893), again at Paris (1900), St Louis (1904), London (1908), Chicago (1933) and Paris (1937).

Organizers must be sure in their minds what *type of exhibition* they intend, whether generalized or specialist, once-for-all or permanent, stationary or mobile. Sweden has a travelling exhibitions organization (STE), which arranges its activities with the cooperation of adult education services and some other agencies. The *arrangement of the exhibits* is another vital aspect. It is important to select visually interesting material, which is also representative of the subject. Nowadays, it may be supported by recorded tapes of description or explanation, and by devices which the public can try out (pressing a button to make a model move, for instance).

Adequate *publicity* should be planned for promoting exhibitions, to attract an encouraging attendance. It is sometimes a good idea to send invitation cards to important personages and usually valuable to invite a local dignitary to perform the opening ceremony. Then *security* must be provided, to ensure the safety of exhibits; some items on show may be irreplaceable if lost or accidentally destroyed. A check should be kept on those going in and out of the exhibition centre, and plain-clothes security men should be brought in to assist the uniformed ones. *Hours of opening and closing* should be carefully worked out. Workers are likely to be free to come only in the evenings, but housewives may prefer the daytime. More people are likely to come at a weekend than during the week (particularly an end-of-the-month weekend!).

The importance of good planning and organization cannot be over-emphasized. D. V. Proctor observes: 'The energy and interest that are longing to be employed can so easily be dissipated, the emotion dulled, by a surly reception, by poor organization and frustrating delays, or even by hunger. . . .'[23]

The adult educator can use exhibitions to promote his programmes, motivate his students and increase their knowledge and interest. But he must work out the details very carefully for maximum educational effect. He will be well advised to enlist the cooperation of other bodies before mounting an exhibition.

Some suggested items for exhibition are:
Crafts of various kinds, including pottery, calabash carving, brass and leather work, blacksmithing, woodcarving. These exhibitions could stimulate interest in crafts in danger of being ignored by the newly literate
Art work, such as painting

Musical instruments, with performances on some of them
Fashion, including textiles and hair-dressing
Writings on particular themes – constitutions, language and litera-
   ture, sporting history
Farm products – cocoa, maize, cotton, fruit, groundnut, eggs
Indigenous games

Sponsorship of exhibitions could be sought from:
Community organizations
Religious bodies
Other voluntary agencies
Private firms
Government ministries, departments, etc.
University institutes and departments
Libraries, including public and university libraries

A checklist of exhibition requirements is:
Site (either a hall or room or piece of open ground)
Pavilions or covered areas for shade (grass mats may be sufficient)
Stands for the various displays
Storage facility
Administrative facility
Toilet arrangements
Refreshment area or restaurant
Loudspeaker for relaying music announcements and speeches
Entrances for exhibitors and visitors

Trade fairs and agricultural shows

Trade fairs are usually 'periodical gatherings of manufacturers or
producers of goods, exhibiting their latest products for promo-
tional and sales purposes'. The emphasis is therefore on commerce
and trade. It is believed that the word **fair** was first used to distinguish a specific trade's gathering from an ordinary market.

   In traditional Africa, trade fairs were held on a limited scale in
the markets, city centres, villages and road junctions. During such
fairs, considerable publicity was given to the produce of particular
families or villages. The plan was that even if little sales were made
during these fairs, participants would be made aware of the quality
and source of certain produce; this was thus a rather sophisticated
marketing technique.

   Modern fairs are a product of the contact of Africa with the
outside world. It is known that Bartholomew Fair was the main

cloth mart of England between 1133 and 1855 and was held annually at West Smithfield on St Bartholomew's Day and for some days after. It is also known that British merchants took their wares to the great fairs all over Europe, such as Cologne, Bruges, Antwerp, Champagne, Milan and Frankfurt.

Trade fairs became elaborate ceremonies in the nineteenth century in Europe, with the growth of the industrial revolution. As early as 1829, the Royal Dublin Society had organized a trade fair to stimulate sales of Irish goods. Later came the Great Exhibition in the Crystal Palace, which we have already mentioned, and the Wembley Exhibition of 1924/25 (which featured the products of the countries of the British Empire) and the annual British Industries Fair from 1915 to 1955.

On the attainment of independence, West African countries began to participate in international trade fairs. They were represented at the World Exposition held in Montreal in 1967, the World Expo held in Osaka in 1970 and the Cotonou Trade Fair in 1970.

Fairs are recommended to adult educators and community developers. Although they have a commercial purpose, they have some of the educational attributes of any other type of exhibition. But where the majority of the population live in rural areas many more people will be affected by agricultural shows. These not only publicize agricultural products, they afford an opportunity to discuss various agricultural techniques and demonstrate improved farming aids. Such shows provide a means of reaching people who will never go near libraries and museums. For this reason, Ahmadu Bello University, Zaria, for some years used to mount educational exhibitions at the main agricultural shows held in the various northern states of Nigeria.

Information on the organization and promotion of exhibitions and trade fairs in West African countries could be obtained from the addresses given below:

Nigeria	The Director, Trade Fairs, PMB 2558, Information Division, Federal Ministry of Information, Ikoyi, Lagos
Ghana	The Director of Trade Fairs, Ministry of Trade Industries and Tourism, PO Box M47, Accra
Sierra Leone	The Permanent Secretary, Ministry of Trade and Industry, Ministerial Building, Freetown

Republic of Gambia	The Gambia Chamber of Commerce, 78 Wellington Street, PO Box 333, Banjul
Bénin	Chambre de Commerce, d'agriculture et d'industrie du Bénin, ave General de Gaulle, BP 31, Cotonou
Liberia	Liberia Chamber of Commerce, PO Box 92, Monrovia
Ivory Coast	Chambre de Commerce de la République de Côte d'Ivoire, BP 1399, Abidjan
Senegal	Chambre de Commerce, d'Industrie et d'Artisanat de la région du Fleuve, rue Bisson, BP 19, St Louis-de-Senegal

Festivals

Festivals are perhaps the most popular feature of the African way of life. The Africans' love for dancing, celebrations, singing and commemoration of events are perhaps exemplary and peculiar to us.

A Nigerian teacher wrote in an essay in the 1930s that 'the government of the town or village was, and still is, incomplete without the drum'. He explained that the beating of the drum was significant because of the message carried by the exercise. 'It was the broadcast of the town hall – the instrument of summons, and everybody on hearing its sound would halt and listen to its heart-searching message as it glided through the still air.'[24] Similarly other forms of festival carried messages. Thus before the introduction of writing, festivals were a form of instruction, a means of disseminating knowledge and information and a vehicle for the conveying of moral values and social codes. Festivals made education a lively exercise; and we should learn from this. Today a good deal of education is very dull. Can we not marry it once more to popular culture and bring back some of the excitement with which learning was brought to our forefathers? This is a time of cultural revival. Serious thought should be given to reviving the use of traditional festivals for adult education.

Festivals are organized by families, social groups, age-grade associations, religious and political groups. Through these, the history of such groups is told; one is made aware that contemporary society has roots and causes.

Most West African countries organize regional and national arts festivals, and in 1977 Nigeria was host to a huge World Festival of Black and African Arts and Culture (Festac). Such major affairs serve to remind the elite of their roots, but for the adult educator, grassroots festivals are of more significance. Local festivals are usually more protracted (perhaps too much so), but they usually involve very many ordinary people. Popular local festivals can be used to generate an awareness of the significance of their culture and to promote a sense of social responsibility and of ethnic and national unity.

Notes and references

1. Information in this section was gained from: W. J. Harris, *Patterns of Library Growth in English-speaking West Africa* (Legon, 1970); J. Parkes, 'The regional library service in northern Nigeria', *West African Libraries*, vol. 1, no. 1 (March 1954), pp. 7–9; S. B. Aje, 'Public libraries in western Nigeria – a general survey', *WALA News*, vol. 2, no. 3 (August 1956), pp. 78–84; and K. Okorie, *Eastern Region Library Survey: A Report to the Eastern Region Library Board* (Enugu, 1956)

2. J. A. O. Payne, *Payne's Lagos Almanack and Diary* (Lagos, 1879), p. 47

3. Western Nigeria Development Project, Project Analysis no. 10: *Western Regional Library* (Ibadan: Economic Department of the Premier's Office, 1962)

4. I. Lieberman, *A Survey of the Lagos City Library* (Lagos, 1964), p. 5

5. E. J. A. Evans, *A Tropical Library Service: The Story of Ghana's Libraries* (London, 1964), p. xiii

6. T. Kelly, *A History of Adult Education in Britain*, 2nd ed. (Liverpool 1970), p. 314

7. John D. Snider, *I Love Books* (Washington, 1966), p. 41

8. *Ibid.*, pp. 28–9

9. *Ibid.*, p. 150

10. *Ibid.*, p. 151

11. P. Hiatt and H. T. Drennan (eds), *Public Library Services for the Functionally Illiterate* (American Library Association, 1967), p. 9

12. Payne, pp. 47, 48

13. Hiatt and Drennan, p. 13. Adults should be educated on the use of libraries. For a discussion of the subject, see M. Omolewa, 'Adult readers in Nigerian Libraries, 1932–60: a study of library use in colonial Nigeria', *Nigerian Libraries*, vol. 10, no. 1 (April 1974), pp. 36–7

14. For example, often the aim of speakers and contributors at literary and debating clubs and societies is to impress the audience with their mastery of grammar, use of language and 'logic' of presentation. They treat facts as of secondary importance, often assuming them without checking them properly.

15. S. Milburn, 'Stone sculptures in Esie (Ilorin province)', *Nigerian Teacher*, vol. 8 (1936)

16. J. D. Clarke, 'These disgusting images', *Nigerian Teacher*, vol. 1, no. 5 (1935), p. 6

17. Kenneth Murray, in *Overseas Education* (1933)

18. Unesco, *Museums, Imagination and Education*, Museums and monuments series no. 15 (Paris: Unesco, 1973), p. 17

19. *Ibid.*, p. 113

20. *Ibid.*, p. 17

21. *Ibid.*, p. 29

22. K. B. Forge, 'Exhibition of school work, Warri province: Warri Government School (22 July 1933), *Nigerian Teacher*, vol. 1, no. 2 (1934), pp. 46–8

23. D. V. Procter, 'Museums – teachers, students, children', in Unesco, *Museums, Imagination and Education*, p. 29

24. 'The all-Nigeria festival of the arts, 1970', *Nigeria Magazine*, nos. 107/109 (1971), pp. 15–19

Suggestions for further reading

Braun, E. *Museums of the World*. Munich, 1973

Lyman, H. *Library Materials in Service to the New Adult Reader*. Chicago, 1973

Ogunsheye, F. A. *Manual for School Libraries in Nigeria*. 2nd ed. University Department of Library Studies and the Nigerian Library Association, Ibadan, 1971

Part Four
Some Varieties of Adult Education Activity

10 Literacy efforts in West Africa
Kwa O. Hagan

Introductory

While world *percentages* of illiteracy are declining, *absolute numbers* of illiterates are actually increasing; and, although the transistor radio and the community television set do provide alternative channels of access to new knowledge and ideas, the printed word is still the cheapest and most practical means of transmitting knowledge and ideas over time and over space. Literacy, as Paulo Freire has suggested, seems to represent a good deal more than just another skill; it is a force for the raising of human consciousness. Up till the present, however, insufficient attention has been paid to illiteracy in West Africa. This chapter first sets the West African problem in an international frame of reference and then looks at the extent of illiteracy in West Africa. It examines the various approaches to adult literacy teaching and then provides some brief case-studies. Finally, it raises the questions of national commitment and shows how the fight against illiteracy is inextricably bound up with language problems.

The problem of illiteracy in West Africa within the context of world illiteracy

Achievement of literacy in West Africa has, over the years, constituted a major social problem. A solution to the problem must be a two-pronged, simultaneous attack, upon child illiteracy and adult illiteracy. Indeed, the greatest wish of every West African country, and also of all independent states of Africa, must be equality of educational opportunity for every child of school-going age. For, if all children of school age could be admitted to school, and there stay on to complete at least the primary level of education, they could then grow into adolescence as literate people. If they are given further educational opportunity with particular emphasis on vocational training, they would then be able to develop skills to fit them, as adults, into gainful employment. But then, education everywhere is a very expensive proposition, more so in West African countries, which are faced with the problems of poverty, ignorance, squalor, disease and idleness.

In 1962, the United Nations launched the first UN Development Decade, during which the areas of the world known as the developing countries were encouraged through international cooperation to devote about 4 per cent of their gross national product to the provision of primary education. It was hoped that by such effort, illiteracy would then be lessened or be completely wiped out at source. Because of scarce resources, however, the developing countries have a very long way to go in order to achieve such a goal, so that the problem of illiteracy has remained in many areas of the world, including West Africa.

The statistics of world illiteracy at the beginning of the Development Decade, according to a survey conducted by Unesco, revealed that there were around the world at that time over 700 million adults who were unable to read and write, and that women formed the majority of these illiterates. Out of the 700 million adults, some 330 million were between the ages of fifteen and fifty; this age group everywhere is regarded as constituting the 'active population', that is, the bulk of people who must be helped to develop basic skills, apart from reading, writing and some reckoning, in order to become productive workers within the development programmes in every country.

The Unesco survey also revealed that out of some 206 million children of school age, only 110 million or about 55 per cent gained admission to school. Thus, some 96 million children, or 45 per cent, were unfortunately destined to grow up into adulthood without the advantage of any formal schooling. Even so, the problem was and still is made more difficult by the stark fact that large proportions of children who are lucky enough to go to school do not complete their primary education, and so as drop-outs very soon relapse into illiteracy. They grow up to swell the adult illiterate population at the rate of some 20 to 25 million every year, to such an extent that, the Director-General of Unesco, in presenting the Literacy Awards for 1974, revealed:

Mankind will enter the year 1975 with 800 million illiterates. Though the percentage of illiterates is falling, their absolute number goes on steadily increasing. In 1960, 58 per cent of illiterates were women, but by 1970 this percentage had risen to 60 per cent; in the course of those ten years the number of illiterate men rose by 8 million, that of illiterate women by 40 million.[1]

In trying to solve the problem, there are those who hold the view that as resources are scarce, it is only realistic to utilize them to educate children; afterwards, if it is at all feasible, some measure of mass education to minimize adult illiteracy can then be devised. But as we have earlier noted, if adult illiteracy is to be wiped out, the attack upon it must be twofold. Child illiteracy and adult illiteracy must both be tackled effectively. This was the conclusion of the world conference of ministers of education on the eradication of illiteracy, held in Teheran, Iran, in 1965, which resulted in the *Declaration of Persepolis*.

Nature and extent of adult illiteracy in West Africa

Literacy rates in the West African sub-region seem very much on the low side. The official figures show only one country, Ghana, as having, like Egypt in North Africa, an adult male literacy rate as high as 30 per cent. Ghana's record has come about as a result of the country's tradition of formal school provision, which has developed since the middle of the nineteenth century, and also as a result of its relative prosperity over a long period.

In seven countries where reasonably up-to-date figures are available, the percentage of illiteracy among people above the age of fifteen was as follows:

Percentage rate of illiteracy

	1960	1974
Ivory Coast	91	80
Liberia	91	85
Sierra Leone	93	85
Togo	90	88
Senegal	95	90
Mauritania	95	90
Mali	95	90

Unfortunately we have no recent comparative figures for Ghana or Nigeria, both of which are recorded as having the notably lower illiteracy rate of 75 per cent in 1960.

All these figures should, of course, be taken with a certain amount of caution; particularly they do not show variation between one part of a country and another – variations which are quite dramatic in Nigeria, where in some areas probably 60 per cent of the people can read and write, while in others only as few as 2 per cent can do so. Another difference hidden in the figures is that between men and women. It seems that, almost always, more men than women are literate. Unesco documents give these rates for the beginning of the 1970s:

Percentage illiteracy rates for men and women

	Men	Women
Liberia	86.1	95.8
Sierra Leone	90.4	96.1
Senegal	89.6	98.1
Mali	96	99.5
Ghana	70	90
Nigeria	76	94

The illiteracy rates in West Africa need to be set within the total illiteracy rates in all Africa. When the overall percentage in Africa

is compared with that of two other developing areas of the world –
Asia and Latin America – the rate is as follows:[3]

Men

1970	literate adults (thousands)	illiterate adults (thousands)	illiteracy percentage
Africa	35,100	60,900	63.4
Asia	393,000	231,000	37.0
Latin America	64,900	16,100	19.9

Women

1970	literate adults (thousands)	illiterate adults (thousands)	illiteracy percentage
Africa	16,000	82,000	83.7
Asia	266,000	348,000	57.7
Latin America	59,700	22,500	27.3

It will be seen from these statistics that the governments of
African states, and more so of West Africa, are faced with a for-
midable task in efforts to eradicate illiteracy in their respective
countries.

Approaches to literacy teaching

Attempts made in the past at literacy education took on a traditional approach to teaching. The primary education approach for
children was the same one used to teach all adults who wanted to
learn how to read and write; and the primary school teachers were,
for the most part, the instructors at adult literacy classes. These
teachers had to introduce the reading primers for the formal school
system at the adult literacy classes. In addition, readers based on
Bible stories were used to lead adults gradually on to the reading
of the Bible in the vernacular. For reading the Bible in one's own
language was considered by many missionaries as an all-important
factor in the development of a fuller life.

In the twentieth century, various new approaches have been tried. For a long time the approach and the literacy techniques of *Dr Frank Charles Laubach,* the 'father of literacy,' were popular. An ordained Congregationalist minister, he initiated successful literacy campaigns in the Philippines in the early 1930s, and from 1935 to 1948 he advised on the eradication of illiteracy in many countries, including Egypt, Kenya, Tanganyika and Zanzibar (now Tanzania), Nigeria, the Gold Coast (Ghana) and Liberia. After his retirement in 1955, Frank Laubach and his son, Dr Robert Laubach, founded the independent Laubach Literacy Fund to promote research and action in combating illiteracy.

Although he developed many variations, the Laubach method had two essential bases. One was the campaign approach known as 'each one teach one'. The other was the use of specially prepared cards, each depicting a familiar everyday object, with the name of the object printed on it. Early cards in a series showed objects were each related to a letter of the alphabet. The learner would thus associate that letter with that picture and be reminded of the relevant word and sound. The cards moved progressively on to words of two, three and more syllables. Such word-pictures proved a useful way of enabling adults to learn easily and quickly how to read and write. This method of building up from single-syllable words to longer ones is called **synthetic** or **phonic**.

Early approaches to literacy education, however, both by the missionary churches, and by the Laubach Card method adopted in the government-sponsored literacy campaigns, presupposed that any literate person was capable of teaching an adult illiterate person the skill of reading and writing; also that primary school teachers, by virtue of their training, occupation and experience, were best suited as instructors at adult literacy classes. This view was held in both English-speaking and French-speaking countries of West Africa.

From traditional to functional

Literacy teaching in the past, either through the use of primers and Bible reading, or by the Laubach Card method, is now often called **traditional literacy**. It was offered to all willing illiterate adults to enable them merely to learn how to read and write.

Since the 1960s, a new approach has been used, commonly termed **functional literacy**. As already mentioned in Chapter 1, this approach attempts to combine the skill of reading with another skill, in a programme related to a specific target group in a particular environment.

A useful description of functionality in adult education, which can also be related more specifically to literacy is:

Functional adult education is that which, founded on the relationship between man and work (taking the word *work* in its broadest sense) and linking the development of the individual with the development of the community, reconciles the interest of the individual with those of society. Functional education therefore is that in which the individual fulfils himself within the framework of a society whose structures and whose superstructural relations facilitate the full development of human personality. Thus, it helps to produce an individual who is a creator of material and spiritual wealth, while at the same time allowing him unrestricted enjoyment of his creative work. Viewed in this way, functional adult education is, to a great extent, the aspiration of educators throughout the world who are concerned with the effectiveness of their work.[4]

Work-oriented functional literacy involves a specific target group, motivation of the learners and skilled literacy teachers. A *target group* could be made up of workers engaged in agricultural projects (see the case-studies on Guinea and Mali later in this chapter), of workers on a construction site or in a group of factories, of farmers or fishermen (preferably organized in some form of co-operative), or of women who need to improve their skills either as traders or home-makers. *Motivation* is assisted where learners soon see results, and work-oriented functional literacy is usually planned as an intensive programme offering several hours a week, so that learners make rapid progress and are able to use their new skills quickly. This encourages them to continue.

The provision of skilled literacy teachers is important. Since functional literacy postulates that literacy education involves much more than the plain mechanics of reading and writing, it demands a thorough understanding of and insight into the problems and learning capacity of the adult. Unfortunately, most West African countries still rely heavily on primary school teachers for literacy work, but such people have no training at present either in methods of adult teaching or in the skills to be woven into functional literacy projects (carpentry, new ways of farming, home economics or whatever). It is desirable that moves towards incorporating adult education methodology into school-teachers' training (such as are under way in Nigeria) should be emulated. Moreover, in-service courses in methods and techniques of functional literacy should be organized for school-teachers already in the field.

Another approach to literacy teaching is that of *Paulo Freire*, the Brazilian adult educator whose psycho-social literacy system is known as **conscientization**. His view is that 'becoming literate implies a transformation of the learner from a passive being to an active, critical, creative one'. The learner, he contends, must be exposed to the use of familiar words of social and cultural import, along with pictures or illustrations; such exposure would encourage the learner's self-discovery and self-expression through speech and writing.

Methodology

Put simply, methodology is the special form or method of approach in any mental activity. Thus, in our own context, the term stands, in the first place, for the form in which the skill of reading and writing is imparted; secondly, it represents how in the process of literacy teaching, other skills can be acquired, especially when the learner is involved in a work-oriented literacy project.

In fact, we have still to learn more about the method of teaching literacy to adults. This is because research on reading and writing has been conducted in the past largely on the method of teaching children how to read and write. As such, instructors in adult literacy programmes have been left free to find out their own approach.

Since the 1940s, and up to the period of functional literacy projects in West Africa during the late 1960s, most countries in the sub-region did generally adopt the Laubach Card method in literacy campaigns, using a local language as the medium of instruction.

The Freirean method differs from the synthetic Laubach method in that it is eclectic; the learner first becomes familiar with the look of a word representing something important to him (often quite a long word, like 'trade-union' or 'election'), which he can later break into parts and from which he can learn other words. Freire has claimed that by such a method adults were able to read and/or write Portuguese quite fluently in six to eight weeks.[5]

The media used in the Freirean method are usually printed cards or primers; for functional literacy, each stage in the primer also represents a stage in the economic task which the learner is being helped to understand and perform better. A good example of such primers is the series prepared at the University of Ibadan for a work-oriented literacy project for tobacco farmers. Month by month, the necessary farming operations are treated. An extract from the diary for the month of December, for instance, shows that the farmers are encouraged as follows:

Nursery Work
1 Collect nursery materials
2 Start shade-making
Field Work
1 Continue ploughing
2 Burn stalks
3 Provide for water
4 Make bricks and fire them
Barnsite Work
1 Transport wood to barnsite
2 Deposit money with bank for necessary crop expenses[6]

In some French-speaking countries of West Africa, particularly in the Ivory Coast, a method known as **radio-vision** was developed in the struggle against illiteracy. This consisted of filmstrips which were shown to adult classes, along with synchronized broadcast lessons. The advantage was that a literacy programme could reach out to widely scattered audiences, but the method turned out to be a rather expensive one, involving the provision of suitable transmitters and receiving sets – the cost of which could hardly be afforded by a good many of the West African states.

Further developments in literacy methodology are being encouraged by the *International Institute for Adult Literacy Methods*, an important organization based in Teheran and sponsored by Unesco and the government of Iran. Among its many useful contributions is a series of training monographs called *Literacy in Development* (see the Suggestions for further reading on page 205).

Evaluation

It is necessary, when a literacy project is in progress, to ascertain what attitudes and behavioural changes have taken place among the group affected by the project, and also what the impact has been on the larger society. In a work-oriented functional literacy project, it is necessary to investigate the economic impact also. In the case of an agricultural literacy programme, one would ask, have farmers produced more crops and better quality crops, have they gained a better income?

The whole subject of evaluation has been treated in detail in Chapter 5. Here, it is simply necessary to point out that Freire's work has affected thinking on the evaluation of functional literacy of all kinds. Freire has postulated that literacy education becomes a process by which the new literate is made aware of his inner creative powers, and so sees through literacy a means of liberating himself and of expressing his powers. Freire, therefore, recognizes in functional literacy a very basic change in the learner's self-image and his view of society, and so of his place and role in that society. In other words, through literacy education the learner, as society's new individual, with a completely changed attitude and outlook, can become a sort of reincarnated being.

Post-literacy

The formative conference of the African Adult Education Association in January 1968 passed this resolution, among others:

> This conference on continuing literacy is of the unanimous opinion that literacy will not be functional or continuing unless it is combined with access to educational opportunities related to all the functions of adults, and it is essential that the artificial distinction between literacy training and the other forms of adult education be brought to an end.[7]

The new stress on functional literacy and on literacy for conscientization reminds us that literacy is not an end in itself; it is the beginning of a continuous process, and it is important that methods and materials be devised to support neo-literates to help them to maintain literacy and to enable them to learn further. This takes us outside the scope of this chapter but must be borne in mind by anyone engaged in literacy programmes.

Case-studies in literacy: some early efforts in English-speaking West Africa

The following case-histories relating to literacy raise certain issues, such as the questions of *script*, of *language* and of *literacy agencies*.

Most **scripts** used in literacy teaching are based on the Arabic or the Roman alphabet. In Muslim areas all over Africa, indigenous languages have been written in Arabic script; for example, 'Hausa' written in this form is designated as *ajami*. There have been, however, several efforts to develop new scripts. In Liberia, it is on record that Dualu Bukate in 1814 developed a script for his own language, Vai, in order to teach his people to read. Scripts were later invented by members of other ethnic groups – the Base, Loma and Kpella. In the twentieth century, much language writing has been influenced by the standard orthography of the International Africa Institute, which is based on the Roman script but uses a number of additional symbols.

There has been a good deal of discussion about **language**. Early teachers of reading sometimes taught a foreign language; for instance, many malams taught Arabic, as the language of the Holy Koran, and some Christian missionaries, such as the Wesleyan Methodists in Ghana, used English. Other missions concentrated on the mother-tongue. In the eighteenth century in Ghana, Jacobus Capitein (1717–47), the African chaplain-schoolmaster of the Dutch Reformed Church, produced the first reading material in Fante (the Lord's Prayer, the Ten Commandments and part of the catechism) and in the nineteenth century the Bremen and Basel missionaries placed a heavy emphasis on indigenous languages. In south-eastern Ghana, between 1835 and 1918 (when work ceased as a consequence of the German defeat), the Basel missionaries produced a significant number of primers and other readers in Ga and Twi, and the Bremen Mission, who operated from 1847 to 1918 in what is now the Volta region of Ghana, worked extensively to study and develop literature in Ewe. Perhaps the most notable linguistic work of the nineteenth century was that done under the auspices of the CMS at Freetown, by W. S. Koelle, who in 1853 produced his *Polyglotta Africana*, with a comparative vocabulary of 300 words and phrases in 150 West African languages.

The main **literacy agencies** in the cases considered were Christian missions and national governments. Most of the early work was done by missions and churches, and it was not until after the Phelps–Stokes reports of 1922 and 1924 that the idea of government intervention in adult education was seriously mooted (this was followed up by a British Colonial Office report of 1925). For various reasons there was actually little government activity in literacy, either in the British dependencies or in Liberia until the 1940s.

Liberia

E. L. Gauto of the Liberian Education Ministry's Division of Adult Education has documented the development of literacy work in his country.[8]

After Bukate, the churches stepped in. Bishop Payne of the Episcopal Church worked on Bible translation and between 1848 and 1868 produced and printed the Book of Genesis and two of the gospels in the Grebo language. Sporadic attempts at adult literacy education were then made by missionary bodies during the next one hundred years.

It was not until the 1940s, during the period of government participation in literacy efforts in Nigeria and Ghana, that the government of Liberia also lent its support to literacy education. This was done through the encouragement of Dr Frank Laubach who, on a visit to Liberia, demonstrated before President Tubman and members of his government how quickly adults could read and write by his Laubach Card method of teaching. Consequently, a budgetary allocation for literacy education was made, and a special fund established for the production of literacy primers in nine principal vernaculars, including Vai, Grebo, and Kru. By presidential proclamation a national literacy campaign started in 1950 which has since been continued rather intermittently.

In 1969 a Unesco-assisted Functional Literacy Programme in English, aimed at mixed ethnic target groups working in the mining concessions, was launched. However, the ultimate aim of the government of Liberia has been to devise a programme to eradicate illiteracy from the country's population of 1.5 million. In furtherance of this aim, it has now become an established custom for the president of Liberia to include a statement in each annual message to the nation encouraging the population to participate in, or give support to, the national literacy programme.

Ghana: the missions

Capitein's work, mentioned above, became the basis whereby illiterate converts of the Fante-speaking coastal areas learnt how to read at the same time as they mastered the rudiments of the Christian faith.

In the nineteenth century, three missions did outstanding literacy work: the Basel Mission, the Bremen Mission and the Wesleyan Methodist Mission. The Basel group insisted that illiterate adults of the church attend weekday evening courses for one year in order to be taught reading and writing and to be given religious instruction, while their successors, the Scottish Mission, organized adult literacy Sunday Schools from 1918 to 1926.

The Wesleyan Methodists were, however, the pioneers of 'Sabbath' or Sunday Schools for illiterate church members. In 1870, these Sunday Schools in the Methodists' West African district had 1082 adult learners taught by sixty-four volunteer teachers in six stations (or 'circuits'), including, at that stage, two in Nigeria —

Lagos and Abeokuta. It was soon discovered that those who volunteered to teach at the Sunday Schools were rather inexperienced and were handicapped by lack of reading material, so the district synod of 1885 decided to organize the work of Sunday Schools on a proper basis. Previous synods had tended to regard the formal day schools as a nursery ground for their young Christians; but since the numbers of children in day schools were few compared with the increasing numbers of adults in the church, the synod of 1885 shifted the emphasis to the adult Sunday Schools. The African ministers and lay leaders of the church seem to have endorsed such emphasis; and by 1905, the Sunday School movement had spread from the coastal areas to up-country places. Its spread posed problems of organization: that of lack of experienced teachers; by the 1920s, that of having to grade learners in the schools; and the perennial one of providing suitable reading material for new literates.

As a result of the reform measures undertaken by the church, great enthusiasm was put into the movement: classes increased throughout the country; numbers of voluntary teachers and superintendents rose, to the extent that there was by 1935 a record number of 49,582 adult learners of both sexes in classes. It is worthy of note that the Methodist Church did keep regular and up-to-date records of its literacy efforts from the very beginning of Sunday School activity in 1870 right up to the 1940s. A summary of statistics on Sunday Schools covering a period of forty years is shown as follows:

Summary return on Sunday Schools, Methodist Church, Gold Coast District, 1905–45[9]

10-year period	Number of circuits	Number of schools	Voluntary teachers	Learners (both sexes)
1905	18	135	679	15,233
1915	23	351	1336	33,340
1925	28	581	2028	46,062
1935	30	664	2877	49,582
1945	30	632	2352	41,397

The work done during the period of seventy-five years, from 1870 to 1945, to make the Sunday School the centre of adult literacy efforts might indeed be regarded as impressive. All the same, the attempt had merely scratched the surface of the problem of illiteracy within the Methodist Church in particular and in the country generally. But by the 1940s it was clear that the colonial government would enter the field, and so the church in 1946 decided on a different role for the Sunday School, and declared that: 'By a gradual guided process during the years ahead, the Sunday School is to be re-organised to fit the needs of children of varying age groups, with worship and lessons suited to the children at each age stage.'[10]

The work of the various missions was of significant help to the government when it embarked on a mass literacy campaign after 1948. It was able to use the linguistic research of the various missions and enlist their help in the production of primers and readers. The Ewe Presbyterian Church, for example, which had grown in the area of the Bremen Mission, had already prepared a mass literacy primer with the help of Dr Frank Laubach before the government campaign.

Nigeria and Ghana: the colonial and successor governments

Participation of Commonwealth West African governments in literacy efforts in the 1940s was an effect of World War II to accelerate the tempo of social development. Such efforts were largely influenced by a report of the Colonial Office Advisory Committee on Education in the Colonies, entitled *Mass Education in African Society*. The report emphasized adult literacy effort in African countries in these terms:

> It has been proved that the attainment of literacy makes people aware of the need for social and economic improvement, and therefore they will cooperate more readily with welfare and other agencies working on these lines. . . . If control in local government is to be on a wide and democratic basis, it cannot nowadays be in the hands of a mass of ignorant and illiterate people.[11]

The report was taken seriously by the colonial governments of Nigeria and the Gold Coast and the two countries were among the first to experiment on it. Their efforts produced quite different results; for the programme in what was then the eastern region of Nigeria started purely as a literacy campaign and turned out in the end to be a great experiment in community development, while in Ghana, what was planned in the Volta region (then British Transvolta Togoland) as an integrated project in adult mass education ended up largely as a literacy campaign.

In Nigeria, by 1949, the government had shown its practical

interest by appointing twelve mass education officers in its Ten Year Development Plan for Education.[12] In the northern region a regional Adult Education Office was opened to plan intensive literacy campaigns; in 1952 it was expanded, with a Vernacular Literature Section to supply reading material in support. By 1954, the North Regional Literature Agency was set up, sited in Zaria and charged with the responsibility of providing reading material for the campaigns on a large scale and of promoting an atmosphere of public awakening and enlightenment during a period of social change.

The agency was also responsible for preparing, publishing and circulating a comprehensive primer for use in the regional literacy campaign. Also, a Hausa newspaper, *Gaskiya tafi Kwabo*, was produced as follow-up reading matter which was topical and so evoked general interest not only among the new literates but also among all literates in the region.

Apart from the literacy projects in the north, the first experimental mass education campaign, as proposed in the report, *Mass Education in African Society*, was carried out in 1949 in the Udi district of what then constituted the eastern provinces of Nigeria, starting as a literacy campaign. Hundreds became literate, but theirs was not functional literacy, which would enable them to engage in development projects within their community. When they clamoured for feeder roads, clinics, additional school buildings for their children and for other amenities, the district officer in charge of the campaign, John Chadwick, did not discourage them. Rather, he rallied the people around to provide by their own initiative the amenities they needed, just as they had themselves endeavoured to read and write. So the people supplied labour and some money for the projects they wanted to undertake. Technical assistance, mechanical equipment and additional funds came from official sources. Then, village rivalry came into full play. Many other villages wanted roads, their own clinics and schools, and so the mass education movement spread throughout the Udi district.

It is necessary to note here that while literacy was in fact *not* what the Igbo people were most interested in at the time, it is possible – perhaps even probable – that without the literacy campaign the people would never have been stimulated to take the initiative in demanding the various projects of community development. Had the district officer discouraged the people's initiative, the whole mass education movement in the Udi district would have collapsed. Indeed, the district officer discovered that one enthusiasm led to the other: an enthusiasm to be literate in the

Igbo language became one for road-making, building of schools and community centres and other projects. The Igbo called the mass education movement in their area 'civilization', which did put a new life and a new energy into them. That civilizing energy was indeed the secret of success of the mass education and adult literacy campaign in the Udi district.[13]

The experiment in the Udi district of Iboland in Nigeria was paralleled in Ghana with a mass education and community project first planned in 1948. Much preparation was put in by the government's pioneer mass education officers, who recruited what came to be known as the 'Wandering Social Development Team',[14] and many organizations in Ghana did help the team to prepare for the experiment. For instance, Achimota School helped in the preparation and printing of reading material (the Laubach Reading Card) at the school's printing unit. Mass literacy was but one of six subjects which the campaigners were to teach the people. Thus it was placed in a wider context within a programme which was planned as a movement in community development; but the campaigners were soon beset by hundreds of women who came forward to be taught how to read and write. So the outcome of a campaign which has been meant as a general mass education movement turned out largely to be a literacy campaign of unusual success.

Unfortunately, without follow-up reading material for the new literates, the campaign lost much of its potential effect. It succeeded, however, in firing the imagination of educated members of the rural community, particularly school-teachers, through the other five subjects which were introduced: first aid and hygiene, discussion group technique, village theatre, community singing and band organization. The subjects were indeed carefully selected for an integrated training course, and after a series of fortnightly courses run for a period of four months by the social development team at various towns in the Volta region, it was evident to everyone that a completely new brand of social welfare service had come to the rural people. Adults, particularly large numbers of women, had learnt to read and write the Ewe language.

Official and public reaction to the campaign, however, which was aptly described in a section of the press as the 'School on Wheels', was rather lukewarm. A leader in one of the papers demanded, and the demand was re-echoed in other quarters, that an attempt be made to assess the benefits bestowed on the rural population other than the somewhat doubtful result of the literacy campaign. Such demands were unheeded, and there were no follow-up campaigns run in other areas. This attitude on the part of the government was in marked contrast to the Nigerian situation where, following the success of the Udi experiment, the government broadened its plans for mass education. On the contrary, the Gold Coast government seems to have been less enthusiastic about furthering a mass education programme. For the government was then preoccupied with the transitional period in which a colonial government was handing over the administration of the country to a parliamentary government of Kwane Nkrumah's Convention People's Party (CPP).

The party, in its election manifesto in 1951, had pledged itself to liquidate illiteracy 'in the shortest possible time'. In fulfilment of its pledge, the CPP government introduced a Plan for Mass Literacy and Mass Education, which was unanimously approved by the National Assembly in August 1951. From 1952, the plan was launched in turn, for a period of four months each, in six language areas – Ewe, Fante, Asante-Twi, Ga-Adangbe, Nzema and Dagbani. Large numbers of adult men and women who enrolled to learn to read and write and do some calculation were provided, for a nominal fee, with a 'literacy kit', comprising a primer, two follow-up reading books, a pencil, a notebook, and a learner's badge. The programme was carried out by the Department of Social Welfare and Community Development during the 1950s and up to the mid-1960s with clearly defined objectives.

The annual literacy campaigns, however, as part of the overall plan of mass education and community development cannot, according to available statistics, be said to have achieved the objective of making a large proportion of the illiterate population literate. Up to 1959, the department apparently kept no proper returns on its literacy efforts while the campaign was in progress, from region to region. Even so, it was able to assert that by 1963 the total number of new literates who thronged the annual campaigns stood at nearly 127,000, of which 60 to 65 per cent were women. Such an aggregate was given against an estimated total of over 3 million adult illiterates at that time. It can be seen, therefore, that the sum total of new literates produced was very low, when it is considered that adults made literate year by year reached only 32,500 in 1955. Even this average was not maintained in subsequent years, and so, by 1964 the average had fallen to 22,500.

Case-studies in literacy: the post-independence era

A few countries in West Africa have made encouraging strides in national literacy projects in recent years. In Ghana, already in

1965, the Department of Social Welfare and Community Development, evidently realizing earlier shortcomings, drew up a detailed 'plan of action'; and although it was shelved after the *coup d'état* of February 1966, subsequent governments have continued to make new attempts to tackle the problem. In Nigeria, after a period of slackening off in the early 1960s, Unesco experts were called in, some of the universities undertook various literacy experiments and recently the 1976 National Policy on Education came up with new plans.

Notable projects, however, have been recorded in Sierra Leone, Guinea and Mali.

Sierra Leone

The 1963 census showed that some 90 per cent of the population of 2,120,873 Sierra Leoneans were illiterate, while only 24 per cent of school-age children were actually in school. The government consequently invited a Unesco planning mission to draw up blueprints for an intensive literacy campaign in the six principal languages of the country. The Ministry of Social Welfare and the Provincial Literature Bureau have been mainly responsible for the project, in which the objective of acquiring the skills of reading, writing and calculation is linked to continuing education in the form of vocational and technical training. Literacy classes in English are also given for specific target groups such as taxi-drivers, industrial workers and domestic servants. Instruction is given by voluntary teachers, supervised by the ministry and bureau. The University of Sierra Leone evaluates the various programmes.

Guinea

Guinea was one of the two West African countries selected for the Experimental World Literacy Programme (EWLP) which was one result of the Teheran World Conference on the Eradication of Illiteracy.

Before then, the revolutionary government had in 1968 launched a national literacy campaign. The objective of the campaign was that *all* illiterates should possess a literacy manual which had been produced in the principal national languages by the National Literacy Service under the general joint supervision of the Ministry of Education and the Ministry of Ideology. Every adult illiterate, armed with a manual, was to seek help from someone literate, in order to learn how to read and write. The cam paign, however, which seems to have relied largely on the learner's own volition, apparently achieved very little success.

Consequently, the government agreed to participate in the EWLP, which was launched for a period of three years up to 1971, as a selective and intensive functional literacy project for a limited number of illiterates and semi-illiterate workers in industrial and agricultural sectors of the national economy. This programme of functional literacy under the UNDP (United Nations Development Programme)/Unesco project had to run, for political and other reasons, alongside the government's own national literacy campaign. This raised, according to the Unesco press critical assessment of the EWLP, some fundamental issues, the foremost of which were:

1 While the UNDP/Unesco Functional Literacy Project aimed at a selective and intensive approach towards development of skills for target groups in agriculture and industry, and so at increased productivity generally, the aim of the government-sponsored literacy programme was merely that of mass approach to literacy.
2 There was no provision for the production of follow-up reading material for the new literates who emerged from either programme.
3 The government showed clearly its commitment to an ideologically oriented nationwide adult education programme with a strong literacy component, and indeed felt an uneasiness over a model project that had been 'imposed' on the country by an international agency.

Mali

This was the other West African country chosen for the EWLP – a vast country, sparsely populated, with a high illiteracy rate.

By 1965, there were, according to Unesco sources, some 600 literacy centres around the country. A supporting National Centre for Literacy Material Production was also set up. Unlike Guinea and other West African countries which had mounted national literacy programmes, using a number of local languages as the medium of instruction, Mali decided to bypass its local languages and, instead, to conduct literacy classes in French, the language of its former metropolitan rulers, in an effort to minimize the high cost of having to run classes in many local languages. This left the people, particularly those in the rural areas, with little opportunity to promote their own indigenous culture. As a result, the literacy effort begun in 1965 in a foreign language had only limited success.

Mali therefore elected to participate in the EWLP. A UNDP/ Unesco Functional Literacy Project was put into operation from 1967 to 1972, with the following two main objectives:

1 To reinforce the National Centre for Literacy Material Production, making it possible to reach 100,000 illiterate rice and cotton farmers and 10,000 illiterate workers in the industrial and commercial enterprises of the state.
2 To explore and test the most suitable methods and techniques for training illiterate farmers and workers with a view to improving their productivity and raising their standard of living.[15]

The UNDP/Unesco Functional Literacy Project was from the outset acknowledged as the only national programme. In terms of numbers made literate, it was not as successful as had been hoped; but it had introduced the teaching of literacy in four Malian languages – Mande, Peul, Tamasheq and Songhai – and retained French only for mixed-language groups at industrial centres. This has had far-reaching repercussions. A national institute for functional literacy and language development has been set up, and is engaged in considering 'possible fundamental reforms of all education in order to give Malian youth [many not in school] an education for life in the context of their natural culture and in their own national language'.[16] Another related policy emerged from the project: the Ministry of Production has integrated functional literacy into agricultural development projects by encouraging literacy programmes in rice, cotton and groundnut schemes.

Nevertheless, the problem that has plagued literacy projects in all West African countries will continue to affect the national literacy programme currently operating in Mali. It is the problem of having to produce adequate follow-up reading material, in four languages, for the many thousands who must be helped to keep up their newly acquired skill of reading and writing.

Some issues for West Africa

The survey made so far in this chapter does show that all the countries of West Africa face an uphill struggle of having to make their large illiterate populations literate. As we have observed, some of the countries have made some efforts, while others have yet to embark upon any literacy plans. The governments of West

Africa should each aim at a serious attempt to devise an all-out, short-term or long-term plan of eradicating illiteracy once and for all. Such an objective ought to be achieved within a period of ten to twenty years.

Within the context of the World Literacy Programme, a plan that is carefully conceived by any West African country could well attract international cooperation and financial assistance from other organizations of the United Nations system, or through other funds-in-trust arrangements by some advanced countries of the world.

But charity would have to begin at home in West Africa. The newly created Economic Community of West African States (ECOWAS) ought to follow the example set by the European Fund of the European Community (EEC), to aid economic activity and development in the African, Pacific and the Caribbean (ACP) countries, and take concerted action to set up a literacy fund with possibly the cooperation of other international financial institutions, such as the World Bank, the United Nations Development Programme (UNDP), the African Development Bank (ADB) and even, perhaps, the newly established International Fund for Agricultural Development (IFAD), whose provisional headquarters is in Rome. Indeed, the concept of functional literacy, insofar as productivity in agriculture is concerned, might well induce IFAD, as the world's newest financial institution, to assist in funding a regional functional literacy programme in West Africa. The objective of such a programme should be that of equipping hitherto illiterate farmers, through the process of literacy education, with modern methods and techniques of farming.

The problems to be faced, as the case-studies show, relate to lack of serious government commitment and lack of motivation on the part of the learners. In the era of the missions, where commitment and motivation were present, work was continuous over long periods and efforts were reasonably successful. In modern times, countries with a strong political drive to literacy have produced massive results. There is the example of the USSR, where at the time of the 1917 revolution some 85 per cent of the adult population were illiterate; twenty-five years later illiteracy was virtually wiped out. Then, there is the success story of Cuba, where in 1961, the 90 per cent illiteracy among the country's population of 7 million was said to have been totally wiped out in a crash programme which took only one year. More recently still, China has achieved spectacular results in its literacy drives.

Besides the need for commitment, there are serious logistical problems. In all the three countries – the USSR, Cuba and China – the overriding factor which must have favoured total or substantial eradication of illiteracy would be the use of *only one major language* in each country: Russian, predominantly, in the Soviet Union, Spanish in Cuba and Chinese in China. In contrast, West African countries have in the past conducted literacy campaigns and projects in many local languages and vernaculars. Some of the countries have had to cope, and still do, with as many as four to six languages in their national literacy campaigns. The poor results shown may have had some connection with the unwieldy use of too many languages. However, a few countries in Africa are making some headway in their efforts by using only *one* national or major language – namely, Arabic in Algeria and Egypt, Amharic in Ethiopia. What is needed in every West African country is then some unity of language in the fight against illiteracy.

Next to the problem of language must be the production and effective system of distribution of adequate reading material. What is needed is the kind of suitable material which serves as a means to utilize and develop the skill of the new literate as well as his day-to-day experience, and is graded to match his progress.

It is vitally necessary that universal literacy should be achieved in every West African country, because a country which achieves universal literacy in the modern world is at once lifted into new social, economic and political dimensions. Therefore, it will be well if the economic advisers and educational planners in West Africa, in making financial allocations for adult education and adult literacy programmes, allow themselves to be guided by a Chinese proverb, which the outline plan for India's post-war educational system (the Sargeant Report) quoted in its final paragraph:

> If you are planning for one year,
>   plant grain;
> If you are planning for ten years,
>   plant trees;
> If you are planning for a hundred years,
>   plant men.

Notes and references

1. *Literacy Work*, vol. 4, no. 3 (March 1975). There are two international literacy awards, made annually to an institution, organization or individual adjudged by an international jury to have made an effective contribution to the spread of literacy in any country: the Mohammed Reza

Pahlevi Prize was instituted in 1967 by HIM the Shahinshah of Iran, and the Nadezhda K. Krupskaya Prize was instituted in 1970 by the government of the USSR. Part of the Krupskaya Prize for 1975 went to the National Service for Literacy in Togo for efficient implementation of a functional literacy programme in rural agricultural development.

2. World Bank, *World Development Report 1978* (Washington, D.C., 1978). The differential rates for men and women are taken from Unesco, *Literacy 1969–71* (Paris, 1972)

3. Unesco, *Literacy 1969–71* (1972)

4. From a report on a Latin-American Seminar on Adult Education held in Havana in 1972, and quoted in Unesco, *Final Report Third International Conference on Adult Education, Tokyo, 25 July–August 1972* (Paris, 1972), p. 18

5. Paulo Freire, *Education, the Practice of Freedom* (London: Writers' and Readers' Publishing Cooperative, 1976)

6. *Tobacco Diary for Flue-Cured Tobacco* (Ibadan: University of Ibadan Institute of African Adult Education, n.d., cyclostyled)

7. Ronald Clarke (ed.), *Continuing Literacy*, proceedings of the conference of the African Adult Education Association held at Makerere University College, Kampala, Uganda, 1–6 January, 1968 (Kampala: Milton Obote Foundation, 1968)

8. E. L. Gauto, *The Status of Literacy in Liberia, from 1814–1950 and from 1950–1975* (Monrovia: Ministry of Education, cyclostyled)

9. Compiled by K. O. Hagan from the *Gold Coast Synod Minutes, 1905–1945* (London: Methodist Missionary Society)

10. *Methodist Missionary Society District Minutes* (Cape Coast, 1946)

11. *Mass Education in African Society*, col no. 186 (London: HMSO, 1943)

12. Reported in *West Africa*, 26 February 1949

13. Article in *West Africa*, 22 January 1949

14. The idea of Mass Education Teams had already been successfully tried out in Latin America, notably in Mexico

15. Unesco, *The Experimental World Literacy Project: A Critical Assessment* (Paris: Unesco, 1976)

16. *Ibid.*

Suggestions for further reading

There is a welter of reading matter about literacy. The most useful is often contained in journals. For earlier periods, there is useful data in: *The International Review of Missions*. More recently, various Unesco journals have appeared, and are strongly recommended, particularly *Literacy Work* and *Literacy Discussion*, both published by the International Institute for Adult Literacy Methods, P.O. Box 1555, Teheran, Iran. Recommended books are:

Bataille, Leon (ed.). *A Turning Point for Literacy = Adult Education for Development: The Spirit and Declaration of Persepolis.* Pergamon, Oxford, 1976

Clarke, Ronald (ed.). *Continuing Literacy*. Milton Obote Foundation, Kampala, 1968 (now obtainable from Centre for Continuing Education, Makerere University, P.O. Box 7062, Kampala, Uganda)

Du Sautoy, Peter. *The Planning and Organisation of Adult Literacy Programmes in Africa*. Unesco, Paris, 1966

Gillette, Arthur. *Youth and Literacy*. Unesco, Paris, 1972

Hagan, Kwa O. *Mass Education and Community Development in Ghana – A Study in Retrospect 1943–1968*. Institute of Adult Education Monograph no. 7. University of Ghana, Legon (Accra), 1975

Jeffries, Sir Charles. *Illiteracy: A World Problem*. Pall Mall Press, London, 1967

Laubach, Frank. *Towards World Literacy: The 'Each One Teach One' Way*. Syracuse University Press, 1960

Singh, Sohan. *Learning to Read and Reading to Learn: An approach to a system of literacy instruction*. Hulton Educational Publications in cooperation with IIALM, Amersham, 1976 (One of a series of IIALM Literacy Training Manuals)

Unesco (ED/217). *Final Report, World Conference of Ministers of Education on the Eradication of Illiteracy*. Unesco, Paris, 1965

Unesco. *The Experimental World Literacy Programme: A Critical Assessment*. Unesco, Paris, 1976

11 Education for rural development
Ashok Kumar

Introductory

Rural development essentially means economic and social development in rural areas. It involves the gradual improvement of subsistence agriculture and the rise of living levels in traditional rural societies. The problem of rural development is thus a multi-faceted one which requires a comprehensive and integrated programme of action, rather than the *ad hoc* methods of the past, if it is to have any significant impact on the rural economy. This chapter focuses attention on the agricultural extension factor, and more particularly, the community development factor in rural development. These are both seen as essentially non-formal educational activities; and while educational revolution is not the single panacea for achieving rural transformation, it is important because rural development is a complex process involving many inter-dependent variables, acting in concert with each other, and agricultural extension and community development are crucial variables in the process.

Rural development – an integrated approach

The role of education in the rural development process in West Africa cannot be properly assessed without some understanding of the rural development programme, and its relationship to the problem of general economic development. The Commonwealth Secretariat defines rural development as:

> a comprehensive mode of social transformation which recognises that national development must involve all elements of the population. It is a socio-economic process which seeks to bring about a more equitable distribution of resources and incomes within a society. It involves the integration of the rural poor, the vast majority of the population of all developing countries, into the national economy.[1]

The objectives of rural development can be identified as follows:

a) improved income distribution
b) full and productive employment
c) increased productivity
d) improved food self-sufficiency
e) the provision of basic needs and amenities = food, housing, health as well as the accompanying infrastructure (physical, institutional, community services).

Only if these objectives be achieved, can the level and standard of living of the rural population be improved.

Relationship between rural development and general economic development

West African economies are predominantly rural in settlement, occupational distribution and the composition of output. In fact, the rural population accounts for about 80 per cent of the total population, and the vast majority of the labour force is engaged in agriculture, where productivity is in general extremely low. Consequently, further economic development hinges largely on raising the productivity and, therefore, the real income of the rural sector. This is so not only because rapid rural development is required to cope with a rapidly expanding rural and urban population, but also because the impetus to socio-economic development and transformation comes from this sector. Agriculture plays a vital role in economic development; it provides food, raw materials and labour to growing indigenous industrial processes and valuable foreign exchange from its exports, necessary to finance imports for further industrial development.

Thus a dynamic rural sector is an essential prerequisite for overall economic growth in developing countries.

Causes of low agricultural productivity

The causes of low agricultural productivity can be broadly grouped into *a*) institutional factors; *b*) technological factors; and *c*) general factors.[2]

Institutional factors. There are two main problems: the organization of land holdings in the countryside and the absence of adequate support services for agricultural development.

West African agriculture at present is characterized by small-sized farms and fragmented holdings. Farms are generally two or three acres or less, and many land-tenure systems encourage fragmentation. It is believed by many economists that small and scattered farms waste resources and impede certain types of development. It is less easy, for example, to invest capital in irrigation, fencing and other lasting improvements, even with cooperatives and similar institutions.

Moreover, agriculture and rural industry are faced with inadequate non-farm support services. There is a paucity of rural finance and often the necessary communications, marketing facilities and storage are not available. Some countries have made strenuous efforts to spread new knowledge through agricultural extension, but the propaganda is ineffective when it is not backed up by supplies of high-yield seeds, fertilizers, insecticides and pesticides.

Technological factors. Over many past centuries, West African farmers developed agricultural techniques suitable for soil and climate, and rural craftsmen such as smiths provided them with implements; but, in spite of the efforts of agricultural extension agencies most farmers and craftsmen have had little access to the new knowledge and technologies which have emerged in the twentieth century and have changed agriculture in other parts of the world. Most farmers still plant only a few varieties of crop and are unaware of high-yield seed varieties, fertilizers and pesticides, and of modern scientific advice on spacing, planting dates and crop rotation (the latter becoming ever more important as there is more pressure on land, and old techniques of shifting cultivation cease to be practicable). Mechanization is limited and rural craftsmen have had little incentive to learn about existing agricultural machinery or to develop new equipment suitable for village use. As we have already noted, little agricultural credit has been available to farmers or craftsmen to encourage them to try new methods and techniques.

Social factors. The rural environment is often seen as depressing in comparison with that of the towns (in spite of the existence of slums and growing urban unemployment). The rural social and cultural environment fails to encourage people to take positive and vigorous action towards raising their levels of living. Farmers still live in a state of illiteracy and unawareness and are thus inhibited from taking risks or adopting potentially profitable innovations. Moreover, many of the more lively minded of the rural population migrate to urban areas or neighbouring countries in search of better education and job opportunities, in order to raise their economic and social status. This drain of human talent and potentialities further hampers efforts at rural development.

Social amenities are generally at a low level when compared with the urban areas and this also provides an incentive for migration to the cities. The rural exodus acts as another barrier to increase of agricultural production and productivity. The unemployed migrants are not only *not* producing food; instead, they contribute substantially to the need for increased food imports of most nations in West Africa.

Inadequate and irregular availability of irrigational facilities also inhibits agricultural improvement. Farmers still depend on the mercy of the 'rain god'. Thus agriculture is beset with a high level of risks and uncertainty. Such an unstable environment naturally influences yields, productivity, costs and profit levels.

Agricultural development and education

The problem of low agricultural productivity, however, does not in any way mean that West African soils or farmers are not capable of producing more and better quality crops. Risk-taking against natural factors like rainfall, drought, disease and insects requires the application of scientific discoveries to agriculture and the provision of irrigation facilities. Similarly, factors like improved seeds, fertilizers, implements, insecticides, credit and marketing can be dealt with by the integrated approach of research station and government machinery. But the most important factors inhibiting agricultural progress are lack of education and want of incentives and thus a lack of desire to produce more. This calls for provision of an organization for bringing about changes in human behaviour resulting in a total and integrated development of the rural population.

The methods adopted to teach people the ways of doing things are those of extension education and persuasion rather than force and pressure.

Extension education

Enabling rural people to improve their level of living by aided self-help education is the object of extension education. Extension education combines adult education and non-formal education; it is concerned with educating the adult farmers not just in letters and words or grammar or language but in the technique of raising better crops and animals in better combinations of subsidiary occupation, etc. It can emphasize agriculture; it can also be veterinary extension, home economics extension, nutrition extension, sanitation extension, etc. Under such programmes the extension agent works with the rural people and helps them to solutions for their own needs and wants; he is concerned with making people understand, accept and put new knowledge to work.

Extension is conceived of as the development of the individual, village leaders and the rural society as a whole and as a continuous education process. In it the people are motivated through a proper and organized approach to help themselves by applying science and technology in farming, home-making and community living. It necessarily involves a two-way channel of knowledge and experience. The problems of the field are brought to laboratories and their results are taken back to farmers and villages. Most importantly, participation in programmes is on a voluntary cooperative basis.

Principles of extension education

Certain rules of conduct guide extension workers towards greater effectiveness. They are of course very similar to the principles of adult learning elaborated in Chapter 2. Dahama in his book *Extension and Rural Welfare*[3] lists the following principles:

1 Extension should be based on felt needs and enlightened desire of the people.
2 It should be according to the local conditions of the people.
3 Extension work starts with the people as they are; it works in harmony with their nature and understands their problems as they see them.
4 There is democratic procedure in the formation and execution of the programme.
5 The programme should be started with the simplest problems of farmers, leaving difficult ones for the future.
6 The programme should be so designed that it can give greater benefit to the greatest number of people.
7 The extension programme should be made in consultation with rural people through their local leaders and organizations.
8 Extension work is always to be based on the principles of helping people to help themselves.
9 Extension work grows with the level of understanding and skill of people and is adjusted on the basis of feedback from them.

Agricultural extension

Of all the extension services, agricultural extension is the most important and may be regarded as the key to integrated rural development, since all increase in agricultural production and productivity will provide the necessary sound base. Increase in production of foodstuffs comes at the hands of the cultivator; and, for achieving the objective, it is the cultivator who must be supplied with scientific and technological information and know-how and convinced that he can use it. The task is complex since it involves communicating with an illiterate majority and involves changing the attitudes and mental outlook of the people to bring about continuous improvements. An extension programme should be an action-oriented process. The agricultural extension workers should be sufficiently trained to identify problems arising in the field on the spot, bring them to the research laboratory and carry the results back to the field. The extension worker should not only provide advice on crop and husbandry problems but also act as a business consultant to the farmer; he should be able to advise on the formation of a cooperative or credit society, as well as on marketing, bank loans, etc.

All this, however, does not imply that *community development* should be replaced or overriden by only agricultural programmes. The programmes should be complementary to each other. Community development is a whole, whereas agricultural development is just a part.

Rural community development

In agricultural change and in all rural development the most important factor is the human element. Material and institutional aid are needed, research and technology are needed, but they will not lead to results unless the rural people are motivated to and educated in ways of improving their farms, homes and community. This is what community development is about.[4]

What is community development?

A short definition is: 'Community development is a movement designed to promote better living for the whole community with the active participation and on the initiative of the community.' A more comprehensive United Nations definition is:

The term community development has come into international usage to connote the processes by which the efforts of the people themselves are united with those of governmental authorities to improve the economic, social and cultural conditions of communities, to integrate these communities into the life of the nation and to enable them to contribute fully to national progress.

This complex of processes is then made up of essential elements: the participation by the people themselves in efforts to improve their level of living with as much reliance as possible on their own initiative and the provision of technical and other services in ways which encourage this initiative, self-help and mutual help and make these more effective: it is expressed in programmes designed to achieve a wide variety of specific improvements.

These programmes are usually concerned with local communities because of the fact that the people living together in a locality have many and varied interests in common. Some of these interests are expressed in functional groups organised to further a more limited range of interests not primarily determined by locality.

Any community development programme has the following basic elements:

Self-help No community development programme can succeed without the active support and participation of the people themselves. Thus, a programme should be so organized as to provide opportunities for maximum self-help. Encouragement should be given for the people to actually plan and work on the solution of their problems themselves; this enables them to develop self-initiative; self-reliance and their own leadership.

'Felt needs' Any development programme must start with what the community needs and knows it needs. It should not be imposed on the community by someone else; otherwise it is not community development.

The whole community Community development cannot take place if it does not look at the community in its entirety and seek to build the community as an integrated unit. This enables the people to regard all aspects of community development as their own concern and thereby develop their capacity and faith in themselves and in the capacity of their own cooperative effort to solve their local problems.

The scope of community development

Community development has a formidably wide scope of activity. We shall here deal with some of its most important aspects. Since agricultural development has been mentioned already we shall now concentrate attention on the non-agricultural aspects of community development, the specific elements of change required to bring improvements in the living conditions and health of people. These include:

Health On account of unhygienic conditions of living, lack of drinking and bathing water facilities, rural populations suffer from many diseases. To ensure better health for all, elementary health education is a necessity for any community development programme. Cleanliness, both personal and communal, the disposal of waste, and removal of causes of water pollution are some of the areas in which a community development officer can easily arouse people's interest and enthusiasm. The good will and cooperation of the government health services is necessary for the programme to succeed.

Home economics This programme deals with improved ways of keeping a home, cooking food, decorating a house, raising children, as well as keeping the house clean and free from insects, gardening and information about nutrition. It also covers family relations. It is thus not a subject for women only. It covers the whole family as the basic unit of the community. It is of particular significance to the community development officer as it involves a number of government departments. The value of home economics training cannot be over-emphasized as it ensures that the children are brought up with the initiative, responsibility and sense of service which will make them leaders of the future.

Cooperatives   A way of strengthening small producers is by the establishment of cooperative marketing, thrift and credit societies. Cooperatives enable resources to be pooled and link farmers with a national movement. Contributions come from the people themselves and funds may be made available for purposes important to them – both for local development projects and for the observance of customary events such as funerals, weddings and the installation of chiefs. This combines the advantage of thrift and credit and the linking of credit with marketing. The rural people, as consumers, may also wish to set up cooperative village shops.

Rural industries   These usually take the form of handicrafts, cottage and small-scale industries. They are likely to be related to agriculture in that raw materials are gained from it or in that they supply goods and services to rural people. They would include such industries as bakery, pottery, soap-making, carving and weaving, metal-working, poultry and rabbitry. They require little capital and have a definite relation to the conditions of the locality – the availability of raw materials, the existence of local demand and the supply of local labour. Community development schemes fostering such small rural industries could be very successful. They could provide alternative types of employment and thus stop the tendency to migrate to the towns, keeping young people in their villages and contributing to village development. They could also improve the quality of rural life by putting a greater variety of goods on the market. Such programmes need to include some provision for training (such as the Vocational Improvement Centres give in Nigeria), for quality control and for marketing.

Housing   Self-help methods are customary among rural people. They need to be applied to simple improvements in ventilation and roofing, in use of traditional materials, in design of cooking stores, in location of latrines. The cooperative approach may be used for the provision of communal amenities.

Public amenities   Increased production and better standards of life are closely linked with better water supplies. Building of feeder roads and construction or expansion of post offices (or postal agencies) can provide greater access to the outside world; roads in particular provide the means for easier marketing of crops and thus increased opportunities for higher income, as well as the means for easier supply of consumer goods and thus for improved levels of living. The provision of clean drinking water for humans and animals is vital for health and comfort. All these amenities, however, only become economic when people are living in fairly concentrated settlements.

Recreation and use of leisure   With the decline and neglect of traditional forms of recreation, there is a danger of rural life becoming dull, and also of such social problems as alcoholism, quarrels, litigation and waste of money. Consequently, community development should include sports and entertainment. Team games may be used to arouse community spirit; and public entertainment, through story-telling, masquerade, dance and drama will serve to enliven village life. Recreation and entertainment are essential elements in any integrated community development programme, not only as a force for keeping the community united, but also to preserve its cultural heritage.

These are some aspects of community development. It will be seen that it is a process of conscientization which involves both organization and education. An integrated community development programme is essentially a programme of education, but may also include specific elements of both non-formal and formal education. As the whole of this book is about the education of adult members of the community, I need not say much about it here, but would like to make two points. One is about *literacy*: people cannot attain the status of a full citizen if they are unable to read or write and literacy work has a better chance of success if it is integrated with civic betterment, since it can be seen to be functional and will thus arouse the interest of the community. The second is about *community development training*. Community development requires certain skills in management, in democratic procedures and in record-keeping, and the animators or opinion-leaders in a community need to be encouraged to develop these skills, both formally and also by practically exercising them. Community development assists people to develop themselves and must depend on the people themselves and not just on paid government officials.

Integrated rural development in West Africa

Integrated rural development is wider than agricultural or community development. It is a systematic and multi-sectional programme to attain the integration of the rural population into the mainstream of income groups in a country. It is useful to state that no West African country, to date, has formulated an all-embracing or coordinated programme of rural development, though there have been some *ad hoc* schemes like the 1963 Western Nigeria Integrated Rural Development Programme. We shall deal here, however, with those aspects of agricultural or community development that have so far contributed to rural progress in selected West African countries.

An historical appraisal of community and rural development in some West African countries

Community development as a method of promoting rural development was only taken up by West African governments after World War II. It was then thought of in terms of social development and emerged from the original idea of 'mass education'. The first country to start this method was Ghana, when it embarked on a Plan for Mass Literacy and Mass Education in 1951 under the auspices of the Department of Social Welfare and Community Development (see pages 196–9). Other West African countries also had small-scale sporadic programmes of mass literacy linked to the social approach, although in the then eastern Nigeria, experiments in the field of self-help building were made earlier than other West African countries.[5]

In Sierra Leone, there have been some community development programmes but they have been rather small in scope and activity. This has been mainly due to shortage of staff and funds. Similarly in Gambia, community development has been concentrated in a few districts only.

Rural development activity in Ghana

Hitherto, Ghana had the most comprehensive community development programme in Anglophone West Africa. Practically every field of community development was covered in some measure – self-help building, agricultural and cooperative extension, village recreation, work with women's organizations and youth clubs. Perhaps the most successful was literacy; in spite of the limitations of the mass education campaigns started in the 1950s (see pages 197–9), it is worth remembering that Ghana achieved a 50 per cent literacy rate, which is the highest in West Africa. Other areas of success have been agricultural extension and work with women and youth. For example, in the 1950s a capsid disease struck cocoa, Ghana's main foreign exchange earner. Joint teams from the Department of Social Welfare and the Department of Agriculture sponsored a massive campaign to get farmers to spray their cocoa trees against the disease. There was initial political resistance, but in the end the campaign was so successful that the supply of sprayers was quite inadequate.

Lately, more women have been attending classes in simple home economics, and women extension workers are also welcomed into village households. Courses in social education and citizenship have been run in some regions of the country, and 'model villages' have been developed which have given the rural population a sense of citizenship and of participation in the movement to progress. The most notable of these model villages were built for the 90,000 people displaced by the Volta River hydro-electric project. Many community development programmes in Ghana, however, have been shelved due to financial constraints; but the spirit of community development is firmly rooted in Ghana and has great potential for the country's rural and economic development.

Rural development activity in Nigeria

The size of Nigeria has made it difficult for any rural development programme to have an impact, and much of the work has been at regional or state level. By 1960, all regions had departments concerned with community development and with agricultural extension. The eastern region built on the Udi experience, the western region borrowed the idea of farm settlements from Israel, while the northern region had a far-reaching programme of 'public enlightenment', which emphasized community development, literacy and women's education. Agricultural extension throughout the country was linked with research by the federal government and by the universities. Churches also took an interest in rural betterment; the Catholic Church still does a great deal of women's club work stressing health and nutrition, while the Protestant *Faith and Farm* worked in the eastern region and the mid-west, and more recently in Plateau state.

After the division of Nigeria into twelve and then nineteen states, there has been greater diversity of programmes. Heavy expenditure on agricultural extension was made in particular by Kano state, while the west and its successor states (Ogun, Ondo and Oyo) have spent extensively on community development training. Rivers and Cross-Rivers states have linked their community development to mechanical units, which can lend equipment for building, road-clearing and farming projects.

University departments concerned with agricultural economics and rural health have in recent years initiated various schemes of guided change. There are major projects by the University of Ibadan (Badeku and Ibarapa), Ahmadu Bello University (Malumfashi) and in various centres by the Universities of Ife and Nsukka. Most of these place emphasis on the training of youths in improving agricultural methods and settling them on the land. They also involve the training of community development workers who will, after the initial training period, be posted to 'model' villages, where they will be concerned with literacy, self-help projects, women's work, village planning and housing, the training of youth, as well as 'first aid' work. They will also act as liaisons between the villagers and the various ministries involved in the integrated rural development programme.

Trends in Sierra Leone and Gambia

Community development in both these countries has yet to make a significant impact on rural development. In Sierra Leone, shortage of funds has limited the scope of community development. Most of the activities have been concentrated on literacy work in local languages, and women's work, which has been viewed as having the greatest potential. There is little self-help construction work, but there is evidence of expansion of agricultural extension activities, particularly with the influence of the University College of Njala. But most of these efforts are frustrated by lack of coordination between the participating departments. Sierra Leone, thus, has no coordinated or all-embracing rural development programme. In Gambia, the picture is no different. Most of the activities are concentrated on literacy work and the coverage is rather limited.

Notes and references

1. Commonwealth Secretariat, Report of the Workshop on Rural Development in Africa, held at Ibadan, 1976 (London, 1976)

2. See any good textbook on development economics. In particular, see UN Economic Commission for Africa, *The Integrated Approach to Rural Development in Africa* (New York: UN, 1971); Uma Lele, *The Design of Rural Development – Lessons from Africa* (Baltimore: Johns Hopkins Press/World Bank, 1975); The Nigerian Economic Society, *Rural*

Development in Nigeria – Report of the 1972 Annual Conference of the Society (Ibadan, 1972)

3. O. P. Dahama, *Extension and Rural Welfare* (Agra, India: Ram Prasam, 1968)

4. T. R. Batten, *Communities and their Development* (London: OUP, 1957) and D. Brokensha and P. Hodge, *Community Development: An Interpretation* (London: International Textbook Co., 1970)

5. I. C. Jackson, *Advance in Africa – A Study of Community Development in Eastern Nigeria* (London: OUP, 1956)

Suggestions for further reading

Callaway, Archibald. *Educating Youth for Rural Development.* NISER, Ibadan, 1968

Commonwealth Secretariat. Report of the Commonwealth Conference on Education in Rural Areas, held in Accra, Ghana, March 1970

Malassis. *Economic Development and the Programming of Rural Education.* Unesco, Paris, 1966

Morris, Jon. *Farmer Training as a Strategy of Rural Development – A Chapter in Education Development.* University College, Nairobi, 1966

Nyerere, Julius K. *Socialism and Rural Development.* Government Printer, Dar es Salaam, 1967

Okedara, J. T., and Stanford, R. *The Role of Adult Education in Community Development.* Report of the NNCAE Conference held in Jos, 1974. Nigerian National Council for Adult Education, Lagos, 1976

Olatunbosun, Dupe. *Nigeria's Neglected Rural Majority.* OUP, Ibadan, 1975

Sheffield, J. R., and Diejomoah, V. P. *Non-Formal Education in African Development.* African-American Institute, New York, 1972

Wilson, Fergus B. *Education and Training for Rural Development in Africa.* FAO, Rome, 1968

International Bank for Reconstruction and Development (World Bank). *The Assault on Poverty.* Johns Hopkins Press, Baltimore, 1975

Part Five
Conclusion

12   Trends and problems
J. A. Akinpelu

Introductory

A chapter on trends and problems may be considered irrelevant in such a book as this if all it achieves is a rehash of what has perhaps been more expertly done by other contributors. On the other hand, it will be considered relevant and desirable if it tries to draw together the major trends and problems that have perhaps been casually raised by them, and tries to focus attention on them. Such a task is necessary because the problems have been raised in different places, by different writers, and for different reasons, and it is just possible for the reader to have forgotten them before coming to the end of the book. The task of this chapter, therefore, is to remind the reader about the major issues, some of which have been raised, that characterize adult education in West Africa, in preparation for the next chapter which will try to predict its future direction and prospects. First, then, let us briefly review the trends.

Trends in adult education in West Africa

Adult education is still in its infancy both as a discipline and as a profession, though certainly not as an educational process. As an educational practice, it is as old as the first adults that walked the surface of the earth. Hence, in West Africa, the introduction of the so-called 'modern' or Western European concept, which was indeed a relatively formal and highly organized system, was a super-imposition on the traditional, less sophisticated but apparently successful system of adult education. As suggested by earlier contributors in this book, there is a great need for the integration of both the African traditional, the Arabic-Islamic and Western/modern modes for maximum effectiveness within the milieux in which adult education is being conducted in West Africa.[1] Our concern with the trends of the development of adult education here will, however, be limited to the movements in the received modern mode. The integration belongs to the future.

World trends in the progress of adult education

In tracing the trend of development of adult education in West Africa, it will be appropriate to touch on the global and international trends in the context of which the West African scene can be best appreciated. On the world scene, the emergence of modern adult education as a profession and a discipline is a twentieth century phenomenon, and the process is still continuing. The progress has, however, been rapid and deliberately planned: at periodic intervals, international experts, high policy-makers and top national political leaders meet at international conferences and seminars to review the progress so far made and outline new directions of aims, objectives and strategies. This is a new and happy procedure which was not characteristic of the formal education system, and its effect has been to prevent out-of-school education from becoming as stratified, rigid and inflexible as the formal education system. It has, on the other hand, made it a most promising alternative to the school system for meeting the pressing needs of man.

The earliest international conferences were those held at *Cambridge* (UK) and *Elsinore* (Denmark) in 1929 and 1949 respectively.[2] The objectives of adult education, as perceived at those times, answered the needs of the times: there was the need in Europe, for example, to bridge the socio-cultural gap between the elite and the masses, and hence it was thought that adult education would help to popularize or democratize the *haute culture* (or high culture) which was formerly the preserve of the upper classes and the bourgeoisie. The spread of liberal education would, it was thought, prevent the sort of dictatorship and tyranny that had just ended with the defeat of Hitler's Germany. In short, the objective was cultural.

By 1960, when the next international conference was convened in *Montreal* (Canada), there had been radical changes in the concept, the objectives, the contents and the implementation strategies of adult education. It was now seen as an instrument for national survival on the social, political and economic planes. The underlying principle was that of social engineering, utilizing human resources for the development and/or sustenance of nationhood.

On the socio-political plane, the developing nations needed it to forge integrated and united nations out of a welter of strong sub-national, ethnical or regional loyalties; while the developed nations needed it to contain the disintegrative socio-political forces that manifested themselves in youth alienation and revolt, and widespread apathy among their electorates. On the economic front, the developing nations needed mass adult education for the take-off of their economies, and especially for facilitating modernization. The developed countries with their highly modernized economies discovered that their scientific and technological civilization demanded *more* rather than less education, if only to sustain their present standards. In short, the emphasis in every instance was on the nation and the use that could be made of the individuals for the survival of the nation.

The next trend was, as it were, a corrective to Montreal's over-emphasis on the nation and the economic utility of the individual in the scheme of things. The 1972 *Tokyo International Conference* restored the balance in the tug between the individual and the claims of the society. While not diminishing the importance of the latter, it pictured education as more for the integrated development of the individuals as human beings than for the economic and political contributions that they could make. While the idea of lifelong education germinated immediately after Montreal, it came into full bloom, at least theoretically, at Tokyo.

A sub-trend of the Tokyo era is the new concept of adult education as enunciated by *Paulo Freire, Ivan Illich* and other humanist/existentialist-oriented educational thinkers. Their message is mainly for the individual but has a strong socio-political bias; it is directed to the 'oppressed peoples' of the world, whatever their forms of oppression. It is extremely difficult to express their philosophy in a single sentence but it may be tolerably described as a call on the individual to be an activist-participant in the shaping of his society through an education that prepares him to play this role. This education Paulo Freire calls '**cultural action for freedom**'.

From this short historical analysis, we could identify four major movements: the era of adult education as a liberal/general/cultural education; followed by the era of positive use of adult education for material and nationalistic ends; next, a third movement, which sought to restore the balance in favour of continuous and integrated development of human beings; while the fourth and a sub-movement emphasizes more the role of the individual as the author of his own and his society's development. These were the movements which form the backdrop of the West African trends to which we now turn.

The West African scene

Adult education in West Africa, as elsewhere in the world in the 1940s, served principally as a cultural vehicle. The illiterates were taught literacy skills of reading and writing so as to enable them to share in the new European culture; while those already literate groomed themselves on literacy and liberal education to make them 'cultivated gentlemen'. The 1950s, however, added political and nationalistic objectives to the originally purely cultural aim. Through the print media, the West African nationalists sought to educate their followers on the struggle for national self-government. They advocated a sort of mass political education rather than a formal or systematized adult education process.

It is appropriate here to sketch the characteristics of this era. Adult education was essentially a non-governmental affair with the voluntary agencies predominating. The media handled mass education. In the area of literacy education, governmental support was sporadic, and focused mainly on literacy education and supervision rather than active involvement. A few classes in literacy were conducted but the impact was slight and negligible. The objectives of the adult education efforts were literacy education as a prerequisite for democratic self-government; liberal education to prepare the indigenous for the social and civic responsibilities into which they were soon to enter; and mass political education to give massive support for the demands for self-government. Economic and functional education hardly existed.

With the attainment of independence by different West African nations there appeared to be a lull in the drive for adult education. Attention was shifted towards expanding the formal education system. In certain countries, especially Ghana, Guinea and Mali, there was a heightened political education, the net effect of which was divisive rather than integrative, because it sought to impose the ruling parties' political manifestoes as the national ideologies, suppressing the voices of dissent instead of arriving at consensus through the democratic process. In other places, like Nigeria, adult education went back to the idea of literacy of the liberal and cultural type. In all, adult education as a functional instrument for socio-economic development or for the survival of the nation was not yet realized.

In the late 1960s and 1970s, however, partly as a result of participation in international conferences on adult education, and partly as a result of the growing awareness of the inadequacies of the formal education system for meeting the needs of a nation in a hurry, the various West African governments began to pay new attention to adult education. For the first time in Nigeria, for example, adult education was given a separate allocation in the National Development Plan apart from unspecific allocations to various forms of adult education undertaken in other ministries. This is a clear evidence of the recognition of adult education for national development and as an instrument of national survival. This is the stage at which we are now: we have subscribed to the theory of lifelong education but we have yet to put this into practice. As to the conscientization theory of Paulo Freire and others, we have still to work out the implications of it for the West African scene, even though I am personally convinced that it has a message for us.

If we may characterize the present position of adult education in West Africa, it would be correct to say that we have just reached the dawn of awareness – an awakened consciousness of the importance of adult education but without as yet the full national commitment to its prosecution.

Problems of adult education in West Africa

Because the modern concept of adult education is a twentieth century phenomenon, its newness gives rise to a large number of problems, some of which had also been raised in respect of formal school education in its early days and been solved in the course of centuries of its development. The problems that are raised are both theoretical and practical, conceptual, technical and administrative. Many of them are internal to its development as a discipline and as a profession, while others are external and posed by circumstances under which it operates. As a very new phenomenon in the modern sense in West Africa, it is clustered with very many problems and it will be possible to mention only a few of them here. Our selection, however, will not be entirely subjective because, as already indicated, some of these problems are perennial and internationally recognized as important, while those that are peculiar to West Africa have been identified as worthy of mention through repeated references to them in the earlier chapters. Also because of the large number of the problems, we shall group them into clusters, of which there are three major ones:

1 Theoretical problems relating to the recognition of adult education as a discipline and a profession;
2 administrative problems of strategies and implementation of adult education policies;
3 pedagogical or andragogical problems of effective delivery of adult education.

Theoretical and conceptual problems

The first problem under the first cluster of conceptual and theoretical problems is that of stabilizing or formalizing the terms and concepts which we use in adult education. This is not merely a question of semantics: its importance lies in the facilitation of communication between theoreticians and practitioners, and between them and outsiders. Besides this practical problem of communication, there has to emerge a corpus of identifiable adult education concepts, so that adult education may be recognized as an **academic discipline** which, in the words of Walton and Kuethe, is 'a body of subject matter made up of concepts, facts, and theories, so ordered that it can be deliberately and systematically taught'.[3] Formal education and other traditional disciplines have undergone similar processes. Suffice it to say here that it is a problem: the Third International Conference on Adult Education held in Tokyo identified it as a major problem, and went on to say 'that an international dictionary of adult education was badly required'.[4] None has emerged so far, but certainly efforts are being made from which such a dictionary could emerge. Chapter 1 gives a representative sample of such terms and concepts[5] – some of them old, others new – which need to be analysed, clarified and established for usage. This is a first prerequisite for any empirical or theoretical research to proceed on even keel.

Redirection of research in adult education

Research is of paramount importance for the development of adult education as a discipline and a profession. Research has often been thought of as an intellectual or academic exercise that is worlds apart from practice. This is a misconception, it is theory that evolves from valid and meaningful practice, whereas practice itself can hardly proceed without one type of theory or another. If one may parody the saying of a famous German philosopher, Immanuel Kant, on the relationship of theory and practice: a theory that is not based on practice is empty just as practice that does not proceed from theory is blind. Thus, for the theoretician and the practitioner, research is most fundamental and they must collaborate in it. The practice has been for research to be identified with the university departments/institutes, but this is a traditional position that needs to be modified. Perhaps large and extensive researches are better done within the universities; but even here collaboration with those in the field has mutual advantages, and the findings are better assured of successful implementation.

But even more important is the need for the field-worker to be competent to conduct by himself some rudimentary action-research alongside his field-work preoccupation. This implies that some basic research skills should be included in the training of adult education and community development organizers, so that they can carry out investigations on matters of immediate urgency. For example, there is nothing preventing an adult literacy teacher or even an organizer conducting an experiment with a new method of teaching that occurs to him in the course of his routine duties as likely to be more successful in teaching adults. The sin is to subject whole classes arbitrarily to a method that has never been tested or experimented with. A way of finding out the potentiality of the new method is to designate a particular class as the 'experimental' group and another the 'control' group, with all other significant variables held constant. The adult educator can introduce his new method into the teaching of a unit to the experimental groups while the current method is used to teach the same unit to the control group. After teaching sufficient units to warrant evaluation, he can test the performances. If he discovers some appreciable differences in favour of the experimental group, then he can proceed to broaden his area of application; and if the success story continues, he can adopt it as a new general method and recommend it to others with some confidence.

This is a hypothetical example which is applicable to all categories of field-workers, be they extension education workers in agriculture and health, or community and social welfare officers. The idea is to have a **pilot scheme** before inflicting a new scheme or method on the whole population. This is the rough and ready village-type research technique which an adult education trainee should be introduced to in the course of his training – otherwise, he will just continue to apply the received method of ideas in a routine fashion. Such studies by field workers are essential in West Africa where statutory allocations to research are regarded as of low priority, and even at times as a luxury.

On the international scene, however, considerable research in adult education has taken place, and one of its fruits is the gradual acceptance of the subject as a budding discipline. The major emphasis of these investigations has been in the area of national and international comparisons of the structures, methods, organization, planning and administration of adult education (see pages 27, 44). Researches into the *foundations* of adult education have been few and far between, and in any case have not been as generously funded. And yet, as another contributor has pointed out, the dark areas of the discipline include investigation the physiological, sociological and psychological factors affecting the adult learner (see pages 31–5). This is especially true of the West African situation. It has been found in research into how children learn that findings in one cultural milieu are hardly transplantable wholesale into another and that even ordinary adaptation is not as good as replicating the experiments with the indigenous population. So also in the sociology and psychology of adult learners in West Africa, research has to be initiated with the indigenous adults as subjects, and similar research in other cultural milieux should provide only necessary insights and guidelines.

The final problem about research into adult education in West Africa is that of financing and encouraging research activities. Due to the present low visibility and narrow conception of adult education in governmental circles, public funds are hardly earmarked for them; but there is no doubt that research and field-work are equally important, each for its own reasons. It is important to be able to count by the droves how many illiterates have been made literate by field-workers: but the method by which they are made literate, and whether the same or larger numbers can be made literate in a shorter time and at half the cost through an alternative method, are equally worth investing in. The anti-intellectual tendency of voting money only for field-work and leaving nothing for research needs to be discouraged. West African governments, aided by international education agencies, have to allocate funds generously to research if adult education is to be virile enough to fulfil the national development objectives which are set out for it.

Problems of administrative strategies for adult education

The second cluster of problems besetting adult education in West Africa is that of administrative strategies for the implementation of adult education policies. By this I mean the problems of organization, planning, administration and financing of adult education in the sub-region. The problems are many and complex and so our treatment necessarily has to be selective; however, as a result of their interconnected nature, one can hardly treat one without touching the others.

Problem of scope and location of adult education

The first problem posed under this heading is that of the wide and diversified scope of adult education.

The Nairobi (Unesco) conference of 1976 defined adult education as denoting the 'entire body of *organized educational processes . . .*' (my italics).[5] This is an invitation to include under adult education all possible relatively organized education processes that are outside the formal school system. The Nigerian National Policy on Education has done some filling in by saying that it 'consists of functional literacy, remedial, continuing, vocational, aesthetic, cultural and civic education for youths and adults outside the formal school system'.[6] This multiplicity of objectives and content should really be the strength of adult education in guaranteeing equality of opportunity for the diverse aspirations of the populace; but, in fact, with the government economic and financial planners, it is a liability. They seem to be looking for specificity and neatness in programmes on which to put government funds. Hence they plump for literacy education which seems nearest to the formal school system in neatness and organization. There the success of the programme can be easily determined, in terms of the numbers made literate, and the expenses thus 'justified'. A discussion with the ministry officials often reveals that the objectives of remedial, continuing, aesthetic, cultural and civic education exist only as policy statements without concrete programmes to point to.

Even where these programmes exist, they are scattered about in many ministries and lumped in with the other programmes in such a way as to lose their very identity. The ministries of information will claim to be responsible for aesthetic and cultural adult education but often all that we see are annual festivals and cultural shows which are meant to entertain, and only incidentally educate; there are no programmes of *systematic* education. A similar fate befalls other aspects of adult education that are given refuge in other ministries and departments. More importantly, when it comes to funding, these educational aspects are given low priority. The solution to the problem of loose organization would seem to lie in the setting up of high-powered, generously funded national boards of adult education which will coordinate, fund and organize adult education programmes of every variety; such boards exist, notably in Kenya and Zambia.

The disposition in some countries to create a specific division of adult education in the national ministry of education (and in the Federal Republic of Nigeria to establish one in the Ministry of Education of each component state) provides only a partial solution. It may solve some of its financial problems since there is then one voice defending its interests instead of the many indifferent voices as before. But, this location is not without its own dangers, the foremost of which is that of getting assimilated into the formal school system, with all its rigidity and inflexibility. There will be the temptation to see adult education mainly in terms of literacy education and remedial evening classes; in short, to diminish or play down that variety and diversity of programmes which has been the major characteristic and strength of adult education.

On the advantages side, the location of adult education in a ministry of education conforms with current ideas of lifelong education. The integration of both formal and non-formal systems is likely to be made easier. There is, however, an anxiety that the integration may in the short run work against the interest of adult education. The idea of lifelong education, as far as educational planning in West Africa is concerned, is still fuzzy; it is still a fashionable theory. For example, the new Nigerian National Policy on Education proclaims it as the foundation and basis of the new educational policy;[7] but the structures, organization and financing are far from adequate to achieve the idea of lifelong education. The danger is simply this: that adult education has hardly been recognized as a distinct entity, autonomous and on a par with formal education, yet its integration into the still fuzzy and vague idea of lifelong education is strongly advocated. The Nairobi Conference of 1976 was aware of this danger when it recommended that adult education should retain its identity in the lifelong education scheme and be accorded equal status with formal school education. In West Africa, adult and non-formal education still have long battles to fight to attain equal treatment with formal education. The attitude of the various governments to it, as I have already described it, is only the beginning or the dawn of awareness – which is still a long shot from complete acceptance and a commitment.

Decentralization and financing of adult education

Another problem under the cluster is the decentralization and financing of adult education. This, in normal circumstances, should be an advantage because adult education by its very nature is best organized and conducted at the local level to make it thoroughly relevant for solving the local community problems. Over-centralization, with a centrally imposed curriculum, organization and even methodology (as in the formal school system) is alien to its natural growth. In Nigeria, for example, the need for decentralization would seem to have been recognized when the instruments setting up the new Local Government Councils vested the organization, financing and control of adult education in each council's committees on education, with supervisory councillors as the chairmen. This is as it should be, if the councils are always financially buoyant. Even when centrally placed, whenever there is any economic or financial 'belt-tightening', adult education votes, along with other activities considered peripheral, are the first to be cut. Now, the problem of local governments in Nigeria is that of perennial shortage of funds to carry out projects. In the circumstances, adult education may be poorly organized and inadequately financed.

There is also the question of the conditions of service of the professional workers in adult education and community development. During the Seventh Annual Functional Literacy Seminar organized by the Department of Adult Education, University of

Ibadan, on the Role of the Local Government Councils in the Promotion of Adult Education, field-workers expressed the fears that, if their conditions of service, etc., are to be decided at the local level, they would be exposed to the local councillors' whims and caprice, which will be aggravated when the country returns to civil rule in 1979; that their salaries might be irregular and/or late since the councils are usually poor; and that in any case, the decentralization was likely to retard the emergence of adult education as a profession since standardization in any form would be difficult to achieve. These are basically human problems which cannot be disposed of by mere rational argument, and hence still pose problems for adult education in West Africa.

Legislating access to adult education

The last problem to touch upon in this cluster is that of *legislation* to ensure equal access to education for all underprivileged or disadvantaged people. It has now become well known that mere quantitative expansion of present facilities does not necessarily democratize the educational system.[8] In fact, it may on the contrary perpetuate the existing inequalities or even widen the gap still further, since those who have already benefited are likely to be more aware of the expanded educational facilities and hence take more than their own proportionate share. Therefore, even if larger resources are made available for adult education, there will still be a problem of the disadvantaged, or the 'forgotten people' (as they were described by the Tokyo conference) not benefiting significantly.

A possible solution is an extensive diversification of adult education opportunities so that all categories of adults could benefit. Investigations should be conducted into the constraining factors that militate against the 'have-nots' seizing the opportunities. One of the most important factors that will be found is the constraint of poverty itself; the people concerned either have no funds with which to attend or have no time to spare from their work-a-day jobs. Here the introduction of appropriate legislation may do the trick; employers may be obliged through appropriate incentives or legislation to guarantee part-time or block-time release for their illiterate and semi-literate employees, and also to set aside a percentage of profits for the appropriate education for them. This is already being done in many Commonwealth countries, including Nigeria, with the setting up of an Industrial Training Fund or similar scheme. The only snags are that the schemes often benefit the workers in the middle-level income group at the expense of the low-income group consisting of the unskilled and illiterate labour hands; and as they are financed by staff development and training funds, the schemes scarcely include the broader general and liberal education of the workers, the training being focused on the employment skill as though that alone defines the whole human being. The true education must aim at the integrated development of all aspects of a person, as the Tokyo conference recognized.

Problems of pedagogy and effective delivery

The third and last cluster of problems is that of pedagogy, or the effective delivery of education to adults. These problems have already been highlighted in many of the earlier chapters, and so we shall not go in depth into them. We shall emphasize only two or three problems considered very significant. The first has to do with the preparation of the adult educator. Adult education, because of its diversified scope, programmes and clientèle, poses a problem for the training of adult educators. Diversified objectives imply diversified teaching methods. Thus, the monolithic teaching method characteristic of the child education process will be out of place in the training of adult educators. The Nairobi Conference recommended that 'Training for adult education should, as far as practicable, include all those aspects of skill, knowledge, understanding and personal attitude which are relevant to the various functions undertaken, taking into account the general background against which adult education takes place.'[9] This multiplicity of teaching methods poses a problem for curriculum design and development.

Training adult educators

Linked with the above is the fact that most of the field-workers in West Africa at present have little formal inductive training for their jobs and less opportunities still for in-service or on-the-job courses. In areas where there is dearth of academically qualified personnel, neo-literates are employed. This does not augur well for the development of adult education in West Africa. A possible solution to the problem of staff shortage and inadequate preparation in the area of adult literacy teaching is contained in the suggestion of the Tokyo conference of 1972 that adult education principles, methods and techniques be integrated into the programme of teacher education at all appropriate levels.[10] A similar recommendation was made by the Nigerian National Council for Adult Education in their proposals for a National Adult Education Programme in 1973;[11] happily, this has been accepted in principle in Nigeria, and the methods of implementation are being worked out by the Federal Ministry of Education. This integration or introjection of adult education into the curricula of teacher training colleges and university faculties of education should release a sizable number of candidates to teach adults on a part-time basis. Their training in adult teaching methods will help them to achieve greater successes as adult educators. Periodic in-service courses would further enhance their performances.

Another major problem is that whatever training exists is given in complete isolation. The social welfare workers, the agricultural and health extension workers, the adult literacy personnel and the community and social development workers are all trained oblivious to the fact that they are all adult educators, modifying and changing the attitudes and behaviours of adults for the better. Again, this is a result of the professions concerned being located in different ministries and isolated from each other. It is therefore essential that coordination should take place at two levels – first, that of possibly a high-powered coordinating national board for adult education, as recommended earlier, and secondly, a jointly organized core curriculum for all adult education workers before they branch into their respective areas of specialization. With this coordination at two levels, it will be possible for all adult education personnel in their various specializations to see their work as aspects of the same system.

Use of mass media as aids in adult education

The next problem relates to the use of mass media for adult education purposes. Due to the multiplicity of the objectives and of the clients of this type of education, the mass media can be effectively used to reach a diversified and widely scattered populace. Indeed, considerable success has been achieved in the use of this vehicle for the delivery of adult education (see pages 149–53). This is not to say that the mass media do not have their own inherent disadvantages such as the fact that their listeners or audiences cannot enter immediately into a dialogue with the source of transmission on any subject being treated; but there is no doubt that the mass media can be effective in the general and civic education of adults.

Apart from these inherent defects, there are some other external constraining factors that constitute a problem to their effective usage. For example, some of the media are still thought of as mainly for entertainment rather than for education. Of course, there is a sense, an extended sense, in which something meant purely for entertainment can be educative (e.g. listening to a piece of music which can be regarded as leisure education); but what we are saying is that programmes can be so designed that while they are entertaining, they are at the same time deliberately educative. If I may illustrate with an American example and from children's education, a TV programme known as 'Sesame Street' was an intensive literacy education for children and yet very entertaining. Again, for maximum effect, the programme receivers must be accessible to all at the cheapest rate possible. Thus, the governments might consider removing all import duties and tariffs on all receivers so that the poorest individual can possess at least a pocket transistorized radio set and have access to television. That this has not been done is again evidence that governments in West Africa are not as yet committed to the idea of adult or mass education. There is, also, the problem of programming, which individual stations have to tackle in such a way that appropriate programmes are slotted for appropriate audiences or viewers at the most appropriate times of the day.

Under this cluster of problems, there is also that of ancillary services, which are not yet being fully exploited for education purposes. We refer to the libraries, museums, multi-purpose adult education centres and so on. These services are few and mostly concentrated in the urban areas where, in most of Africa, only a fraction of the population reside. Mobile library services which could reach the neo-literates in the rural areas hardly exist. Newspapers specifically geared to the interest of the rural neo-literates are few and relatively expensive for the average rural inhabitants. Instead of taking over urban wide-circulating English language papers, the governments can leave these to the private entrepreneurs, and spend their resources on mass production and circulation of vernacular newspapers, pamphlets and bulletins among the neo-literates. The problem here, as I see it, is a misplaced priority and also a lack of public commitment to the idea of mass adult education.

Evaluation in adult education

Finally, there is the problem of evaluation, which has hardly been seriously tackled in West Africa. The problem is actually twofold: the evaluation by the project sponsors or organizers to assess the progress of projects and final achievements; and the personal self-assessment by an individual learner of his own progress. Most of the writings on evaluation have emphasized only the first one, which possibly stems from the need to justify to the sponsor of the programme that his money has been well spent. I shall not dwell on the problems that may arise from this, but will rather emphasize that for the development of independent learning (which is the major aim of adult education), the learner has to be taught some rudimentary or village-type self-evaluation procedure. This will enable him to monitor his own progress in as simple a way as possible. This is hardly practised anywhere in West Africa but it is worth considering. To design such a simplified evaluation procedure for the adult in each adult education project is a problem to be added to the macro-evaluation problems which are well known and well highlighted in this book.

Conclusion

This chapter has been an attempt to raise, selectively, current problems facing adult education in theory and practice in the sub-region of West Africa. We have not made any systematic attempt to solve them; it would be presumptuous to try to do so, apart from the fact that doing so will be outside the topic. Nor can the selection or the treatment of the problems here pretend to be exhaustive; but it is sufficient if they are considered important enough to merit attention or significant enough to constitute a hurdle in the path of the progress of adult education in West Africa.

Notes and references

1. See Chapters 1 and 3
2. Unesco, *A Retrospective International Survey of Adult Education, Montreal 1960 to Tokyo 1972* (Paris, 1972)
3. J. Walton and J. Kuethe (eds), *The Discipline of Education* (Madison: University of Wisconsin Press, 1963), p. 5
4. Unesco, *General Report, Third International Conference on Adult Education, Tokyo 25 July–7 August, 1972* (Paris, 1972), p. 13
5. Unesco, *Recommendation on the Development of Adult Education* adopted by the General Conference at its nineteenth session, Nairobi, 26 November, 1976. For the rest of the chapter, this meeting is referred to simply as the Nairobi conference.
6. Federal Republic of Nigeria, *National Policy on Education* (Lagos: Federal Ministry of Information, 1977), p. 21
7. *Ibid.*, p. 5

8. George Z. F. Bereday, *Essays on World Education: The Crisis of Supply and Demand* (London: OUP, 1969), p. 53 ff.
9. Unesco, Nairobi Conference (1976), p. 34
10. Unesco, *General Report* (1972), p. 14
11. NNCAE, *Proposal for a National Adult Education Programme for Inclusion in the Third National Development Plan* (Ibadan: Nigerian National Council for Adult Education, 1973)

Suggestions for further reading

Bergevin, Paul. *A Philosophy of Adult Education*. Seabury Press, New York, 1967
Bown, Lalage (ed.). *Adult Education in Nigeria: The Next Ten Years*. Nigerian National Council for Adult Education, 1972
Freire, Paulo. *Education: The Practice of Freedom*, Writers' and Readers' Publishing Cooperative, London, 1976
Hall, B., and Remtulla, K. (eds). *Adult Education and National Development*. Proceedings of the Third Conference of the African Adult Education Association. East African Literature Bureau, Nairobi, 1973
Lawson, K. H. *Philosophical Concepts and Values in Adult Education*. University of Nottingham, 1975
Lowe, John (ed.). *Adult Education and Nation Building*. Edinburgh University Press, 1970
Lowe, J., Grant, N., and Williams, T. D. *Education and Nation Building in the Third World*. Academy Press, Edinburgh, and Onibonoje Press, Ibadan, 1973
National Adult Education Association of Tanzania, *Adult Education and Development in Tanzania*, vol. 1. NEAT, Dar es Salaam, 1975

13 The future

Lalage Bown and Michael Omolewa

Introductory

A major question broached in Chapter 12 is that of how we translate the idea of lifelong education into practice. Indeed, we believe that the realization of lifelong education is the crucial issue for the future of adult education since, without it, adult education is likely to remain marginal or fragmented at best. We will look at the immediate prospects for the development of West African adult education within a fabric of lifelong education; then at the likely long-term needs of and challenges to adult education within that fabric; and lastly at possible goals for lifelong education which may be taken up by planners and policy-makers, by educators and learners.

Some of the problems and challenges have been discussed in earlier chapters. They are restated here for emphasis. Throughout we have stressed that adult educators themselves, in partnership with adult learners, will need to resolve the various issues raised. If they do so, adult education will have a bright and promising future in West Africa. But decline may set in if the various problems are not tackled with zeal and determination.

Futures and plans

Among a number of useful verbal and written guides, we have derived especial help from the report of the Unesco international commission on the development of education, *Learning to Be,* often known as the Faure Report, after the commission's chairman. It must be seen as a pivotal document, since it was the first coherent international attempt to study the implications for the whole of education of modern social, economic and scientific trends, and the application, in their light, of the concept of lifelong learning. Readers are advised to study thoughtfully the section in the Faure Report on 'Futures'.[1]

It may seem presumptuous, of course, to try to predict the future and we are not here attempting to prophesy or practise divination. Our purpose is to observe existing patterns of adult education and estimate how they may reshape themselves in the light of known problems and trends.

Most West African countries have national development plans; and modern planning strategies make some kind of forecasting necessary. Professional planners work out lines of development with regard to current trends and official policies. Among other matters, they look at manpower statistics to see how many adults (of what ages and sex) there are likely to be in the population from year to year, what levels of education they have and what skills they will need. They are not, of course, watching undirected development; the very idea of a plan is that it is an effort to *shape* development, including educational development. Consequently, we do not regard it as out of place if we here suggest possible ways of integrating adult education into development plans and into possible policy choices for adult and lifelong education.

Immediate prospects

A criterion that could be used to predict the future of adult education in West Africa is the scope of development and growth up to date. As demonstrated in earlier chapters, adult education has recorded appreciable progress. It has a multiple heritage – traditional, Islamic, Christian, 'Western' and post-colonial – and the combination of all these forms has given it a richness greater than that of any one of them. Traditional methods of communication are used to convey new messages. Literacy is no longer the preserve of select Muslim or Christian converts, of chiefs and sons of chiefs; it is now assumed to be the right of all men and women. Indeed, the whole of adult education is regarded as such a right, and there are new ideas about provision of educational opportunities, curricula for adults and the access of mature persons to various types of learning.

Favourable forces at work

There are various forces making for increased recognition of adult education by West African governments and people. For the most cynical, adult education is a safety valve, to 'create an illusion of opportunity for all'. For others, it is an alternative to formal schooling, which most countries simply cannot afford to provide for all. Moreover, it is a political necessity in situations where some first-level schooling is being provided on a large scale and where there is likely to be only limited access into the higher levels for some time to come. For instance, it is estimated that in the 1980s in Nigeria, some 1.6 million children annually will leave primary schools without any prospect of going into any formal post-primary institution; it will inevitably take time before the formal secondary system can be expanded to keep pace. In such circumstances out-of-school education for youth and young adults will have to be provided.

As the Faure Report points out, the second half of the twentieth century has brought a great leap forward in science and technology and the application of scientific invention is now very rapid. Any country that wants to 'keep up' will need to devise means for all workers to be kept in touch with new ways of using their skills. Hence the interest in many countries in programmes of industrial and agricultural training and retraining, and in the idea that work and study should be linked together.

At the same time, there is a growing disenchantment with the 'Western' system of education, with its emphasis on the acquisition of the certificate. Certificate worship, which Dore describes as 'the creeping disease',[2] clearly negates the objectives of traditional African adult education, with its emphasis on the acquisition of morals, the transmission of national culture and the inculcation of socially acceptable attitudes to work and life. While very many people, including policy-makers and senior educationists, still confuse certification with education (and need to be helped to rethink their whole position, perhaps in high-level policy seminars), there are signs of unease with this approach. For instance, some governments have been constrained to set up committees on education for citizenship and education for moral values.

All these factors have led to a general consensus in West African countries that adult education is indispensable to economic development and to the establishment of a just and democratic society. Some constitutions enshrine the commitments to eradicate illiteracy. The 1979 constitution of Nigeria lists this and the provision of 'equal and adequate educational opportunities at all levels' as among the fundamental objectives and guiding principles of state policy.[3]

At the same time, the circumstances of political struggle in some countries have led to the evolution of a political philosophy which stresses popular education. In West Africa, the most notable example is Guinea-Bissau (Guiné). Because it achieved independence through prolonged guerrilla war, the nationalist leaders had to win the hearts and minds of their followers, so that everyone understood what they were fighting for. Amilcar Cabral laid stress on the importance of popular knowledge and understanding:

> Let me point out, though, that one type of struggle which we think basic has received no mention ... I mean *the struggle against our own weaknesses*. ... Experience in Guiné has shown us that in the general framework of the daily struggle, this battle against ourselves – no matter what difficulties the enemy may create – remains the most difficult of all, whether for the present or the future of our peoples. ...
> When Africans say in their proverbial language that 'no matter how hot the water from your well, it will not cook your rice', they express a fundamental principle of physics but also one of political science. We know that the evolution of a phenomenon in movement, no matter what its external appearance may be, depends upon its internal characteristics. And we know that on the political level our own reality – can only be transformed by detailed knowledge of it, by our own efforts, by our own sacrifices.[4]

Having hammered out a set of principles based on self-reliance and indigenous resources and on a broad provision of political education, the leaders of Guinea-Bissau have continued to hold to them after independence and have become the first West African government to try out on a large scale the adult educational principles of Paulo Freire.[5] At the time of writing this chapter, no evaluation of the experiment is yet available.

While increasing national recognition is being given to adult education by governments and peoples in West Africa, there is also an increasing international interest. Several UN bodies, including Unesco, the Economic Commission for Africa and the Education Division of the Commonwealth Secretariat[6] have spread ideas and information about adult education and have fostered conferences and seminars at which persons from various countries can exchange experiences and draw common conclusions.

All this augurs well for the future of adult education.

Obstacles to the development of adult education

In spite of the relatively favourable climate which is likely to exist in West Africa for the development of adult education in the last two decades of the century, we must guard against over-optimism. The previous chapter has alerted us to some important problems: the lack of clarity in the thinking of some adult educators about their own work, our occasional lack of imagination about content, andragogical method and delivery systems, and the administrative difficulties caused by the looseness of adult education organization.

The most obvious practical obstacle to progress in adult education is scarcity of resources. While lip-service is paid to the idea of lifelong education, few governments provide adequate funds for it. The proportion of national education budgets allocated to adult education in West Africa is seldom up to 1 per cent. Real improvement could be made if West African countries were to follow the example of India, which launched a National Adult Education Programme (NAEP) in October 1978 and uses 10 per cent of the government's education budget to finance it.

An effort has to be made to wrestle more funds from national and local governments for adult education programmes. National governments must also be made aware of the pivotal role of agricultural extension, health education, industrial training, forces education, literacy and other varieties of adult education in national development. This will not happen if adult educators fold their arms and expect funds to rain down from the authorities. They must make a concerted effort to obtain them. Additional money can also be raised by enlisting the continued support of international agencies such as those mentioned in Chapter 3 and Appendix 1; but this should be in addition to internal effort.

Meanwhile, we need to make the most of what we have. First, let us recognize that the head, 'Adult Education' (or Adult Literacy or Non-Formal Education), in a national education budget is by no means the sole financing available for adult educational activity broadly conceived. Often large amounts are devoted elsewhere in the budget to agricultural extension or health education or the women's bureau or to a special campaign such as Operation Feed the Nation in Nigeria. If there is greater cooperation between all agencies and workers whose task includes enlightening the public, existing resources would go very much further.

Second, as we noted in Chapter 1, many forms of education can unlock their own resources and generate income for the learners and for programmes. In their interesting book of case-studies of non-formal education in Africa, Sheffield and Diejomaoh give several examples of schemes in which learners acquire new skills and are able to sell their products – for instance the Buseko Home Industries project for young women on the Copperbelt in Zambia.[7]

Third, adult education is a field for voluntary endeavour, and very often voluntary agencies can outstrip governments because they are more flexible in their approach and can more readily risk experiment. There may be a case for more government-grant aid to voluntary bodies for adult education programmes. This was the view taken by a Commonwealth specialist conference on non-formal education in development held in Delhi in 1979 and attended in the main by representatives from developing countries.

A more fundamental obstacle, of which limited government budgets are a symptom, is lack of whole-hearted commitment on the part of rulers and leaders. The case of Guinea-Bissau is exceptional. In most West African countries, policy-makers talk about adult education as a useful activity, but usually do not seem to give their hearts to it. They will not change their attitudes without help. As mentioned in Chapter 3, adult educators need to organize themselves to advise governments locally and nationally and also to publicize the potential of adult education for national development. We must, of course, be seen to live up to our claims. This is one reason why record-keeping and evaluation, mentioned in Part 2 of this handbook, are important. Our own demonstrable achievements will provide our best argument. All our adult students should be our allies in any venture to gain more recognition and hence more resources for adult education.

Realistically, looking at the main obstacles we face, we need not be discouraged. They can be effectively tackled if we have the courage of our convictions.

Adult education within the context of lifelong learning – the next stage

Many adult educators have always placed emphasis on the active role of the adult learner and the need for the learner's full participation in his own education. It has always been regarded as unsatisfactory to 'decree' adult programmes from some official quarter, without consultation, and it has been tacitly accepted that no person can learn on behalf of another. Now such ideas are permeating the whole of education. In a number of countries, the accepted goal is to make all education *learner-centred* and to make learning *student-centred*.

This has been accompanied, and in part stems from, some shift in thinking about child education and development brought about by new trends in *physiology* and *psychology*. As the Faure Report says: 'the human brain has a very large unused potential', and awareness of this potential, following from recent scientific research, has put a new challenge to educators. Only by starting from an assumption of the individual learner's possible capacities can education enable him to develop. At the same time, there are changes in psychology. For over half a century, educational psychology, as applied to child education, has been heavily influenced by *behaviourist psychology,* which in its cruder forms can lead to a view of the human being as a creature to be manipulated and controlled.

Behaviourist psychology is associated with the important American psychologists, J. B. Watson and B. F. Skinner; it basically rejects the concept of 'mind' and of 'ideas' and emphasizes the control of behaviour through 'conditioned responses'. Education is thought of as a matter of providing the right stimulus or push to bring about a foreseeable reaction in the pupil. Behaviourism has brought many useful ideas to psychology and is a first-class tool for the study of animal behaviour, but in the hands of some educators it has led to a narrow and dehumanizing view of education. It has little to tell us about human creativity or the place of the individual will and imagination in learning. Recently thinking about child education has shifted to place more emphasis on the young learner as a person.

Further, psychologists interested in human development have increasingly carried out studies of older persons, as well as of children and adolescents. Chapter 2 was based in part on conclusions about adult learning drawn from these studies.

All these developments have brought educators of adults and educators of children closer together and should make it easier for child education and adult education to come together and be seen as parts of a whole lifelong learning system. We are thus likely to see ever more emphasis in the immediate future on the individuality and autonomy (self-guidance) of the learner, young or old.

In adult education, we would therefore expect to see ever more enlistment of the learners *to plan and shape their own learning* and thus more use of systems of programme design and methods of education which encourage active participation and independent learning.

If adults are given more say in their programmes, we would expect an increased variety of subject-matter in adult education in West Africa. The *content* of adult education might be expected to satisfy a great many demands of the learners. There will continue to be demands to improve economic skills as well as to satisfy scientific curiosity. Learners will also want to satisfy their natural pride in their own culture and society, to understand politics better and to develop their own individual talents. We will therefore have to turn our attention to providing education in basic scientific principles, in indigenous languages, arts and religions, in the study of society, in political science and in a whole range of subjects that encourages an individual's own creative efforts.

With regard to *methodology,* group and discovery methods, as well as individual learning, seem to be the modes of the future. To keep abreast, we must discard the old 'authoritarian' (dictatorial, dominating) methods and techniques associated with the old-fashioned school classroom, and fully *involve* our adult students. Many of the methods and techniques suggested in Chapter 6 will help us to do this.

The *sources of help* for the individual learner seem likely to increase. Distance teaching opportunities are already noticeably increasing in West African countries. Not only do we see an improvement in correspondence education, but there are signs that the mass media will be available to play a larger role in providing learning opportunities to more men and women in West Africa. Forecasts of scientific developments in the 1980s say that electronic communication is likely to become more cheaply available; this should put more radio and television sets in the hands of ordinary people and might even give us working telephone systems sufficiently widespread to be used for educational purposes, as they already are in such countries as Australia and the USA.

Long-term needs and challenges

These are some immediate expectations. What about the longer term?

While most adult educators have some personal views on their profession and while a handbook like this implies a certain set of *values* (such as the worth of the individual, the importance of forms of development which improve society), our profession still lacks an adequate and expressed philosophy. The last chapter has challenged us with the fact that we are still often rather vague about the ideas underlying our work. Much **fundamental thinking** still remains to be done; and in the next twenty years we will have to tackle this task. We will have to ask ourselves such questions as:

What views of man, and what views of human behaviour, underlie our work?

What is our understanding of social, economic and political development and how adult education fits into it?

How does adult education relate to such other professions as community development and social work?

As the last chapter has shown, to answer such questions, we need much more *research*. An American educationist, writing of his own country, has said:

one problem seems to be the weak research base. The field should not become overly academic ... much of its strength lies in its practical turn. But every specialty needs a strong scholarly foundation and adult education has not yet achieved this.[8]

If it is true of the USA, it is equally true of adult education in West Africa. Countries such as India and the USSR have national directorates and institutes charged with adult educational research on a national scale. May we look forward at least to national research networks in our own countries, giving overall direction to the data collection and research which can be done by all adult educators in the field, and also endowed with resources for some major projects?

New concerns: environment and leisure

The problems of basic philosophy and of adequate research have long been with us. We may also expect to face problems which have not yet been taken seriously – either because they do not now exist or because, though present, they have not yet loomed large to us.

Our concern as educators at present is for the human being *in his socio-economic setting.* We will one day have to become concerned for the human being *in his physical environment.* The United Nations has already become worried about the destruction and spoiling of man's environment, to the extent that it has set up the UN Environment Programme based in Nairobi; but most people in West Africa have not yet taken environmental problems seriously. The signs are that we will have to before very long. We are yearly losing productive land to the desert on the edge of the Sahel; and a city like Lagos is already polluted by filth on land, sewage in the lagoon and motorcar fumes in the air! A new task of education, both of children and of adults, must be to teach the conservation of our natural resources and the avoidance of worse pollution. As has been said, we have 'only one earth', and if we destroy our part of it, we have nowhere else to live. So **environmental education** may be expected on our agenda for the future.

In our concern for social and economic needs in developing countries, we are preoccupied unavoidably with production and employment. We have to educate people for work skills which will bring them a living. But the signs from Western Europe are that advancing technology means that less and less time is spent working. Machines do the work and few people are needed to tend them. Thus more and more men and women have more and more spare time or leisure. **Education for leisure** has looked ridiculous in West Africa in the past, but it is an idea which we may have to take up before too long, if our countries take up advanced technology. We can already see how few people are needed to man an oil industry such as Nigeria's. If citizens are not to become bored and frustrated (and young and energetic ones delinquent), we will have to provide educational programmes to enable them to fill their spare time satisfyingly. This will require such provision as **sports and physical education for adults,** which is virtually undeveloped among us at present.

Some suggested goals for adult educators

So far, we have talked of likely developments in philosophy, content and methodology of adult education, within the overall lifelong learning pattern. We have talked of forces shaping development, of possible obstacles, of ideas about learners' capacities which will affect the content and methodology of adult education. We have mentioned the effect of technological invention on electronic communication. We have also tried to look beyond immediate prospects to longer-term needs (for more philosophical exploration and more organized research) and challenges to be expected from environmental decay and shorter working time.

All of these developments and predictions must also take account of our actions as adult educators. We will have to play our part in making the future.

What goals may we set for ourselves?

Apart from doing all we can to overcome the difficulties placed in our way by lack of funds and absence of commitment, we must also take account of new ideas in adult educational planning (see Chapter 4) and in teaching methodology.

Additionally, we need to strive to achieve the administrative and structural changes mentioned in Chapter 12. Every pressure should be exerted on policy-makers to make a reality of two sorts of integration – *the integration of all education into a lifelong learning system* and *the integration of adult education into national development planning.*

Many recommendations have been made internationally for the coordination of the whole education system. The present fashionable idea is to put all forms of education together in one ministry. This looks an easy answer, but what has tended to happen is that adult literacy education is put under the jurisdiction of the education ministry and given a marginal place. Other important and often better funded forms of adult education remain (and obviously always will remain) within other ministries. Some inter-ministerial coordination, such as has been advocated in Chapters 3 and 12, must be worked for. The trend is in favour of this solution. We have the backing for it of ECA and the Commonwealth and we also have examples from other African countries. It is a solution worth fighting for.

Equally, we need to fight for a recognized place for adult education in national plans. Among current ideas as to how this can be done are:

the training of adult educators themselves in planning techniques;
the analysis by adult educators of the adult education components
   of their country's plan;
the monitoring of those components by adult educators;
the formation by adult educators of their own professional bodies
   to offer advice on planning to governments;
pressure for the inclusion of adult educators and educationists in
   bodies responsible for national planning;

pressure for the inclusion in national censuses of questions to provide information on adult education.

Greater integration and improved links with other educational and development bodies should allow us to expect better support services. Adult education work depends not only on cooperation with development ministries and voluntary bodies; its ultimate effectiveness is tied up with the services mentioned in Chapter 9, such as libraries, museums and agricultural shows. While literacy remains an important priority for adult education, all services relating to the production and distribution of books and newspapers must claim our interest. We must hope for and encourage the number of book, magazine and newspaper publishers, of bookshops and travelling book salesmen, as well as the growth of the printing industry. Without all these, our libraries cannot function. In addition, we must attempt to come closer to our colleagues in the librarianship profession, so that we may use their professional advice in providing book collections at adult education centres and may keep them informed of places where their services are needed.

Some preoccupation with planning and organization is necessary if we are to attain the future for adult education which we can all see is possible. Once again, however, *all our planning must be done with the human element in mind.* While there is a constant emphasis on rural development, let us not forget the needs of particular groups of adult learners. Women, both rural and urban, have been largely neglected by adult educators in the past, for example. Also little has been done to help the low-income urban worker to survive and to control his fate.

Such guidelines are recommended for adult educators to adopt. If we work towards the sorts of integration and support services mentioned, and bear in mind constantly the special needs of special groups of learners, we will be able to come in sight of the lofty goal described in the Faure Report:

> The physical, intellectual, emotional and ethical integration of the individual into a complete man is a broad definition of the fundamental aim for education.[9]

Conclusion

It is generally recognized that 'adult education as an apolitical pressure of adult educators' is desirable. Our pressures will be accorded respect in so far as we show ourselves true professionals worthy of that respect.

The rationale for greater professionalization has been given in Chapters 1 and 12; the uses of professionalization in teaching and motivating adults are discussed in Chapters 2, 6 and 8; while Chapters 4 and 5 give some guidance on the operational strategies of the adult educator. For the future, there will have to be greater emphasis on the development of adult education as a profession.

Adult education training will have to be extended and refined; adult educators will need to take more advantage of existing professional bodies and periodicals; and there may be a case for a West African organization of adult educators with its own journal as a medium for discussion, exchange of views and spread of information on adult education problems.

As in most modern professions, adult educators must be prepared to work hard. We must be resourceful, forward-looking and dynamic. We must not remain wedded to tradition or bound by conventional approaches. Our primary task should be to experiment and initiate new programmes, using new methods to hand and, in particular, grasping the exciting possibilities open to us through the mass media. We should be ready to try new ways of planning and administration and should make the best use of national and international resources. Above all, we must constantly adjust ourselves to changing times in our various communities.

Adjustment, for ourselves as for other learners, requires constant refreshment of knowledge and ideas. A famous Indian poet once said: 'A lamp cannot light another lamp unless it continues to burn its own flame.' As apostles of adult learning, we need to follow our own advice and continue reading and learning and thinking about our own work and about our profession. If we do so, we will have done our part towards the attainment of a 'learning society'.

This book is a first learning resource for West African adult educators. While the writers hope it will be useful throughout an educator's working life, its value will only be fully realized if those who read it and put it on their shelves put other books beside it and continue reading to extend the knowledge, skills and ideas which it has tried to teach.

We wish all who read it good luck in this exciting, strenuous and important profession.

Notes and references

   1. Edgar Faure *et al.*, *Learning to Be: the world of education today and tomorrow* (Paris: Unesco, 1972), pp. 87–165
   2. Ronald Dore, *The Diploma Disease: Education, Qualification and Development* (London: Allen & Unwin, 1976)
   3. Federal Military Government of Nigeria, *The Constitution of the Federal Republic of Nigeria 1979* (Lagos Federal Ministry of Information Printing Division, 1979), ch. 2, sect. 18.
   4. Quoted in Basil Davidson, *The Liberation of Guiné: Aspects of an African Revolution* (Harmondsworth: Penguin, 1969), p. 74
   5. Paulo Freire, *Pedagogy in Process: The Letters to Guinea-Bissau* (London: Writers' and Readers' Publishing Cooperative, 1978)
   6. The address of the Secretariat, an inter-governmental (but not UN) agency, is: Marlborough House, London sw1y 5hx United Kingdom
   7. James R. Sheffield and Victor P. Diejomaoh, *Non-Formal Education in African Development* (New York: African-American Institute, 1972), p. 4
   8. F. H. Harrington, *The Future of Adult Education* (San Francisco: Jossey-Bass, 1977), p. 187
   9. Faure, p. 156

Appendices

Appendix 1 Addresses of major relevant organizations

Information about membership subscriptions and cost of publications may be obtained by writing to the addresses given. Where a publication is free of charge, this is indicated here. All publications mentioned are in English or have English editions.

United Nations agencies

United Nations Educational Scientific and Cultural Organization (Unesco)

a) Adult Education Section
Division for Structures, Content, Methods and Techniques of Education
Unesco, 7 Place de Fontenoy
75700 Paris, France

Publishes a quarterly journal, *Adult Education Information Notes*. Free of charge; essential for all adult educators.

b) Mass Communication Centre
Division of Free Flow of Information and Communication Policies
Unesco, 7 Place de Fontenoy
75700 Paris, France

c) BREDA (Unesco Regional Office for Education)
BP 3311
Dakar
Republic of Senegal

Publishes *NEIDA Information* (Network of Educational Innovation for Development in Africa), occasional, free of charge.

d) International Bureau of Education (IBE)
Palais Wilson
1211 Geneva 14
Switzerland

Provides various important documentation and abstracting
services.

e) International Institute for Adult Literacy Methods
PO Box 1555
Teheran
Iran

Publishes *Literacy Discussion* (quarterly); *Literacy Work*
(quarterly); and *Literacy Documentation* (three times a year).

Economic Commission for Africa (ECA)

a) Manpower, Training and Public Administration Section, ECA
PO Box 3001
Addis Ababa
Ethiopia

b) Training and Research Centre for Women, ECA
PO Box 3001
Addis Ababa
Ethiopia

Food and Agriculture Organization (FAO)

Economic and Social Policy Department, FAO
Via delle Terme di Caracalla
Rome
Italy

Publishes *Food and Nutrition* (quarterly).

*International Bank for Reconstruction and Development (World
Bank)*

Headquarters
1818 High Street NW
Washington, DC
USA

Publishes annual reports, free of charge; sector reports,
occasional, free of charge.

International Labour Organization (ILO)

a) Workers' Education Branch, ILO
CH-1211, Geneva 22
Switzerland

b) Training and Development Publications, ILO
CH-1211, Geneva 22
Switzerland

Publishes Training and Development Abstracts (bimonthly)

World Health Organization

Headquarters
1211 Geneva 27
Switzerland

Publishes *WHO Chronicle* (monthly).

International non-governmental agencies

Associated Countrywomen of the World

50 Warwick Square
London SW1V 2AJ
United Kingdom

International Confederation of Free Trade Unions

Headquarters
rue Montagne aux Herbes Potagères
3741–1000 Brussels
Belgium

International Congress of University Adult Education

c/o Hon. Secretary, Department of Adult Education
Faculty of Education
University of Lagos

Publishes *ICUAE Journal* (quarterly).

International Cooperative Alliance

11 Upper Grosvenor Street
London W1
United Kingdom

Publishes *Review of International Cooperation* (monthly)

International Council for Adult Education

c/o Ontario Institute for Studies in Education
252 Bloor Street West
Toronto
Canada M5S 2V6

Publishes *Convergence* (quarterly). This is the major

Publishes Convergence (quarterly). This is the major
international journal in the field. There are special low-price
subscriptions for students. Editorial and subscription address:
PO Box 250, Station F
Toronto, Canada M47 2L5

International Council for Correspondence Education

Membership and Recruitment Services
5B Francis Grove
London SW19 4DT
United Kingdom

Publishes quarterly newsletter.

International Council of Museums

Maison de l'Unesco
1 rue Miollis
75015 Paris
France

International Council on Social Welfare

345 East 46th Street
New York, NY 10017
USA

International Extension College

131 Hills Road
Cambridge CB1 1PD
United Kingdom

Publishes occasional *Broadsheets on Distance Education*.

International Federation of Library Associations

IFLA Secretariat
Netherlands Congress Building Tower, 3rd floor
PO Box 9128,
The Hague, Netherlands

International Federation for Parent Education

4 rue Brunel
75017 Paris
France

International Federation of Workers' Educational Associations

Wipplingerstr. 35
1010 Vienna
Austria

League of Red Cross Societies

17 Chemin des Crêts
Petit – Saconnex
Geneva, Switzerland

Publishes *Red Cross World* (three times a year).

World Confederation of Organizations of the Teaching Profession

5 avenue du Moulin
1110 Morges
Switzerland

Publishes *Echo* (quarterly), free of charge.

World Council of Churches

a) Headquarters
17 route de Malagnon
Geneva
Switzerland

b) Commission on the Churches' Participation in Development
PO Box 66,
150 route de Ferney

1211 Geneva 20
Switzerland

Publishes *CCPD Newsletter*

World Education

1414 Sixth Avenue
New York, NY 10019
USA

Publishes *World Education* (mainly concerned with family planning, health and nutrition education).

World Federation of Trade Unions

Nam. Curieovych 1
Prague 1
Czechoslovakia

Inter-African non-governmental agencies

African Adult Education Association

Kenyatta Conference Centre
PO Box 30746
Nairobi
Kenya

Publishes *Journal of African Adult Education*

Afrolit Society

PO Box 72511
Nairobi
Kenya

Arab Literacy and Adult Education Organization (ARLO)

a) Headquarters
1 Shihab Street
Dokki Giza
Egypt

Publishes *Education of the Masses*

b) ASFEC (Regional Centre for Adult Education and Functional Literacy in Rural Areas in the Arab States)
Sirs-el-Layyan
Menoufia
Egypt

CREAA (Regional Council for Literacy and Adult Education in Africa)

PNA
Ministère de La Santé Publique et des Affaires Sociales
Lome, Togo

Foreign non-governmental agencies, regional and national

Adult Education Association of the USA

810 18th Street NW
Washington, DC 20006
USA

Publishes *Adult Leadership* (monthly) and *Adult Education*.

Asian and South Pacific Bureau of Adult Education

c/o Centre for Continuing Education
Australian National University
PO Box 4
Canberra ACT 2600
Australia

Publishes *ASPBAE Courier*

British Committee on Literacy

c/o Agriculture and Rural Development Centre
University of Reading
16 London Road
Reading RG1 5AQ
United Kingdom

Canadian Association for Adult Education

29 Prince Arthur Avenue
Toronto, Ontario
Canada

Council of Europe Committee for Out-of-School Education and Cultural Development

Strasbourg
France

Publishes various important reports.

Dag Hammarskjöld Foundation

Övre Slottsgatan 2
752 20 Uppsala
Sweden

Publishes *Development Dialogue* (biannually), free of charge.

European Bureau of Adult Education

Nieuwe Weg 4
PO Box 367
Amersfoort
Netherlands

Publishes *Notes and Studies* (bimonthly).

European Centre for Leisure and Education

Prague 1
Jilska 1
Czechoslovakia

Publishes *Society and Leisure* (quarterly). This centre is linked with Unesco.

Friedrich Ebert Foundation

Kolnerstrasse 149
53 Bonn-Bad Godesberg
German Federal Republic

German Adult Education Association (DVV)

a) Department for Adult Education in Developing Countries
Konstantinstr. 100
5300 Bonn Z
Federal Republic of Germany

Publishes *Adult Education and Development* (biannual), free of charge, in English, French, Spanish.

b) Africa Bureau, DVV
PO Box 9298
Kotoka International Airport
Accra
Ghana

German Foundation for International Development

Postfach 120518
D53 Bonn 12
Federal Republic of Germany

Publishes *Development and Cooperation* (quarterly), free of charge.

Indian Adult Education Association

17-B Indraprastha Marg
New Delhi 110002
India

Publishes *Indian Journal of Adult Education* (monthly).

National Institute of Adult Education (England and Wales)

19B de Montfort Street,
Leicester LE1 7GE
United Kingdom

Publishes *Adult Education* (bimonthly).

Organization for Economic Cooperation and Development

2 rue André-Pascal
75775 Paris
France

Scottish Institute of Adult Education

57 Melville Street
Edinburgh EH3 7HL
Scotland
United Kingdom

Publishes *Scottish Journal of Adult Education* (three times a year).

African national organizations

Kenya Board of Adult Education

PO Box 30547
Nairobi
Kenya

Nigerian National Council for Adult Education

PMB 1001
UniLag Post Office
Akoka, Yaba, Lagos, Nigeria

People's Educational Association of Ghana

c/o Institute of Adult Education
PO Box 31
Legon
Ghana

Tanzania Institute of Adult Education

PO Box 20679
Dar es Salaam
Tanzania

Zambia Adult Education Advisory Board

PO Box RW93
Lusaka
Zambia

Appendix 2 Unesco Recommendation on the Development of Adult Education

The General Conference of the United Nations Education, Scientific and Cultural Organization, meeting in Nairobi from 26 October to 30 November 1976, at its nineteenth session.

Recalling the principles set forth in Articles 26 and 27 of the Universal Declaration of Human Rights, guaranteeing and specifying the right of everyone to education and to participate freely in cultural, artistic and scientific life and the principles set forth in Articles 13 and 15 of the International Covenant on Economic, Social and Cultural Rights

Considering that education is inseparable from democracy, the abolition of privilege and the promotion within society as a whole of the ideas of autonomy, responsibility and dialogue,

Considering that the access of adults to education, in the context of lifelong education, is a fundamental aspect of the right of education and facilitates the exercise of the right to participate in political, cultural, artistic and scientific life,

Considering that for the full development of the human personality, particularly in view of the rapid pace of scientific, technical, economic and social change, education must be considered on a global basis and as a lifelong process,

Considering that the development of adult education, in the context of lifelong education, is necessary as a means of achieving a more rational and more equitable distribution of educational resources between young people and adults, and between different social groups, and of ensuring better understanding and more effective collaboration between the generations and greater political, social and economic equality between social groups and between the sexes,

Convinced that adult education as an integral part of lifelong education can contribute decisively to economic and cultural development, social progress and world peace as well as to the development of educational systems,

Considering that the experience acquired in adult education must constantly contribute to the renewal of educational methods, as well as to the reform of educational systems as a whole,

Considering the universal concern for literacy as being a crucial factor in political and economic development, in technological progress and in social and cultural change, so that its promotion should therefore form an integral part of any plan for adult education,

Reaffirming that the attainment of this objective entails creating situations in which the adults are able to choose, from among a variety of forms of educational activity the objectives and content of which have been defined with their collaboration, those forms which meet their needs most closely and are most directly related to their interests,

Bearing in mind the diversity of modes of training and education throughout the world and the special problems peculiar to the countries whose education systems are as yet underdeveloped or insufficiently adapted to national needs,

In order to give effect to the conclusions, declarations and recommendations formulated by the second and third international conferences on adult education (Montreal, 1960; Tokyo, 1972) and, as far as the relevant paragraphs are concerned, by the World Conference of the International Women's Year (Mexico, 1975),

Desirous of making a further contribution to putting into effect the principles set forth in the recommendations addressed by the International Conference on Public Education to the Ministries of Education concerning the access of women to education (Recommendation No. 34, 1952), facilities for education in rural areas (Recommendation No. 47, 1958), and literacy and adult education (Recommendation No. 58, 1965), in the Declaration adopted at the International Symposium for Literacy in Persepolis (1975) and in the Recommendation concerning Education for International Understanding, Cooperation and Peace, and Education relating to Human Rights and Fundamental Freedoms adopted by the General Conference at its eighteenth session (1974);

Taking note of the provisions of the Revised Recommendation concerning Technical and Vocational Education adopted by the General Conference at its eighteenth session (1974) and of resolution 3.426 adopted at the same session with a view to the adoption of an international instrument concerning action designed to ensure that the people at large have free democratic access to culture and an opportunity to take an active part in the cultural life of society.

Noting further that the International Labour Conference has adopted a number of instruments concerned with various aspects of adult education, and in particular the recommendation on vocational guidance (1949), the recommendation on vocational training in agriculture (1956), as well as the convention and recommendation concerning paid educational leave (1974), and of human resources development (1975),

Having decided, at its eighteenth session, that adult education would be the subject of a recommendation to Member States,

Adopts this 26th day of November 1976, the present Recommendation.

The General Conference recommends that Member States apply the following provisions by taking whatever legislative or other steps may be required, and in conformity with the constitutional practice of each State, to give effect to the principles set forth in this Recommendation.

The General Conference recommends that Member States bring this Recommendation to the attention of the authorities, departments or bodies responsible for adult education and also of the various organizations carrying out educational work for the benefit of adults, and of trade union organizations, associations, enterprises, and other interested parties.

The General Conference recommends that Member States report to it, at such dates and in such form as shall be determined by it, on the action taken by them in pursuance of this Recommendation.

I.   DEFINITION

1.   In this Recommendation:

the term 'adult education' denotes the entire body of organized educational processes, whatever the content, level and method, whether formal or otherwise, whether they prolong or replace initial education in schools, colleges and universities as well as in apprenticeship, whereby persons regarded as adult by the society to which they belong develop their abilities, enrich their knowledge, improve their technical or professional qualifications and bring about changes in their attitudes or behaviour in the twofold perspective of full personal development and participation in balanced and independent social, economic and cultural development;

adult education, however, must not be considered as an entity in itself, it is a sub-division, and an integral part of, a global scheme for lifelong education and learning;

the term 'lifelong education and learning', for its part, denotes an overall scheme aimed both at restructuring the existing education system and at developing the entire educational potential outside the education system;

in such a scheme men and women are the agents of their own education, through continual interaction between their thoughts and actions;

education and learning, far from being limited to the period of attendance at school, should extend throughout life, include all skills and branches of knowledge, use all possible means, and give the opportunity to all people for full development of the personality;

the educational and learning processes in which children, young people and adults of all ages are involved in the course of their lives, in whatever form, should be considered as a whole.

II.   OBJECTIVES AND STRATEGY

2.   Generally speaking, the aims of adult education should be to contribute to:

(*a*) promoting work for peace, international understanding and cooperation;

(*b*) developing a critical understanding of major contemporary problems and social changes and the ability to play an active part in the progress of society with a view to achieving social justice;

(*c*) promoting increased awareness of the relationship between people and their physical and cultural environment, and fostering the desire to improve the environment and to respect and protect nature, the common heritage and public property;

(*d*) creating an understanding of and respect for the diversity of customs and cultures, on both the national and the international planes;

(*e*) promoting increased awareness of, and giving effect to vari-

ous forms of communication and solidarity at the family,
local, national, regional and international levels;
(*f*) developing the aptitude for acquiring, either individually, in
groups or in the context of organized study in educational
establishments specially set up for this purpose, new knowledge, qualifications, attitudes or forms of behaviour con-
ducive to the full maturity of the personality;
(*g*) ensuring the individual's conscious and effective incorpora-
tion into working life by providing men and women with
an advanced technical and vocational education and developing the ability to create, either individually or in
groups, new material goods and new spiritual or aesthetic
values;
(*h*) developing the ability to grasp adequately the problems
involved in the upbringing of children;
(*i*) developing the aptitude for making creative use of leisure
and for acquiring any necessary or desired knowledge;
(*j*) developing the necessary discernment in using mass communication media, in particular radio, television, cinema
and the press, and interpreting the various messages
addressed to modern men and women by society;
(*k*) developing the aptitude for learning to learn.

3.   Adult education should be based on the following principles

(*a*) it should be based on the needs of the participants and
make use of their different experiences in the development
of adult education; the most educationally underprivileged
groups should be given the highest priority within a perspective of collective advancement;
(*b*) it should rely on the ability and determination of all human
beings to make progress throughout their lives both at the
level of their personal development and in relation to their
social activity;
(*c*) it should awaken an interest in reading and develop cultural
aspirations;
(*d*) it should stimulate and sustain the interest of adult learners,
appeal to their experience, strengthen their self-reliance,
and enlist their active participation at all stages of the educational process in which they are involved;
(*e*) it should be adapted to the actual conditions of everyday
life and work and take into account the personal characteristics of adult learners, their age, family, social, occupa-

tional or residential background and the way in which these interrelate;

(*f*) it should seek the participation of individual adults, groups and communities in decision making at all levels of the learning process; including determination of needs, curriculum development, programme implementation and evaluation and should plan educational activities with a view to the transformation of the working environment and of the life of adults;

(*g*) it should be organized and operated flexibly by taking into account social, cultural, economic and institutional factors of each country and society to which adult learners belong;

(*h*) it should contribute to the economic and social development of the entire community;

(*i*) it should recognize as an integral part of the educational process the forms of collective organization established by adults with a view to solving their day-to-day problems;

(*j*) it should recognize that every adult, by virtue of his or her experience of life, is the vehicle of a culture which enables him or her to play the role of both learner and teacher in the educational process in which he or she participates.

4.   Each Member State should:

(*a*) recognize adult education as a necessary and specific component of its education system and as a permanent element in its social, cultural and economic development policy; it should, consequently, promote the creation of structures, the preparation and implementation of programmes and the application of educational methods which meet the needs and aspirations of all categories of adults, without restriction on grounds of sex, race, geographical origin, age, social status, opinion, belief or prior educational standard;

(*b*) recognize that although, in a given situation or for a specific period, adult education may play a compensatory role, it is not intended as a substitute for adequate youth education which is a prerequisite for the full success of adult education.

(*c*) in eliminating the isolation of women from adult education, work towards ensuring equality of access and full participation in the entire range of adult education activities, including those which provide training for qualifications leading to activities or responsibilities which have hitherto been reserved for men;

(*d*) take measures with a view to promoting participation in adult education and community development programmes by members of the most underprivileged groups, whether rural or urban, settled or nomadic, and in particular illiterates, young people who have been unable to acquire an adequate standard of general education or a qualification, migrant workers and refugees, unemployed workers, members of ethnic minorities, persons suffering from a physical or mental handicap, persons experiencing difficulties of social adjustment and those serving prison sentences. In this context, Member States should associate themselves in the search for educational strategies designed to foster more equitable relations among social groups;

5.   The place of adult education in each education system should be defined with a view to achieving

(*a*) a rectification of the main inequalities in access to initial education and training, in particular inequalities based on age, sex, social position or social or geographical origin;
(*b*) the assurance of a scientific basis for lifelong education and learning as well as greater flexibility in the way in which people divide their lives between education and work, and, in particular, providing for the alternation of periods of education and work throughout the life span, and facilitating the integration of continuing education into the activity of work itself;
(*c*) recognition, and increased exploitation, of the actual or potential educational value of the adult's various experiences;
(*d*) easy transfer from one type or level of education to another;
(*e*) greater interaction between the education system and its social, cultural and economic setting;
(*f*) greater efficiency from the point of view of the contribution of educational expenditure to social, cultural and economic development.

6.   Consideration should be given to the need for an adult education component, including literacy, in the framing and execution of any development programme.
7.   The objectives and goals of adult education policy should be incorporated in national development plans; they should be defined in relation to the overall objectives of educational policy and of social, cultural and economic development policies.

Adult education and other forms of education, particularly school and higher education and initial vocational training, should be conceived and organized as equally essential components in a coordinated but differentiated education system according to the tenets of lifelong education and learning.

8.   Measures should be taken to encourage the public authorities, institutions or bodies engaged in education, voluntary associations, workers' and employers' organizations, and those directly participating in adult education, to collaborate in the task of defining further and giving effect to those objectives.

III.   CONTENT OF ADULT EDUCATION

9.   Adult education activities, viewed as forming part of lifelong education and learning, have no theoretical boundaries and should meet the particular situations created by the specific needs of development, of participation in community life and of individual self-fulfilment; they cover all aspects of life and all fields of knowledge and are addressed to all people whatever their level of achievement. In defining the content of adult education activities priority should be given to the specific needs of the educationally most underprivileged groups.

10.   Civic, political, trade union and cooperative education activities should be aimed particularly towards developing independent and critical judgement and implanting or enhancing the abilities required by each individual in order to cope with changes affecting living and working conditions, by effective participation in the management of social affairs at every level of the decision-making process.

11.   While not excluding approaches intended to achieve a short-term solution in a particular situation, technical and vocational education activities should as a general rule emphasize the acquisition of qualifications which are sufficiently broad to allow of subsequent changes of occupation and a critical understanding of the problems of working life. It is necessary to integrate general and civic education with technical and vocational education.

12.   Activities designed to promote cultural development and artistic creation should encourage appreciation of existing cultural and artistic values and works and, at the same time, should aim to promote the creation of new values and new works, by releasing the expressive capabilities inherent in each individual or group.

13.   Participation in adult education should not be restricted on grounds of sex, race, geographical origin, culture, age, social status, experience, belief and prior educational standard.

14. With regard to women, adult education activities should be integrated as far as possible with the whole contemporary social movement directed towards achieving self-determination for women and enabling them to contribute to the life of society as a collective force, and should thus focus specifically on certain aspects, in particular:

(a) the establishment in each society of conditions of equality between men and women;

(b) the emancipation of women from the preconceived models imposed on them by society in every field in which they carry responsibility;

(c) civic, occupational, psychological, cultural and economic autonomy for women as a necessary condition for their existence as complete individuals;

(d) knowledge about the status of women, and about women's movements, in various societies, with a view to increased solidarity across frontiers.

15. With regard to settled or nomadic rural populations, adult education activities should be designed in particular to:

(a) enable them to use technical procedures and methods of individual or joint organization likely to improve their standard of living without obliging them to forgo their own values;

(b) put an end to the isolation of individuals or groups;

(c) prepare individuals or groups of individuals who are obliged, despite the efforts made to prevent excessive depopulation of rural areas, to leave agriculture, either to engage in a new occupational activity while remaining in a rural environment, or to leave this environment for a new way of life.

16. With regard to such persons or groups as have remained illiterate or are experiencing difficulty in adjusting to society because of the slenderness of their resources, their limited education or their restricted participation in community life, adult education activities should be designed not only to enable them to acquire basic knowledge (reading, writing, arithmetic, basic understanding of natural and social phenomena), but also to make it easier for them to engage in productive work, to promote their self-awareness and their grasp of the problems of hygiene, health, household management and the upbringing of children, and to enhance their autonomy and increase their participation in community life.

17. With regard to young people who have been unable to acquire an adequate standard of general education or a qualification, adult education activities should, in particular, enable them to acquire additional general education with a view to developing their ability to understand the problems of society and shoulder social responsibilities, and to gaining access to the vocational training and general education which are necessary for the exercise of an occupational activity.

18. If people wish to acquire educational or vocational qualifications which are formally attested by certificates of education or of vocational aptitude and which, for social or economic reasons, they have not been able to obtain earlier, adult education should enable them to obtain the training required for the award of such certificates.

19. With regard to the physically or mentally handicapped, adult education activities should be designed, in particular, to restore or offset the physical or mental capacities which have been impaired or lost as a result of their handicap, and to enable them to acquire the knowledge and skills and, where necessary, the professional qualifications required for their social life and for the exercise of an occupational activity compatible with their handicap.

20. With regard to migrant workers, refugees, and ethnic minorities, adult education activities should in particular:

(*a*) enable them to acquire the linguistic and general knowledge as well as the technical or professional qualifications necessary for their temporary or permanent assimilation in the society of the host country and, where appropriate, their reassimilation in the society of their country of origin;

(*b*) keep them in touch with culture, current developments and social changes in their country of origin.

21. With regard to unemployed persons, including the educated unemployed, adult education activities should be designed, in particular, to adapt or modify their technical or professional qualification with a view to enabling them to find or return to employment and to promote a critical understanding of their socio-economic situation.

22. With regard to ethnic minorities, adult education activities should enable them to express themselves freely, educate themselves and their children in their mother tongues, develop their own cultures and learn languages other than their mother tongues.

23. With regard to the aged, adult education activities should be designed, in particular:

(*a*) to give all a better understanding of contemporary problems and of the younger generation;

(*b*) to help acquire leisure skills, promote health and find increased meaning in life;

(*c*) to provide a grounding in the problems facing retired people and in ways of dealing with such problems, for the benefit of those who are on the point of leaving working life;

(*d*) to enable those who have left working life to retain their physical and intellectual faculties and to continue to participate in community life and also to give them access to fields of knowledge or types of activity which have not been open to them during their working life;

IV.   METHODS, MEANS, RESEARCH AND EVALUATION

24.   Adult education methods should take account of:

(*a*) incentives and obstacles to participation and learning specially affecting adults;

(*b*) the experience gained by adults in the exercise of their family, social and occupational responsibilities;

(*c*) the family, social or occupational obligations borne by adults and the fatigue and impaired alertness which may result from them;

(*d*) the ability of adults to assume responsibility for their own learning;

(*e*) the cultural and pedagogical level of the teaching personnel available;

(*f*) the psychological characteristics of the learning process;

(*g*) the existence and characteristics of cognitive interests;

(*h*) use of leisure time.

25.   Adult education activities should normally be planned and executed on the basis of identified needs, problems, wants, and resources, as well as defined objectives. Their impact should be evaluated, and reinforced by whatever follow-up activities may be most appropriate to given conditions.

26.   Particular emphasis should be placed on adult education activities intended for an entire social or geographical entity, mobilizing all its inherent energies with a view to the advancement of the group and social progress in a community setting.

27.   In order to encourage the broadest possible participation, it

may be appropriate in some situations to add, to locally based adult education, methods such as:

(a) remote teaching programmes such as correspondence courses and radio or television broadcasts, the intended recipients of such programmes being invited to form groups with a view to listening or working together (such groups should receive appropriate pedagogical support);
(b) programmes launched by mobile units;
(c) self-teaching programmes;
(d) study circles;
(e) use of voluntary work by teachers, students and other community of members.

The various services which public cultural institutions (libraries, museums, record libraries, video-cassette libraries) are able to put at the disposal of adult learners should be developed on a systematic basis, together with new types of institutions specializing in adult education.

28. Participation in an adult education programme should be a voluntary matter. The State and other bodies should strive to promote the desire of individuals and groups for education in the spirit of lifelong education and learning.

29. Relations between the adult learner and the adult educator should be established on a basis of mutual respect and cooperation.

30. Participation in an adult education programme should be subject only to the ability to follow the course of training provided and not to any (upper) age limit or any condition concerning the possession of a diploma or qualification; any aptitude tests on the basis of which a selection might be made if necessary should be adapted to the various categories of candidates taking such tests.

31. It should be possible to acquire and accumulate learning, experiences and qualifications through intermittent participation. Rights and qualifications obtained in this way should be equivalent to those granted by the systems of formalized education or of such character as to allow for continued education within this.

32. The methods used in adult education should not appeal to a competitive spirit but should develop in the adult learners a shared sense of purpose and habits of participation, mutual help, collaboration and team work.

33. Adult education programmes for the improvement of technical or professional qualifications should, as far as possible, be organized during working time and, in the case of seasonal work,

during the slack season. This should, as a general rule, be applied also to other forms of education, in particular literacy programmes and trade union education.

34. The premises necessary for the development of adult education activities should be provided; depending on the case, these may be premises used exclusively for adult education, with or without residential accommodation, or multi-purpose or integrated facilities or premises generally used or capable of being used for other purposes – in particular, clubs, workshops, school, university and scientific establishments, social, cultural or sociocultural centres or open air sites.

35. Member States should actively encourage research in all aspects of adult education and its objectives. Research programmes should have a practical basis. They should be carried out by universities, adult education bodies and research bodies, adopting an interdisciplinary approach. Measures should be taken with a view to disseminating the experience and the results of the research programmes to those concerned.

36. Systematic evaluation of adult education activities is necessary to secure optimum results from the resources put into them. For evaluation to be effective it should be built into the programmes of adult education at all levels and stages.

V. THE STRUCTURES OF ADULT EDUCATION

37. Member States should endeavour to ensure the establishment and development of a network of bodies meeting the needs of adult education; this network should be sufficiently flexible to meet the various personal and social situations and their evolution.

38. Measures should be taken in order to:

(a) identify and anticipate educational needs capable of being satisfied through adult education programmes;

(b) make full use of existing educational facilities and create such facilities as may be lacking to meet all defined objectives;

(c) make the necessary long-term investments for the development of adult education: in particular for the professional education of planners, administrators, those who train educators, organizational and training personnel, the preparation of educational strategies and methods suitable for adults, the provision of capital facilities, the production and provision of the necessary basic equipment such as visual aids, apparatus and technical media;

(d) encourage exchanges of experience and compile and disseminate statistical and other information on the strategies, structures, content, methods and results, both quantitative and qualitative, of adult education;

(e) abolish economic and social obstacles to participation in education, and to systematically bring the nature and form of adult education programmes to the attention of all potential beneficiaries, but especially to the most disadvantaged, by using such means as active canvassing by adult education institutions and voluntary organizations, to inform, counsel and encourage possible and often hesitant participants in adult education.

39.   In order to achieve these objectives it will be necessary to mobilize organizations and institutions specifically concerned with adult education, and the full range, both public and private of schools, universities, cultural and scientific establishments, libraries and museums, and, in addition, other institutions not primarily concerned with adult education, such as:

(a) mass information bodies: the press, radio and television;
(b) voluntary associations and consortia;
(c) professional, trade union, family and cooperative organizations;
(d) families;
(e) industrial and commercial firms which may contribute to the training of their employees;
(f) educators, technicians or qualified experts working on an individual basis;
(g) any persons or groups who are in a position to make a contribution by virtue of their education, training, experience or professional or social activities and are both willing and able to apply the principles set forth in the Preamble and the objectives and strategy out-lined in the Recommendation;
(h) the adult learners themselves.

40.   Member States should encourage schools, vocational education establishments, colleges and institutions of higher education to regard adult education programmes as an integral part of their own activities and to participate in action designed to promote the development of such programmes provided by other institutions, in particular by making available their own teaching staff, conducting research and training the necessary personnel.

VI.   TRAINING AND STATUS OF PERSONS ENGAGED
       IN ADULT EDUCATION WORK

41.   It should be recognized that adult education calls for special skills, knowledge, understanding and attitudes on the part of
those who are involved in providing it, in whatever capacity and
for any purpose. It is desirable therefore that they should be
recruited with care according to their particular functions and
receive initial and in-service training for them according to their
needs and those of the work in which they are engaged.
42.   Measures should be taken to ensure that the various
specialists who have a useful contribution to make to the work of
adult education take part in those activities, whatever their nature
or purpose.
43.   In addition to the employment of full-time professional
workers, measures should be taken to enlist the support of anyone
capable of making a contribution, regular or occasional, paid or
voluntary, to adult education activities, of any kind. Voluntary
involvement and participation in all aspects of organizing and
teaching are of crucial importance, and people with all kinds of
skills are able to contribute to them.
44.   Training for adult education should, as far as practicable,
include all those aspects of skill, knowledge, understanding and
personal attitude which are relevant to the various functions
undertaken, taking into account the general background against
which adult education takes place. By integrating these aspects
with each other, training should itself be a demonstration of sound
adult education practice.
45.   Conditions of work and remuneration for full-time staff in
adult education should be comparable to those of workers in similar posts elsewhere, and those for paid part-time staff should be
appropriately regulated, without detriment to their main occupation.

VII.   RELATIONS BETWEEN ADULT EDUCATION AND
        YOUTH EDUCATION

46.   The education of young people should progressively be
oriented towards lifelong education and learning, taking into
account the experience gained in regard to adult education, with a
view to preparing young people, whatever their social origins, to
take part in adult education or to contribute to providing it. To this
end, measures should be taken with a view to:

(*a*) making access to all levels of education and training more widely available;

(*b*) removing the barriers between disciplines and also between types and levels of education;

(*c*) modifying school and training syllabuses with the aim of maintaining and stimulating intellectual curiosity, and also placing greater emphasis, alongside the acquisition of knowledge, on the development of self-teaching patterns of behaviour, a critical outlook, a reflective attitude and creative abilities;

(*d*) rendering schools, institutions of higher education and training establishments increasingly open to their economic and social environment and linking education and work more firmly together;

(*e*) informing young people at school and young people leaving full-time education or initial training of the opportunities offered by adult education;

(*f*) bringing together, where desirable, adults and adolescents in the same training programme;

(*g*) associating youth movements with adult education ventures.

47.   In cases where a training course organized as part of adult education leads to the acquisition of a qualification in respect of which a diploma or certificate is awarded when the qualification is acquired through study in school or university, such training should be recognized by the award of a diploma or certificate having equal status. Adult education programmes which do not lead to the acquisition of a qualification similar to those in respect of which a diploma or certificate is awarded should, in appropriate cases, be recognized by an award.

48.   Adult education programmes for youth need to be given the highest priority because in most parts of the world the youth form an extremely large segment of society and their education is of the greatest importance for political, economic, social and cultural development of the society in which they live. The programmes of adult education for youth should take account not only of their learning needs, but should enable them to orient themselves for the society of the future.

VIII.   THE RELATIONS BETWEEN ADULT EDUCATION AND WORK

49.   Having regard to the close connexion between guaranteeing the right to education and the right to work, and to the need

to promote the participation of all, whether wage-earners or not, in adult education programmes, not only by reducing the constraints to which they are subject but also by providing them with the opportunity of using in their work the knowledge, qualifications or aptitudes which adult education programmes are designed to make available to them, and of finding in work a source of personal fulfilment and advancement, and a stimulus to creative activity in both work and social life, measures should be taken:

(a) to ensure that, in the formulation of the curriculum of adult education programmes and activities, the working experience of adults should be taken into account;

(b) to improve the organization and conditions of work and, in particular, to alleviate the arduous character of work and reduce and adjust working hours;

(c) to promote the granting of educational leave during working time, without loss of remuneration or subject to the payment of compensatory remuneration and payments for the purpose of offsetting the cost of the education received and to use any other appropriate aid to facilitate education or updating during working life;

(d) to protect the employment of persons thus assisted;

(e) to offer comparable facilities to housewives and other homemakers and to non-wage-earners, particularly those of limited means.

50.   Member States should encourage or facilitate the inclusion in collective labour agreements of clauses bearing on adult education, and in particular clauses stipulating:

(a) the nature of the material possibilities and financial benefits extended to employees, and in particular those employed in sectors where rapid technological change is taking place or those threatened with being laid off, with a view to their participation in adult education programmes;

(b) the manner in which technical or professional qualifications acquired through adult education are taken into account in determining the employment category and in establishing the level of remuneration.

51.   Member States should also invite employers:

(a) to anticipate and publicize, by level and type of qualification, their skilled manpower requirements and the methods of recruitment which are envisaged to meet such needs;

(b) to organize or develop a recruitment system such as will encourage their employees to seek to improve their occupational qualifications.

52.   In connexion with adult training programmes organized by employers for their staff, Member States should encourage them to ensure that:

(a) employees participate in the preparation of the programmes;

(b) those taking part in such programmes are chosen in consultation with the workers' representative bodies;

(c) participants receive a certificate of training or paper qualification on completion of the programme enabling them to satisfy third parties that they have completed a given course or received a given qualification.

53.   Measures should be taken with a view to promoting the participation of adults belonging to labouring, agricultural or craft communities in the implementation of adult education programmes intended for such communities; to this end they should be granted special facilities with the aim of enabling the workers to take those decisions which primarily concern them.

IX.   MANAGEMENT, ADMINISTRATION, COORDINATION AND FINANCING OF ADULT EDUCATION

54.   There should be set up, at all levels, international, regional, national and local:

(a) structures or procedures for consultation and coordination between public authorities which are competent in the field of adult education;

(b) structures or procedures for consultation, coordination and harmonization between the said public authorities, the representatives of adult learners and the entire range of bodies carrying out adult education programmes or activities designed to promote the development of such programmes.

It should be among the principal functions of these structures, for which resources should be made available, to identify the objectives, to study the obstacles encountered, to propose and, where appropriate, carry out the measures necessary for implementation of the adult education policy and to evaluate the progress made.

55. There should be set up at national level, and, where appropriate, at sub-national level, structures for joint action and cooperation between the public authorities and bodies responsible for adult education on the one hand and the public or private bodies responsible for radio and television on the other.

It should be among the principal functions of these structures to study, propose and, where appropriate, carry out measures designed to:

(*a*) ensure that the mass media make a substantial contribution to leisure-time occupations and to the education of the people;

(*b*) guarantee freedom of expression, through the mass media, for all opinions and trends in the field of adult education;

(*c*) promote the cultural or scientific value and the educational qualities of programmes as a whole;

(*d*) establish a two-way flow of exchanges between those responsible for or those professionally engaged in educational programmes broadcast by radio or television and the persons for whom the programmes are intended.

56. Member States should ensure that the public authorities, while assuming their own specific responsibilities for the development of adult education:

(*a*) encourage, by laying down an appropriate legal and financial framework, the creation and development of adult education associations and consortia on a voluntary and administratively independent basis;

(*b*) provide non-governmental bodies participating in adult education programmes, or in action designed to promote such programmes, with technical or financial resources enabling them to carry out their task;

(*c*) see that such non-governmental bodies enjoy the freedom of opinion and the technical and educational autonomy which are necessary in order to give effect to the principles set forth in paragraph 2 above;

(*d*) take appropriate measures to ensure the educational and technical efficiency and quality of programmes or action conducted by bodies in receipt of contributions from public funds.

57. The proportion of public funds, and particularly of public

funds earmarked for education, allocated to adult education, should match the importance of such education for social, cultural and economic development, as recognized by each Member State within the framework of this Recommendation. The total allocation of funds to adult education should cover at least:

(a) provision of suitable facilities or adaptation of existing facilities;
(b) production of all kinds of learning materials;
(c) remuneration and further training of educators;
(d) research and information expenses;
(e) compensation for loss of earnings;
(f) tuition, and, where necessary and if possible, accommodation and travel costs of trainees.

58.   Arrangements should be made to ensure, on a regular basis, the necessary funds for adult education programmes and action designed to promote the development of such programmes; it should be recognized that the public authorities, including local authorities, credit organizations, provident societies and national insurance agencies where they exist, and employers should contribute to these funds to an extent commensurate with their respective responsibilities and resources.

59.   The necessary measures should be taken to obtain optimum use of resources made available for adult education. All available resources, both material and human, should be mobilized to this end.

60.   For the individual, lack of funds should not be an obstacle to participation in adult education programmes. Member States should ensure that financial assistance for study purposes is available for those who need it to undertake adult education. The participation of members of underprivileged social groups should, as a general rule, be free of charge.

X.   INTERNATIONAL COOPERATION

61.   Member States should strengthen their cooperation, whether on a bilateral or multilateral basis, with a view to promoting the development of adult education, the improvement of its content and methods, and efforts to find new educational strategies.

To this end, they should endeavour to incorporate specific clauses bearing on adult education in international agreements concerned with cooperation in the fields of education, science and culture, and to promote the development and strengthening of a special division for adult education in Unesco.

62.   Member States should put their experience with regard to adult education at the disposal of other Member States by providing them with technical assistance and, in appropriate cases, with material or financial assistance.

They should systematically support adult education activities conducted in countries so wishing, through Unesco and through other international organizations, including non-governmental organizations, with a view to social, cultural and economic development in the countries concerned.

Care should be taken to ensure that international cooperation does not take the form of a mere transfer of structures, curricula, methods and techniques which have originated elsewhere, but consists rather in prompting and stimulating development within the countries concerned, through the establishment of appropriate institutions and well coordinated structures adapted to the particular circumstances of those countries.

63.   Measures should be taken at national, regional and international level:

(*a*) with a view to making regular exchanges of information and documentation on the strategies, structures, content, methods and results of adult education and on relevant research;

(*b*) with a view to training educators capable of working away from their home country, particularly under bilateral or multilateral technical assistance programmes.

These exchanges should be made on a systematic basis, particularly between countries facing the same problems and so placed as to be capable of applying the same solutions; to this end, meetings should be organized, more especially on a regional or sub-regional basis, with a view to publicizing relevant experiments and studying to what extent they are reproducible; similarly, joint machinery should be set up in order to ensure a better return on the research which is undertaken.

Member States should foster agreements on the preparation and adoption of international standards in important fields, such as the teaching of foreign languages and basic studies, with a view to helping create a universally accepted unit-credit system.

64.   Measures should be taken with a view to the optimum dissemination and utilization of audio-visual equipment and materials, as well as educational programmes and the material objects

in which they are embodied. In particular, it would be appropriate:

(a) to adapt such dissemination and utilization to the various countries' social needs and conditions, bearing in mind their specific cultural characteristics and level of development;

(b) to remove, as far as possible, the obstacles to such dissemination and utilization resulting from the regulations governing commercial or intellectual property.

65.   In order to facilitate international cooperation, Member States should apply to adult education the standards recommended at international level, in particular with regard to the presentation of statistical data.

66.   Member States should support the action undertaken by Unesco, as the United Nations Specialized Agency competent in this field, in its efforts to develop adult education, particularly in the fields of training, research and evaluation.

67.   Member States should regard adult education as a matter of global and universal concern, and should deal with the practical consequences which arise therefrom, furthering the establishment of a new international order, to which Unesco, as an expression of the world community in educational, scientific and cultural matters, is committed.

Appendix 3 About the authors of this handbook

J. Ade Akinpelu, MA (London), PhD (Columbia). Reader in the Philosophy of Education, Department of Adult Education, University of Ibadan, and Acting Head of the Department from October 1977.

E. Kwasi Ampene, BA (London), PhD (Chicago). Director, Institute of Adult Education, University of Ghana. Associate Honorary Secretary-Treasurer, International Congress of University Adult Education. Honorary Secretary, 1976–8, African Adult Education Association.

Lalage Bown, MA (Oxon), Dr Univ (Open University). Professor and Head, Department of Adult Education, University of Lagos. Previously Chief Extension Coordinator, Ahmadu Bello University and Director of Extra-Mural Studies, University of Zambia. Board Member, International Council for Adult Education; Honorary Secretary-Treasurer, International Congress of University Adult Education. Honorary Secretary, 1968–73, African Adult Education Association.

C. R. Abiose Cole, MA, Dip Ed (Dunelm). Director of Extra-Mural Studies, Fourah Bay College, University of Sierra Leone. National President, People's Educational Association of Sierra Leone. Member, Sierra Leone National Literacy Committee.

Kwa O. Hagan, BLitt (Oxon). Formerly National Secretary People's Education Association (Ghana) and Deputy Director, Institute of Public Education, University of Ghana. Lately Senior Resident Tutor, Institute of Adult Education, University of Ghana. Member during 1960s of Unesco international committees on Adult Education and Literacy.

E. A. Haizel, BA, CertEd (London). Deputy Director, Institute of Adult Education, University of Ghana. Interim President, Ghana National Council on Adult Education. Member-evaluator, Ghana National Working Party on Literacy.

Ashok Kumar, BSc Econ (Ghana), MA (Leic). Lecturer in Economics, Department of Adult Education, University of Ibadan. Formerly Lecturer, Department of Economics, University of Ghana, Legon.

Madu Garga Mailafiya, Dip Ad Ed (Manc), MSc Educ Studies (Edin). Director, News and Current Affairs, Nigeria Television, Kano. Formerly Lecturer, Centre for Adult Education and Extension Services, Ahmadu Bello University, Zaria.

Joseph Taiwo Okedara, BA (Alaska), MA, PhD (Oregon). Senior Lecturer, Department of Adult Education, University of Ibadan. Honorary National Secretary, Nigerian National Council for Adult Education, from its foundation in 1971 until the present.

E. Odinakachuku Okeem, BSc Econ, MSc Econ, PhD (London). Senior Lecturer in Adult Education, University of Nigeria, Nsukka. Formerly Senior Lecturer in Social Studies, Liverpool Polytechnic (England).

Michael Omolewa, BA, PhD (Ibadan). Lecturer in the History of Adult Education, Department of Adult Education, University of Ibadan.

S. H. Olu Tomori, MA, PhD (London). Formerly Staff Tutor, Department of Extra-Mural Studies, University of Ibadan. Now Professor and Head, Department of Adult Education, University of Ibadan. Specialist in English as a Second Language.

Index

adhesive aids: *see* flannelgraph; magnetic board
administration, concept of, 64–5
Adult Basic Education (ABE), American, 16, 105–6
adult education in West Africa: and development, 23–5, 241–5; as a profession, 25–7, 252; definition, 13–18; forms, 73; future, ch. 13; history, 19–23; long-term needs, 248–9; methods, 73; obstacles to, 244–5; organization and planning, 64–7; problems, 228–37; scope and purpose, 13ff.; structures, 43ff.; trends, 223–7
adult education libraries, 165–70
adult educator, 25–7, 30, 32–3; goals, 249–52; qualities, 107–8; role, 41–2, 66–7, 168–9, 252; training, 26–7, 83, 102, 106, 235–6
adult illiteracy, 183–7
adult learner characteristics, 31–5
adult learning, conditions promoting, 35–6, 38–41
adult learning needs, 30–1, 246–7
African Adult Education Association, Kenya, 27, 192
African Institute for Economic and Social Development (INADES), 23
Aglionby, the Rev. John, Lord Bishop of Accra, 161
agricultural extension, 18, 44, 208, 212–13, 244, 245
agricultural productivity, 209–11
agricultural shows, 176–8, 251
Ahmadu Bello University, 154, 177, 219
aids, teaching and learning, 121–42
'Ananse' (spiderman) stories, 116
ancillary services: *see* libraries; museums
animators, 17
apprenticeship, 68

assessing progress, 90–3
assessment, forms of, 93–6
attendance register, 76, 97
audio-visual aids, 92, 126; *see also* stimulus modes

behavioural changes, 35–6, 88–9, 93, 96, 236
behaviourist psychology, 246–7
Botham, C. N., 131; quoted, 130, 133, 139
Boy Scouts movement, 54
British Council, 161, 162
British government, 21–2, 48, 49, 196–7
broadcast media, 146–53
budgeting, 81–3, 244–5
Buseko Home Industries project, Zambia, 245

Cabral, Amilcar (quoted), 243
Capitein, Jacobus, 21, 193, 194
Carnegie Corporation, 162
casual observation, 94; *see also* assessment
Catholic Church, 218
Central Bureau of Literacy, Nigeria, 153
Chadwick, John, 197
chairman, 117–18, 119
chalkboard, 127–32, 133, 136
charts, 132–5
choosing media, 126–7
Christianity, 21, 44, 241
cine film, 139–40
civic education, 16
Civil Aviation Training School, Zaria, 114
Clarke, J. D. (quoted), 171
class facilities, 73–4
colloquy, 119
colonial administrative systems, 47